150 Canadian
Stories of Peace

To Dennis
Happy Birthday!

May you
experience
much joy
and Peace!
Love,
Anne

Cover Design: Alberto Agraso
Original Illustrations: Alberto Agraso

Walking for Peace Publishing
2017

150 Canadian Stories of Peace

Anthology compiled by:
Gordon Breedyk
Mony Dojeiji
Koozma J. Tarasoff
Evelyn Voigt

Dedication

This book is dedicated to the Canadian children, women and men
who work towards a peaceful society.

Table of Contents

Introduction

The idea to compile an anthology of Canadian stories of peace came about at an Ottawa Peace Festival meeting when four individuals – Evelyn, Gordon, Koozma and Mony – expressed the importance of recognizing the contributions of Canadians to peace, as part of the country's larger efforts around its 150th year of Confederation.

Stories of notable Canadians who have dedicated their lives to the pursuit of peace are well documented, but we wanted to hear the personal stories, the more intimate reflections, experiences, struggles and triumphs that make up this journey towards the culture of peace we are collectively building.

Thus began the process of gathering the stories, forming an independent review committee, choosing the stories and, finally, editing and publishing them.

We kept the definition of peace as broad as possible, and welcomed variety in perspectives and voices. Our core criteria was that the story be true, and concise. We welcomed poetry, essays, letters and personal notes.

What you see in this book are the efforts of those men, women and children who took a moment to share with us a personal experience and what peace means to them. They come from varied walks of life and diverse political, social and cultural backgrounds.

Some stories reflect the struggle to find inner peace. Others reveal individuals willing to risk their lives to bring about peaceful solutions. Many are written by those who have lived in conflict areas, including those courageous Canadians who have dedicated their lives to being on the front lines to ensure peace is maintained. We see on-the-ground experiences of what means to work in international development, and contribute to the social and economic structures that form the foundations of peaceful existence within, and among, nations.

Finally, there are stories written by young children who, in few words, capture the essence of peace.

Weaving them together into a beautiful tapestry is the thread of authenticity, words spoken from the heart. Like a diamond, each story reveals a facet of peace and stands complete in its own right. Collectively, they shine brilliantly.

We hope these stories inspire you to think differently, show you a way towards peaceful resolutions, provoke you into action, and perhaps even bring a smile to your face. Above all else, we hope they leave you reflecting on what peace means to you and how you can be its agent in the world.

Peace is not for the weak, as advocates of war may suggest, but truly for the courageous of mind, heart and spirit.

It's been said that you can't hate people once you've heard their stories. Whether or not that's true, what cannot be denied is that stories give us the sacred space to reflect on who we are as individuals and on the fabric of the society we wish to weave. Stories have the power not only to inspire and unite, but to heal divisions and transform hearts and minds. They unite us in our search for a common humanity, crossing boundaries and going straight to the deepest place of truth that dwells within us.

We are grateful to be doing our part to bring this vision of peace to life.

The Planning Committee
Gordon Breedyk, Mony Dojeiji, Koozma J. Tarasoff, Evelyn Voigt

Note from the Editors

First, we wish to acknowledge and thank all the individuals who submitted their stories and gave us their permission to publish them.

The views expressed are those of the authors.

In order to conserve the integrity and tone of each story, we chose to keep editing to a minimum. We added commas, fixed basic grammatical errors, but on the whole, kept the story in the words of its author.

For French-language submissions, we reached out to francophone colleagues to support us in our editing efforts.

Some stories were submitted by Selection Committee members, in which case they recused themselves and allowed other members of the Committee to evaluate and decide the story's fate.

The stories in this anthology are purposely not grouped by theme, in part because most stories fall into more than one category, enriching the experience of reading them without strictures. However, we have included an index at the end of the book that places the stories into seventeen categories. These include Restorative Justice, the Environment, First Nations, Inner Peace, the Arts and many more. We have also included an alphabetical list, by title.

We decided to begin and end this anthology with the voices of Canada's indigenous people and its youth. The call to reflect on, and heal, our past shows us the way towars a future of peace, led by our children.

Although what you see in this collection are the 150 stories chosen by the review committee, it is important to stress that there is not one story that is more valuable than another. It is for this reason that we are making available on our website www.150CanadianPeaceStories.com ALL the stories that were submitted. We hope you enjoy them, and please, continue submitting your stories to 150peacestories@gmail.com to add to the site.

Finally, this project wouldn't be possible without the efforts of our Selection Committee who devoted time, energy and passion to this effort. Our thanks go to Jim Carmichael, Varavadi Monaghan, Yves Morneau, Jamie Swift and group facilitator Harry Monaghan. Thanks also to "eagle-eye" Agnes Cassellman.

Gordon, Mony, Koozma, Evelyn

The Stories

Red Stone Snake Woman

We all at some point in our lives come to a fork in the road, where we are called to make a choice. Every day a more urgent Grandfather Sun greets us than the day before, as it is the time of the 8th fire prophecy. A decision must be made: we can continue on this road of chaos or we can choose the path of peace. I am *Mihko-Asiniy*-Ginebik-*Iskwew*, *Omushkegowuk* from Moose Cree First Nation although I now reside in Ottawa, the unceded territory of the Algonquins. I am an advocate and educator on truth and reconciliation.

As a youth, I quickly discovered deep seeded racism toward Indigenous people in this country, and was heartbroken by the stereotypes and accusations. I was defensive for the suffering of my people and the destruction to our beautiful culture, and dedicated my education to better understand Indigenous issues, such as residential schools. Learning more about this part of Canadian identity shattered parts of me that I did not know could be broken.

You see, when my ancestors were no longer needed in this country for the fur trade or as military allies, and were outnumbered by settlers who needed land, we were seen as "impediments to Canadian progress", as Indigenous versus Western ideas on how you treat the Earth are very different. And because Canadian leaders did not feel like they were making enough headway with our elders, it decided to target our most vulnerable.

While Canada was in the process of confederation, it was also stealing Indigenous children from their parents, forcing them to live in boarding schools created to destroy the Spirit of the Indian. Love and wellbeing were replaced with trauma and shame, and the "kill the Indian, save the man" mentality at these schools was horrific and often killed more than just the Spirit, and took the lives of thousands.

These schools existed until 1996, and leaders in this country have tried to keep this a secret, so our suffering is compounded by a country that does not acknowledge this part of our collective Canadian story.

And this ignorance continues to feed misconceptions, and inhibits us from doing the work we need to do as a country to heal. I work in the field of child welfare, and half the youth in care are Indigenous because of this legacy, and the current systemic racism that puts our most vulnerable at a disadvantage. We are meant to raise our children, to relate, connect, love, and nurture them, and to receive their love as well. It is the essence of the human experience.

How can a parent or child find peace when forced to live with such pain?

I have learned to allow this pain to ignite in me a fire for a torch worth its weight in carrying. A torch lighting the way for reconciliation and peace in this Nation. It is time to inherit the beautiful parts of who we are culturally and spiritually.

In this journey of healing, I received my Spirit name, which is the name Creator has for us, and the path he intended for us to walk. As Red Stone Snake Woman, I have been called to represent the sacred hoop of life, and so part of my purpose here is to guide others to reconnect with our Earth and our interconnection to each other. I aim to bridge relationships so we can gather together in unity. I aim to facilitate the understanding and compassion needed for us to come together because there is still so much ignorance, racism, anger and hurt out there creating walls that must be broken down.

Red Stone means I am strong, and when I am on stage knees shaking and voice trembling as I speak of our suffering, I am reminded that it is in embracing these moments of vulnerability that may make us feel weak, that is in fact a strength. We all must make a choice where we step out of our comfort zones, and step up and do what is right. It is the path of the Rainbow Warriors, where we all come together in harmony.

If this country indeed stands for peace, then we must all gather in compassion to protect our most precious resources, and that is our beautiful Mother Earth and our most beloved children. And we must gather now.

All My Relations. *Gitchi-Meegwetch.*

By: Jenny Sutherland M.S.W., R.S.W., Indigenous Treatment Program Coordinator, Connor Homes.

Nature is my Peace

I love Canada...

It is a peaceful country. I find Canada peaceful because you don't have to worry when you step out of your house that there is danger outside. Also, there is no war in our country. Another part of what makes Canada a peaceful place is that there is a lot of free space with no homes or buildings, so the animals get to live in peace without being disturbed.

When I am at home, I find my peace by getting outside. I also feel peaceful when I spend time with my family. We get to play board games and watch movies together. My parents seem happy and relaxed. We all enjoy spending time together away from work and school.

This summer, I explored the peace and beauty in the nature of Canada. I felt most at peace when I was swimming and going on hikes with my family. I enjoyed these hikes because I got to see the lovely nature of Canada with my own eyes and ears. When I am in nature, I feel happy and I let go of all my worries. I love hearing the sounds of animals. I feel brave and strong when I climb the rocks and trees. It makes me feel more positive about myself and my abilities.

My wish is for people to stop hurting nature and to start appreciating it. Some people may not realize that nature can bring them peace as well. I want everyone to have the chance to enjoy nature and find their peace. This will help to make our world a better place.

By: Kyla McDowell, Age 9

The Banana Tree Case

The conflict was between two neighbors in Sri Lanka, whose houses and land were separated by a live tree fence. A dispute arose when a neighbour with a kitchen compound started to dump all her kitchen waste and other garbage into Chandra's garden space. Several complaints by Chandra brought only temporary relief, after which the routine would start again. Chandra finally got fed up with all the quarrels, but was very cautious not to involve their men folk. After much thought, a fine idea stuck to her mind one day.

On her way back from the market, she bought a banana plant and planted it in her home garden space where the neighbor would dump her garbage. Now, whenever garbage was dumped Chandra would carefully space out the garbage so that it turned into compost for her banana plant. Day by day she would do this and keep watching the banana plant growing healthy and strong. She was so happy to see that banana tree growing tall and, one fine day, she saw the buds forming. She was excited and could not wait until the fruit started growing.

After a period of seven months she saw bananas on her tree. She could not wait until it matured and ripened. Finally, when she found out that it was the time to bring down the bunch of bananas, she sought her husband's help. She very carefully cut the bananas and separated the good half, nicely packed them into a box and took them to the neighbor who dumped garbage into her home garden compound.

When Chandra with a broad smile offered the bananas, the neighbor was surprised and asked "why this is?" Chandra. even with a broad smile, said, "If not for your help I would not have grown the banana tree that gave these fruits. All the compost that went into the growth of the tree was the garbage that you put into my home garden compound. I have brought half of the first harvest to you in appreciation of your cooperation and to say thank you for your help."

The neighbor was in tears. She embraced Chandra and hugged her. She apologized for what she had done and promised not to do so in the future. It was the end of a conflict that led to a strong neighborhood relationship. These two are now in leadership roles in the township in negotiating in other people's conflicts and providing advisory services.

This example is now being shared by many social activists and government officials, all thanks to an initial workshop by SAMADANA/M (the Centre for promoting Nonviolent Conflict Resolution, Peace Building, Conflict Handling and Human Rights). SAMADANA/M was funded by the Canadian International Development Agency in its initial stage to build the capacity of SAMADANA/M when we were struggling to establish ourselves on firm ground. If not for that and other funding, SAMADANA/M would not be in existence today.

Since 1993, it has conducted training programmes, workshops on Conflict Resolution and Handling nonviolent methods and skills in various parts of Sri Lanka, as well as different types of action oriented activities that promote reconciliation, national integration and harmony.

Normally, our training ends up with follow-up activities that would be evaluated and assessed at the follow-up workshops or trainings. This particular training workshop, in Ambantota town concluded with follow-up assignments. One was to identify existing conflicts in the area and to employ some of the learnings to bring the conflict towards a win-win solution.

Nine months later, at a follow-up assessment and a feedback meeting, one of the many report cases was the particularly innovative and creative Banana Tree example mentioned above.

By: Dr. Muzzammil Cader, Moderator/Executive Director, SAMADANA/M, Chairperson, Zonal Task Force - Central Province, Consultation Task Force on Reconciliation Mechanism.

Water Flows Downhill

I am an anti-social old biddy who lives in idyllic tranquillity on a hill at the foot of Mont St Hilaire.

Monsieur V and his wife, a respectable retired couple, built their house next to mine about twenty years ago. Their property begins downhill from my studio. Monsieur V spends most of his waking hours tirelessly adjusting stones, weeding, mowing, renovating and building in his garden. Madame V seldom leaves the house. It seems that she has a great fear of cats of which there are an over-abundance in the neighbourhood. I have never seen either one of them take a walk.

Until the ice storm of 1998 brought it down, a large weeping willow that stood behind my studio.

It must have absorbed a lot of water because I think it was shortly after its demise that V approached me with his complaint that this property was leaking too much water onto his. He asked that I have a concrete channel built along the border to take the water to the road.

I didn't see how it was my responsibility, there was no water visible, and the cost of such a project was more than I could afford anyway. I declined as politely as I could.

A few years went by. Our relations remained polite but distant.

This year, when the snow melt was followed by a very wet spring, I walked into the studio one morning to find a wall of sand bags placed on my side of "the Border".

I thought I would wait a week or two to see if "the Wall" would come down of its own accord, when the ground dried out a bit.

It didn't.

Now, all my adult life, I have been a passionate advocate of peace, so I thought I should try practicing what I preach.

First I "opened a diplomatic channel". I went over to his house and asked him if he would please remove the bags from my property as the ground was drier now. He refused and asked me once again to pay for a viaduct. I did not lose my temper, but just told him I was sorry he was having this trouble.

The next day, I walked down to the municipal town hall and enquired of a clerk what the regulations say about water run-off.

Armed with this by-law, which clearly states that water does indeed tend to flow downhill unaided and life on a mountain can get damp, I came home to find "the Wall" still in place.

My feeling was that it would be better not to wave this paper under his nose in triumph. So I wrote a note to the effect that I was going to plant another weeping willow to replace the fallen tree, plant a thirsty bush and plants along "the Border", in the hope that this would help his problem. I included this note with the by-law and put the envelope in his mailbox.

The next morning "the Wall" had disappeared.

Life is once more tranquil and the garden outside my studio window looks very nice.

By: Ingrid Style

Akwesasne Community Mediates Peace & Ends Deep-Rooted Civil Strife (1990-1992)

"Is Everyone at the Table?" When the world is no longer under your feet, all you have left to stand on is what you stood for.

In1989, the people of the Mohawk territory of Kanesatake were outraged to learn that the neighbouring town of Oka, Quebec planned to expand a golf course onto land the Mohawks considered their sacred burial ground. After trying for a year to stop the golf course expansion through the courts, the Mohawks barricaded the land. In late April 1990, as the nation waited for the next chapter at Oka to unfold, 90 minutes away in the Mohawk territory of Akwesasne the long-simmering internal strife had boiled over, touched off by a gaming licence on the American side of the territory.

During five days of violence that some likened to a civil war, two young Mohawk men were killed. The Canadian side of Akwesasne was evacuated to Cornwall, Ontario, and approximately 900 police officers descended on Akwesasne to attempt to restore order. Akwesasne had always been very complex politically, divided by the Canada-U.S. border, split into numerous different factions, and governed by three separate bodies: the elected Mohawk Council for Akwesasne (MCA) on the Canadian side, an elected tribal council on the U.S. side, and the self-governing traditional Longhouse chiefs. Following the evacuation, I was invited to meet with the grand chief and other leaders in an attempt to mediate a solution.

Thus begins Chapter 1 of my book, "Is Everyone at the Table? 18 Life Lessons in Problem Solving". Mohawk Elders gave me permission to write my stories after 18 years so that one generation could grow from wartime with the peacemaking seeds planted during 1990-1992.

During initial discussions with MCA, I discovered that every major Alternative Dispute Resolution (ADR) organization in North America was interested in providing services. At the time, I was co-founder and Executive Director of the Ottawa Canadian Institute for Conflict Resolution. It was selected as the conflict resolution consultant with me "on the ground." The foundation of their training today is from Mohawk teachings on community-based conflict resolution approaches. Two years of consultation led to Akwesasne creating its own precedent community-based mediation centre, Sken

Nen Kowa - Organization for Great Peace, with Joellene Adams selected by the community as Executive Director.

Traditional teachings, combined with the principles of ADR and conflict resolution, seemed to give the Mohawk leadership the endurance they needed to survive the destabilizing forces. After months of negotiations the various factions finally gathered for their first meeting to discuss implementing a rumour control system to reduce the violence within the community. This was an idea from my colleague Tom Colosi to prevent the process from being disrupted by destabilizing forces, troublemakers, misunderstandings, or inadvertent information.

Each faction, and each police force, would designate a representative. Before anyone acted on information circulating in the community they would check it out with the other representatives and the police to be sure the situation was not worsened by incorrect information, gossip or false rumours planted to stir up trouble. This system did help with conflict prevention and maintenance. It was also a unique way to build on the common ground that we had identified at the beginning of the process: ensuring a better future for the next seven generations.

A leader of the Warrior Society later told me that he believed success had been possible because, for the first time in 100 years, the Mohawks in Akwesasne had been given the opportunity to do something by and for themselves. An Akwesasne Mohawk Chief at the Oka Crisis said, "The Creator gave ADR to the western mind in order to heal with all other communities and cultures in the world."

I believe the Akwesasne mediation centre is a process design model for the world, "not for what they did which is unique to their people and territory"; but, "for the process on how they did it". The former is 'distinct', the latter is 'universal'. My personal and professional problem-solving toolbox expanded in ways I could not have imagined. Ancient and spiritual teachings, traditional dispute resolution, and wisdom from Mohawk Elders and community underpin the innumerable cases settled and my views.

By: Ernest G. Tannis, President, Global ADR Strategies
Doreen Kahalé (Editor)

Femmes au Cœur du Développement et de la Paix

En 2017, la campagne de Développement et Paix avait pour thème : Les femmes au cœur du changement. Je veux à cette occasion célébrer ces femmes championnes de la justice sociale et de la paix au sein de leur famille et de leur communauté. Ce sont elles qui travaillent pour la dignité humaine, le bien commun, la subsidiarité et la solidarité, les quatre principes de la justice sociale. Je voudrais partager avec vous quelques souvenirs qui me reviennent aujourd'hui de ces femmes courageuses que j'ai vues et côtoyées dans différents pays africains où j'ai voyagé et vécu durant 40 ans.

En Zambie, j'étais en attente de leaders d'une association avec qui je devais avoir une réunion. Je m'étais assis à l'ombre d'un manguier. Tout près, il avait une vieille grand-maman entourée de petits enfants du village qu'elle surveillait pendant que les parents étaient aux champs. C'était tout un enseignement qu'elle leur prodiguait à travers des histoires et des proverbes qui avaient trait à la vie au sein du village. Elle était la gardienne de la tradition.

Un autre jour, je circulais à bicyclette à travers des villages en milieu rural. Je suis arrivé au moment où une villageoise venait de tuer seule, un mamba noir, un serpent très mortel. Que de risques pour sa vie elle venait de prendre pour la protection des habitants de son village. Même mort, long de plus de deux mètres, ce serpent m'inspirait la crainte.

En Tanzanie, en mai 1986, des politiques gouvernementales incompréhensibles avaient fait qu'il était difficile de trouver des produits frais à Dar-es-Salaam. Dès que ces règlements ont été révoqués, des femmes ont animé des marchés dans la capitale tanzanienne en s'assurant de faire venir fruits et légumes de partout à travers le pays, résultats du travail de centaines de milliers de femmes, mères nourricières de la nation.

Quel bonheur de fréquenter ces marchés avec ces pyramides de fruits de toutes couleurs où les marchandes, vêtus de pagnes multicolores souriaient à pleines dents.

Un matin, très tôt, alors que je voyageais dans le nord de la Tanzanie, j'ai été confronté à une scène déplorable: un groupe de femmes et de fillettes qui puisaient l'eau souillée à même les cratères dans la route boueuse. Les hommes autour de moi semblaient tout à fait insensibles devant ce qu'ils voyaient. J'ai réussi à convaincre mes supérieurs de dégager des fonds pour construire un pipe-line pour amener l'eau du mont Hanang aux différents villages dans la plaine. Bonheur pour les femmes...

Au Bénin, en1996, l'école primaire est devenue gratuite pour les filles. Quel spectacle que ces petites filles, le long des routes en marche vers l'école, fières et vêtues de leur uniforme impeccable, sac d'école à l'épaule. Plus tard, Lise et moi avons eu l'occasion d'assister à la graduation de groupes de femmes qui avaient suivi des cours d'alphabétisation et s'étaient initiées au micro-crédit.

Des femmes à qui on avait donné l'opportunité de devenir des entrepreneures. Elles ont pu éventuellement alphabétiser leurs maris et contribuer à améliorer la vie de leurs familles et du village tout entier.

J'espère que ces quelques souvenirs pourront démontrer que le développement de l'Afrique passe nécessairement par les femmes et qu'il faut les aider, afin de créer des situations de paix et sécurité.

By: Yves Morneau, professionnel de la paix, CPSC
www.civilianpeaceservice.ca

1996 Peace Work: Chugging Along

In October of 1996, Canada had set up an international meeting of governments to discuss a landmine ban. There were no firm strings attached although there was broad agreement that the weapon caused large numbers of civilian casualties long after conflicts had ended. Even the United States sent a representative to Ottawa in 1996.

Civil society people were invited to attend and I went with UN Association branch member Diana Armour. The main event was at the old Union Train Station across from the Chateau Laurier, transformed into the Conference Centre. It was an impressive venue, several winding stairways, dark wood and marble, a closed underground passageway to the Chateau.

Government delegates collected around a long table in the Hall surrounded by those in theatre seating. Diana and I sat up high, just behind the Egyptian delegation, looking down from the back. The closing meeting rolled on. Words, not deeds. Lloyd Axworthy took over at the microphone.

Then, a remarkable thing happened. He declared, without agreement from attending foreign delegates, that Canada was calling on states to return to Ottawa in a year to sign a new treaty banning anti-personnel mines.

There was a short silence - a gasp? - and then all around, people started applauding loudly and getting to their feet. It was obvious that the support was spotty because there were large blocks of people, including those at the table, still sitting.

I looked at Diana. "Did you hear what I heard?" We stood and cheered but we were as surprised as most everyone.

We learned later that key members of the International Campaign to Ban Landmines had been told privately by the Canadian delegation that the Foreign Minister was going for a new treaty. So get ready for it! (The Egyptians weren't ready either; they weren't standing, and still haven't signed the treaty.)

It would turn out that the landmine effort by Canada was one of several progressive initiatives of that era - "human security", the International Criminal Court, a child soldiers protocol, the responsibility to protect doctrine to prevent genocide and major war crimes. Later would follow the cluster munitions convention that came out of the Ottawa Treaty critique of weapons triggered by civilians. Axworthy also made a gallant effort to pressure NATO members to drop the nuclear weapons component of the alliance's strategic concept. For that, Canada became known as the "nuclear nag".

For all of this effort, you need pesky civil society activists to keep pushing, but you also need a friendly government and a leader within ready to take risks. Much of the dramatic shift in foreign policy was possible because of the end of the Cold War, but practically speaking, it started in a train station in Ottawa.

A colleague was visiting from out of Canada a few years ago, and I pointed out the building where the Ottawa Treaty started. He was thrilled, and insisted I take a picture of him with the façade in behind. He wanted to share a piece of our history too.

By: Robin Collins, Chair of the Group of 78's Working Group on Nuclear Disarmament and Arms Control, Secretary of the Board for the World Federalist Movement – Canada, and former Chair of Mines Action Canada (1998-2002).

Marking Time

The boy swings back and forth,
a pendulum marking time,
as his lungs synchronized with air
inaugurate an arc of song.

His hands grasp rough bark,
the limb of a pomegranate tree
barren as the land

behind him. Up a steep incline
shards of askew rocks
mark the graves of Afghans
slaughtered over years
of conflict. Here and there,

red cloth, worn by the veneration
of wind, oscillates from poles
bleached white as the bones
of martyrs ensconced
below. The boy's feet

against the fixed point of trunk
push him back into the space
that takes on the contour
of his supple body. To and fro,

to and fro, denoted by his innate rhythm,
by the instinctive delight in his voice,
he flies past the scarred landscape,
toward that opening, his future.

By: Blaine Marchand, award winning poet, author and program
manager.

An Intellectual Peace

Peace has many components both physical and mental. Canadians do not have war-torn villages, minefields or the like, to remind us of the physical aspects of war. My sense of peace, and that of many Canadians I'm sure, involves the non-physical elements of freedom of speech and freedom of thought, two of the basic pillars of peace around which, currently, a largely unrecognised war appears to be raging.

History tells us that the objective of war has rarely been peace. Expansion of power, more land, independence from oppression, food supply, religion, family quarrels, moral imperatives, and now eradication of terrorism, all have caused or been the excuse for war.

On the political level, nations are currently struggling to maintain or achieve peace, in the focus on the production, use, prevention of use, and destruction of nuclear weapons.

But while our national attention is focused on these admittedly important issues, we have seemingly lost sight of threats to what has made Canada and other western cultures so desirable to immigrants like myself.

I have during my life woken each day in the happy knowledge that my thoughts and feelings are free, untrammeled and open for discussion. This is my mental peace. It is in a way dependent upon my physical peace; that is, freedom to walk about freely, to have my family sleep at night safe from violence, to have my grandson play safely in a park, to carry out mundane tasks free from threat.

This safety has been achieved through the slow accretion of social, spiritual and cultural norms, not only during the last 150 years, but since settlers began structuring their lives in the New World.

This has not been without strife, but it has seen increasingly open discussion addressing solutions to strife. We see this as a process that will continue, in which Canada moves towards a state not unlike the Garden of Eden, where everyone lives in harmony.

But let us not forget who was the final arbiter of the rules in that garden.

What I am witnessing today is the appearance of a new arbiter in the garden, an inversion of the traditional dictatorships of the past where power was grabbed from the people by a powerful elite, to a new paradigm in which the people cede their independence, unwittingly, to a new form of thought-government.

This is the information technology equivalent of nuclear warheads. This is the era of the sheep or lemming wars, where social media gives the impression of freedom of expression for all.

Social media is like the overloaded passenger ship where everyone runs to one side to see the whale, resulting in the inevitable sinking of the ship. Social media owners are already beginning to censor content in the name of the public good, unfortunately with general public approbation.

Extreme or hate speech may not easily be defined or recognized for what it is, but should the new arbiters in the garden be our new moral guides? Are the adverts that pay for free social media availability becoming our new bible?

If your morning skies are still blue you may not bother checking the weather forecast. If you see the emerging clouds on the horizon, find out what this portends. Will it be a shower or a flood?

Here's the paradox – if you want your personal peace to continue, you may have to fight for it.

But the fight is with thoughts and words – free speech and ideas. That is what WWI and WWII were ultimately about. Let us not end up in a new-style WWIII because we thought appeasement was a weapon.

By: Harry Monaghan

Arriving at Consensus – Peaceful Productivity

Imagine twenty passionate and dedicated nurses from CVAA, Canadian Vascular Access Association, in a conference room for one beautiful weekend in Ottawa.

Their mission? To come to group consensus on hundreds of clinical best practice guidelines that they had drafted in pairs, to be applied to healthcare, Canada-wide.

Weeks before, when I was approached to help the group, I had asked the leader, "Why are you engaging a facilitator for your workshop?" The answer was typical, "There are some powerful personalities with strong opinions so we expect there could be some heated discussions". Wonderful! Passion ... caring ... dedication ... let's do it, let's create peaceful productivity!

Setting up the workshop for success involved planning with the leadership team on two aspects: (1) Tangible: clearly articulate attainable objectives and design processes to achieve them; and (2) Intangible: create an environment where participants feel safe to speak their mind and are open to hear and understand each other's perspectives.

Starting with objectives, the common ground on which to build peace, I asked the leaders, "What does consensus mean to you?" They responded, "Maybe 75%?" I asked, "What about the other 25%? What will happen in implementation if ¼ of your group don't agree with a particular guideline?"

I shared my definition of consensus: Everyone can live with it and will support it outside the room.

They were incredulous, "Impossible! How?"

We decided to use green, yellow and red cards that participants held up after the reading of every guideline. I explained that red cards are gifts: "There is something that needs to be changed or a question I need to ask before I can support it".

When a red card appeared, it was an opportunity to open everyone's mind to see a little broader. I asked, "What gift do you have for us?" Often it was something simple that only one person saw, or a situation unknown to the rest of the room, that required a change.

I then asked for another poll, until all the cards were either green, "perfect", or yellow, "I can live with it and will support it outside this room", group consensus. There were some guidelines that were a little more complex or challenging and we persisted through the process, systematically creating consensus while maintaining an environment of harmony and peace.

What about the intangibles? Creating a safe, peaceful working environment started with clear communications about the objectives and agenda. As participants arrived, they saw a room set up in five round tables of four, instead of a board room table. After introductions, the group co-created Rules of Engagement, which they embraced using the consensus cards. Their rules included "seek to understand", a cornerstone to peaceful productivity.

By the end of the weekend, they had achieved consensus on guidelines with peace and harmony, more than they expected. They learned valuable processes and developed a level of trust and understanding that allowed them to continue their work via teleconference, an idea that they had previously found too difficult to imagine possible.

These special nurses continued to volunteer their time to achieve group consensus on the remaining guidelines, in the peaceful and productive atmosphere that was created that first weekend in Ottawa.

By: Cille Harris, retired engineer, Out Living the Dream with her husband Rob. (www.ra.ca).

A Most Glorious Journey
(How I Became a Peacenik)

To honour the people who have taught me to live by peaceful means and more recently to lead through a lens of peace.

Peace to me is love lived. Since a young age I felt deeply, as I imagine all children do, the harsh, cruel words, the violent emotions and actions, in contrast to the joyful loving moments, the dedicated work that my family undertook to provide us with our needs. I was hurt by the tears and desperation that we expressed with no resolution being achieved. We just endured and were compelled to meet each day's tasks.

Much later in my life I could begin to connect to my family members in a meaningful way and to reconcile some of the hurts. In reflection, I assume these challenges created radar in me for conflict and how it is resolved.

I was often in conflict in school consistently the one having a different view on things, challenging authorities with what I perceived as injustice. I was criticized and disciplined for my views and belligerent behaviour, often called an idealist and bold and brash. I didn't even know what I was looking for so how could I know what to ask for of people.

I am sure no one thought I was open to learning but I was soaking up what people said and did in regard to the conflict at hand. I noted what worked to make things better and what made things worse for the people involved. I unconsciously tested each limit for resiliency and integrity.

It has been a long journey and I am thankful to all my teachers who showed me what heals the hurt generated or expressed by many conflicts. Now I am a senior. I have lived through relationships and institutions, pushing limits, continuing to verbally challenge and often feeling a lack of belonging.

Yet, there are two groups who at first meeting I knew I had found what I was looking for.

The Society of Friends (Quakers) taught about a loving simple God who created us to love all of Creation unlike other faith communities, ideologies or peace groups I explored that used divisive dogma and life instructions based on fear. I was searching for peaceful ways to live. Quakers had found it by Stop killing, Love all beings, Listen deeply to the voice of God in our own hearts.

My second source of evolution came through a note in my email suggesting Canada needed a Department of Peace. While this news felt like water to a shriveling soul there was no space in my life to do anything about it.

Then one day a dear friend sent me an email saying someone was speaking on a Department of Peace in our neighborhood. Bill Bhaneja spoke about this group that had formed in Victoria BC to begin a campaign for a Department of Peace. I have been a member for eleven years since that first meeting.

What have I learned? One day at a Canadian Peace Initiative meeting we reflected on our challenges that seemed much larger than our achievements. I shared with them that I appreciated them and my Quaker community for a deep personal reason. I explained that in the life circumstances I face I start from a familiar emotional behavioural place.

Yet my teachers, and especially my two communities, continue to show me the essence of nonviolence for myself and others that does not deny pain, requires a creative heart and always Love. Regardless of our tasks, that inspires me to continue participating.

I am truly thankful for the individuals and communities who have shown me through positive and negative examples how to live through Love. I live free to be who I am and am committed to pass this gift on to others.

By: Theresa Dunn

A Veteran's Thoughts about Vimy Ridge

Vimy Ridge has been in the news continuously for many days, remembering the 3600 Canadian soldiers who were killed in three days in a battle on that ridge in France in World War I, 100 years ago.

We have built a beautiful monument in remembrance of the soldiers who lost their lives in that unfortunate conflict.

However, I can't help but wonder whether, by putting so much emphasis on this event, by mentioning, repeating and being proud of our military successes, or by seeing war as a means of finding the identity of our country, we are actually glorifying war itself.

When speakers at the remembrance ceremony propound that 'our men' laid down their lives that we can live in freedom or a member of the royalty of a 'colonial' power suggests that those who died were 'fighting against oppression,' one wonders whom they are actually talking about. Who was threatening our freedom and who was oppressing whom during the time of WWI?

Would we honour those who died in that battle more if we quietly remember them, the great loss their death caused to their families, without making so many 'exclamations' about it?

Wars are terrible. The American general Sherman is quoted to have said 'I am sick and tired of killing, war is hell'.

My father was in the medical corps in WWI. He hardly ever spoke about the horrors of that war, but it affected him for some time in his life and led to PTSD, which later may have been a cause for his suicide.

I was not alive during World War One but I am a veteran of World War Two and was conscripted to fight on the Russian Front.

I, and I think many other veterans, would not like to be remembered in such a 'pronounced' way.

All soldiers, no matter from which country, were trained and ordered to kill and they did so.

However, it is not easy, even for a soldier, to kill another human being whom he does not know, just because he wears another uniform.

Are we really heroes for killing each other?

Historically, Canada had a noteworthy way of remembering the ones who died in recent wars. They were asking the still surviving veterans of WWII and other wars, if they would be willing to share their war experiences with a generation of high school students. The students wanted to know what war was really like, after they had studied it in their classroom.

I was invited to several schools and tried to take the listeners with me through a day on the front lines. They were very attentive and involved, which I observed from the thoughtful questions they asked.

A teacher who had invited me to her school wrote to the Historical Canada Memory Project organizer:

"The first-hand accounts of his experience as a soldier on the front allowed us an incomparable and invaluable view into the effects of war on real individuals and their families. ...his visit far exceeds that of any textbook or film I could have offered my students leading up to Remembrance Day this year."

I hope that my experience will encourage these young people to promote and work for peace.

By: Helmut Lemke, Burnaby B.C., member of Point Grey Inter-Mennonite Fellowship, Vancouver.

A Pilgrim for Peace

When I began my 5000-km pilgrimage, I had grand ideas for how I would bring peace to Jerusalem, a region dear to my heart.

I was born and raised in Canada, but my family's roots run deep in Lebanon. I grew up watching The National on CBC every night at 10:00pm, waiting for news that would indicate resolution of any form to the conflicts that plagued the region. I listened from the sidelines as men gathered in our small living room debating the latest happenings in the area, fascinated by the complexity of it all, the friend one day becoming foe the next.

I embraced without question this idea, popular at the time, that there could be no peace without justice. To me, that meant outer action, be it as demonstrations or non-violent resistance.

After 9/11, my pilgrimage fromRome to Jerusalem became my action for peace. I was going to walk to Jerusalem and I was going to call on Palestinians, Israelis and Arabs across all religious and political lines to join me in this Utopian walk for peace and, in one large demonstration, call for unity in a land divided.

I began walking alone in November of 2001, and was joined by a Spanish pilgrim. A deeply spiritual man – a bit of a modern mystic – Alberto would challenge my ideas and intentions for this walk. Sure he cared about peace, but he looked upon our pilgrimage as a quest to uncover our hidden beliefs and expectations and, in healing them, create inner peace.

I agreed with him, of course, but was intently focused on outer action.

"We need to tell people to work for peace in their communities and not wait for someone to create it for them," I insisted. "We need social activists, people creating bridges with those whose ideas differ from their own."

I spoke with great conviction about personal responsibility in creating peace with whomever I met, from Italy to the former Yugoslavia, Albania and Greece. Entering Turkey, and having now walked seven months, several encounters forced me to re-examine this inner aspect of peace.

I met individuals who lived in peaceful settings but who were deeply conflicted and hate-filled, speaking only of revenge and an eye-for-an-eye justice. I met others coming out of civil war, whose communities were still unstable, who spoke of reconciliation and whose hearts were filled with hope and optimism despite the atrocities they had lived through.

Could inner peace, despite the political or social climate, be the key to creating outer peace?

How could I work for agencies or create programs dedicated to reconciliation and peace when my own heart was divided? When I still held so much anger and resentment? When I saw certain groups as "right" and others as "wrong"? When I still had expectations of how peace should look like? What kind of peace was I bringing?

That became my true journey: peeling back those layers that, like a cloak, covered the peace within me, reconciling with my personal demons and standing in confident stillness in the peace that was emerging and entrenching within me.

No, I didn't have the massive peace march of my dreams when I arrived in Jerusalem thirteen months later. But I did have something infinitely more powerful: a roadmap for being peace in the world, which I carry with me to this day.

By: Mony Dojeiji, author, social entrepreneur and pilgrim (www.walkingforpeace.com).

An Excerpt from "Erratic North"

In March of 2003, the Dalai Lama said: "Today, the world is so small and so interdependent that the concept of war has become anachronistic, an outmoded approach. ... War ... should be relegated to the dustbin of history. Of course, the militaristic tradition may not end easily."

However, it is easy to convince people to go to war if you are first able to convince them that they have something to fear. The following appears in Gustave Gilbert's Nuremberg Diary and involves a conversation he had with Herman Goering during the Nuremberg trials. Goering was chief of the Gestapo and second only to Hitler during the Nazi regime.

"Why, of course, the people don't want war. Why would some poor slob on a farm want to risk his life in a war when the best that he can get out of it is to come back to his farm in one piece. Naturally, the common people don't want war; neither in Russia nor in England nor in America, nor for that matter, in Germany. That is understood. The people can always be brought to the bidding of the leaders. That is easy. All you have to do is tell them they are being attacked and denounce the pacifists for lack of patriotism and exposing the country to danger. It works the same way in any country."

Peace is not something that will come from the top down. It cannot come from governments, or the U.N., or religion, from political or social movements, or from anyone outside ourselves. It can only come from finding peace – the dissolution of fear – in each human heart. Peace on earth is intimately connected to peace of mind.

By: Mark Frutkin, award winning author of four books of poetry, three non-fiction works and eight novels.

The Painting for Peace

I walked into my Art class with my binder in hand and took my usual seat. My teacher had said last class that we'd be starting a new Art project, and it'd be our biggest assignment of the year. So I sat at my desk, anxiously waiting for what she had in store for us for the next few weeks.

It turned out our new project was called the Painting for Social Change assignment. We had to pick a recurring problem in our world that we felt strongly about and create a painting on its impact against humanity.

Once my Art teacher disclosed all the information on our project, I began to think. There were so many global problems that I was passionate about. There was poverty, war, politics— the list went on!

Yet as I let my mind wander, I discovered that I couldn't paint any of those issues in the way I'd like to. If I was going to pick a large problem in our world, I wanted to serve it justice on my canvas.

I pondered some more until it came to me.

Racism, my conscious told me. Do a painting on the racism that's been going on in our world. I had come up with an idea and I intended to stick with it.

The next few days were spent collecting images for my painting and finding a good message to convey. I wanted to show the racism that was currently happening, then have some quote or phrase to tell my classmates that we can all come together and promote peace.

The only problem was that I didn't have anything.

As I was gluing some more printed pictures onto my canvas, my mind went back to one of the days during Black History Month. We had sung Oh Canada, prayed, then the announcements came on. There was something that one of the announcers had closed off with on the intercom. The person had said that there was only one race and that was the human race.

Suddenly, the last piece of the puzzle came to me and I knew exactly what I wanted to do.

The time to reveal our paintings arrived and I lifted mine up with trembling fingers. My entire class stared at it either in curiosity or in awe. I looked back at each of my classmates with a small smile on my face.

I didn't know whether or not my painting had an effect on all 27 of the people in my class. However, I knew that all I really needed to do was change the perspective of one of them, and show that person the peace that isn't far away if we reach for it.

My painting could go on to change an entire school population, or maybe just a few people.

But those few people could go on to change the entire world. I glanced at my class one more time, and with that fact in mind, I smiled all the more brightly.

By: Shauna Ndoping.

Le dialogue, un outil de paix

J'imagine que l'on vous a souvent demandé: que voulez-vous faire dans la vie? À cette question, lorsque nous étions plus jeunes, Alain et moi répondions : « être acteur de paix ». Depuis, nous portons un rêve: celui de la paix, un être humain à la fois. Pourquoi cela? Parce que, comme vous, nous constatons combien le monde actuel s'enlise dans la violence des préjugés et, pis encore, dans celle des conflits armés dont les principales victimes sont des femmes et enfants. Comment vivre ici quand là-bas tant de gens souffrent ou meurent? Devant ces lourdes inégalités, nous avons cherché un chemin pouvant apaiser notre douleur intérieure et porter plus loin notre rêve de paix. Du coup, ce chemin s'est ouvert à nous: animer des processus de paix en République centrafricaine (RCA), un pays peu connu, dévasté par les conflits armés depuis la crise de 2013.

Voici notre histoire. Prêts à faire face à notre propre angoisse de travailler dans un contexte tendu, nous avons facilité cinq ateliers dans le but de promouvoir les méthodes de résolution des conflits axées sur le dialogue communautaire comme alternative à la violence. Offerts en collaboration avec l'Institut canadien pour la résolution des conflits (ICRC), ces ateliers s'inscrivaient dans les programmes de la réduction de la violence et de la préparation aux activités de désarmement, de démobilisation et de réintégration de la MINUSCA en RCA.

Au cours de ces ateliers, nous avons été témoins de changements d'attitudes et de comportements; des êtres meurtris par la guerre ont retrouvé la force de parler à nouveau; des ex-combattants ont vu poindre à l'horizon l'espoir de se pardonner. Plusieurs ont appris ou réappris à s'écouter plutôt qu'à juger ou à dominer. Les participants ont repris le dialogue pour imaginer une Centrafrique renouvelée. Ces ateliers ont été pour nous l'occasion d'accueillir la souffrance à la fois des victimes et des acteurs du conflit. Bien que les rôles des participants étaient différents, chacun avait sa place; c'était là notre engagement : une écoute en respectant l'histoire de chacun. Nous avons la conviction qu'une ouverture à l'autre porte le germe de la réconciliation.

Nous avons travaillé afin de lever le voile sur les racines profondes du conflit, liées à l'identité, dans le but d'engager une réflexion collective sur les alternatives à la force et à la violence. Les questions fusaient de toutes parts. C'est alors qu'ont commencé à émerger, sur le ton de la confidence et dans le respect, les perceptions que chacun avait de son pays à partir de sa propre histoire:

« *On sent la douleur de chaque participant. On veut voir la paix revenir en RCA.* »

« *Tout le monde en a marre de notre conflit.* »

Victimes et acteurs des conflits ont transformé leur expérience par une quête de conscience de soi, par la reconnaissance des besoins menacés et la recherche d'humanité en chacun comme si un mouvement collectif de bienveillance progressive les avait conviés à imaginer la RCA autrement. Certains leaders de groupes, au départ opposés les uns aux autres, se sont assis côte à côte, se sont parlé et se sont écoutés. Certains d'entre eux ont commenté:

« *Nous avons ouvert le chemin de la paix dans cet atelier.* »

« *J'ai changé mon comportement et désarmé mon cœur.* »

Nous avons observé une diminution de la tension et un sentiment renforcé d'unité centrafricaine. Un désir de réconciliation a clairement été exprimé et des gestes concrets ont été posés en ce sens dont celui de créer des comités de tierce partie neutre immédiatement après les ateliers. Pour nous, l'un des principaux acquis de la formation en est un d'humanisation des participants et de redéfinition même de leur identité pour certains, passant d'acteurs du conflit et d'ex-combattants à artisans de paix.

Par: Nicole Charron (Praticienne de la paix en collaboration avec l'ICRC) et Alain Paulin (Médiateur agréé).

Behind Those Eyes

During the '80s, I was an English teacher at a refugee camp, Panat Nikhom, Chonburi, Thailand. All refugees there were either Vietnamese, or minorities from Laos, who escaped from Communism in their own countries. Thailand wasn't their destination. Our Thai government had an agreement with the United Nations High Commission for Refugees (UNHCR) to prepare secured places, or 'camps', for them on the condition that they would finally be sent to another country, in this case, the U.S.A. Such 'camps' were all over Thailand, but my camp was the transit point. They would be 'made ready' here, before leaving for their final destination, the 'war free' home where they would be able to establish a peaceful life.

How did we do it? In a very systematic and well organized way. In the 6-month term known as a 'cycle', all adults would attend three types of training: English as a Second Language (ESL), Cultural Orientation (CO), and Work Orientation (WO). Children were put into a Preparation for American Study System (PASS) class, so that they could go to school immediately upon arrival in the U.S. They also had to attend the CO class, while a Learning Disability (LD) class was always there for those who needed it, young or not so young.

My 'students' were all adult hill tribes people: Hmong, Mien, and Lahu. They were, more or less, excited for the new life ahead, except for one. He was always quiet, his eyes often wandered out somewhere, and when caught not paying attention, he just guiltily looked down at the floor.

I had been wondering for a long time what was really hidden behind those eyes.

All of the staff knew that, to the students, the ESL teachers were 'angels'. Often in the CO class, especially when it came to culture shock lessons, we could always guarantee that many students, if not all, would run to us with fear, complaining that the CO teachers were so mean. Of course, they were mean. They had to play the part. The angels' job, then, was to give them comfort, and let them know it was just a simulation.

All my students, men or women, would often seek comfort with me, except for one. Didn't he need help too? I wondered.

One day, I bumped into him after class. I took a chance to greet him in Thai, though we weren't allowed to speak Thai to the students in the class, but this wasn't in the class, was it? He seemed more relaxed. After a little chit-chat, I found out that he was once in the Hmong army, trained by the US to fight the communists. He had nobody left – not even one.

"I can't be American", he said, "What should I do, teacher?"

That was it, I thought. That's what's hidden behind those eyes: confusion and suffering!

The first few seconds, I didn't know what to say. How could a 23 year old 'teacher' advise a 40 year old 'student'? But when I saw him looking at me with full respect and hope, I automatically said to him,

"Find peace in your heart first, then you'll find an answer to all questions in life."

I was stunned by my own words, and so was he! How could I say such a thing? Perhaps I felt his suffering? Or perhaps that's the way I was brought up as a Buddhist? Peace in your heart is the key, understanding the cause of your suffering is next, then solve it with your intellect, not emotion.

Many years later, I still occasionally received letters from students, telling me how their lives were in America. I was happy to know that they were happy too.

To my surprise, I received a letter from my 'wandering eyes' student. Unlike the others who got their letters written for them in perfect English, this one was written in his own handwriting. It read, "I carpenter now. I happy. I American. Thank you teacher, signed...."

Attached to the letter were two twenty-dollar bills. I guessed he'd like to show his gratitude to me. That letter really made my day! I didn't even know my tears were running down my face, but I knew for sure those eyes of his weren't wandering anymore.

By: Varavadi Monaghan (M.Ed, M.A.).

Books not Guns

In 1995, I was then working as Logistics Specialist for UNICEF in Uganda. The presence of the rebel group LRA (Lord Resistance Army) in northern Uganda was a challenge to International Humanitarian agencies. The LRA was engaged in armed conflict with Government forces in many parts of northern Uganda making it logistically difficult to deliver aid to the affected population.

We were on one such 'Humanitarian Mission' to distribute school text books in two primary schools in a rebel-held area. While going for such mission, we were required to take several security measures. The vehicle had to have 'UN' written in large letters bold enough to be visible from a distance. The bullet proof vehicle carried a UN and white flags to indicate the nature of our mission.

The driver was cautious and moved slowly while keeping a watchful eye on the road. Both sides of the road were overgrown elephant grass; who knew when a stray bullet from the bush could hit the vehicle.

We came to a military checkpoint. The driver slowed down. Soldiers at the checkpoint signaled us to stop.

One of them came forward and talked to the driver in a local language. Later we came to know the soldier was asking about our identity, destination and purpose of mission etc. etc. They asked the driver to open the rear door to check what we were carrying.

We saw a few 'Child Soldiers' in the group, carrying guns and staring at our vehicle with a blank look. Usually these children were abducted from different parts of the country. When they saw the vehicle loaded with text books, they just dropped their guns and ran for the books; picked up a few, started flipping and smelling the pages of the new books.

I have been short of words to describe the excitement we saw on their faces!

I felt their eyes were sending a message of peace to us saying 'we want books not guns!'

UNICEF, along with its International partners, was engaged in the rescue and re-unification of those abducted children with their families. I was involved in arranging supplies and logistics in the implementation of these programs; setting up temporary shelter, providing emergency household supplies, and primary health care medication to children until they were reunited with their loved ones.

The questions remain: why these children were carrying guns instead of books?

Why the armed conflict, abductions, violence, political instability in many countries in Africa had taken away the childhood of innocent children and pushed them into the deadly game of war?

By: Kiriti Pal Chowdhury, Supply & Logistics Manager (Retired) UNICEF (Kiritic@gmail.com).

Cosco Family Reunion 2017

The Cosco family reunion has been going on since 1969, every 5 years or so, in Sioux Lookout, Ontario, where 13 of the 14 children were born to Frank Cosco and three successive wives.

Papa entered Canada from Italy in 1898, and later brought over his first wife, Savaria and young son Peter, to establish the first grocery store in Sioux Lookout, Ontario.

Savaria birthed six more children, and when she died, Papa married Katy. My Mom was the first born to Katy, who looked after the children and birthed six children of her own until her premature death.

Papa married Frances who had one more child. It's a long and tough story of hardship and love.

Where is the peace story? The Cosco family is a peace story in itself.

From difficult beginnings, with strong personalities that led to conflict and lingering hard feelings, the original family drew compassion and peace from their faith to create the Cosco Family Reunion legacy that continues after 11/14 of the original family have passed, and 3/14 remaining are not able to attend.

The second generation recently stepped up to continue the legacy. Cousins and offspring came from far and wide and here we are, back again discussing the future and what is possible, in peace, harmony and love.

I've been to about half of the Cosco family reunions, getting here by car, plane, train and motorhome twice – once with our four sons and this year with my husband, Rob. Yes, it's an effort; over 24 hrs of driving from Ottawa, costly both in time and resources, and mentally/emotionally draining.

The rewards? Reconnecting and strengthening relationships with extended family from as far away as Hawaii, LA and BC, as well as Sioux Lookout and closer cities like Winnipeg.

This year is no exception. Three days of driving to be greeted by two dozen excited cousins and their offspring, which was just the beginning of four days of gathering, talking, laughing, crying, caring and loving.

What did we do? Lunches and dinners together, especially Italian night - making the pasta and sauce from scratch, and a pig roast on a spit, Mass, spirit walk in the cemetery, beaches, fishing, bonfires, shopping, golf, hike, auction, float plane rides and a family meeting to name a few of the activities.

I was moved in Mass with the words, "Peace be with you, and with you. Let us offer each other a sign of Peace".

After kissing my husband on my right, and my brother-in-law on my left, I turned around to see a dozen cousins' smiling faces.

I was, and still am, overwhelmed with gratitude for our relationships and our family.

By: Cille Harris, "Real Alternatives for Out Living the Dream!"

Co-operatives and Peace

Co-operatives were not intended as a tool to promote peace or reduce conflict, but in a world where international development is often taking place against a backdrop of conflict, or in post-conflict environments, co-operatives have proven to be a remarkably effective tool in promoting peace. In thinking about this, a couple of simple truths emerge. First – poverty and conflict are inextricably linked. Conflict often starts because of poverty, and conflict inevitably causes poverty. Co-operative development is all about finding long term solutions to poverty and that process, intentionally or unintentionally, reduces the frictions that cause conflict.

The second truth is that where people find a new common purpose, where they work together for the benefit of all, the tensions that linger long after a conflict ends are reduced. Conflict comes in many forms and under many guises – war between nations, war within nations, sectoral or religious strife within societies, and the insidious conflict that gender and other inequalities create within communities and families. In the words of Historian Ian MacPherson, "Human Beings have always been buffeted by conflict, the all-too-frequent extension of unrestrained competition."

In his view this leads to "inequality, discrimination, oppression, and the dark consequences of these behaviours – poverty, deprivation, underemployment and unemployment, despair and death." Conversely, the values that define and drive co-operatives and co-operation work in direct opposition to those "dark consequences" through a focus on the fair and equitable utilization and distribution of resources, a focused realization of human potential through collective action and mutual support.

For many co-operative leaders around the world, the idea that co-operatives and co-operation can be specifically used as tools in building and maintaining peace is still a relatively new idea. Most co-operatives are created for the practical purpose of generating income and improving livelihoods for their members. Yet there are many examples where co-operatives, through accident or design, have proven to be highly effective at all stages of conflict amelioration – from prevention, through to reduction of outright conflict, to the peace making and maintenance phase. Not surprisingly, this success has resulted in an increase in co-operatives as tools for peace. There are many examples to choose from.

In the Israel-Palestinian conflict – perhaps the most intractable on the planet-- co-operatives offer a glimmer of hope. For many years, Israeli co-operators have supported the Palestinian movement through training and market access. A recent example is a joint marketing venture called Co-operative Produce for Peace. Yhuda Paz, the Chairman of the Negev Institute for Strategies of Peace and Development, has promoted co-operatives as a tool for peace in the region for decades.

In Aceh, following 30 years of civil war, co-operatives were one of the first, and most successful, tools used to bring fractured communities together. It wasn't a fast process. First, a co-operative community radio station was created with support from the Canadian Co-operative Association (CCA) to open dialogue within the communities. At the same time, small agriculture or production groups were formed, eventually emerging as true co-operatives supported by a second-tier marking co-operative.

In northern Ghana, where a simmering land dispute would sporadically erupt into violence, the creation of a mutual agricultural co-operative finally brought peace bringing people together to work toward a new set of common, economic objectives.

In El Salvador, following that civil war, the thorny issue of agrarian reform was managed by redistributing land through co-operatives. And in Colombia, a country buffeted by political and narcotics related violence, co-operatives are helping farmers move away from conflict-prone coca production to other legal crops.

It would be misleading to suggest that co-operatives offer a solution to every conflict, but where groups in conflict share a common goal that can be best reached together, the co-operative model offers a set of guideposts that help to change the focus from the wrongs of the past to the possibilities of a peaceful future.

By: John Julian (revised from his Huffington Post article, 2012).

Discovering the Nonkilling Paradigm

One of the joys of acknowledging world citizenship and travelling abroad is the gems we find in getting to know the stranger. For me, an invitational trip in 2007 to Hawaii was an eye-opener about a unique way of looking at peace, peace-making, and nonviolence.

The gem was called nonkilling. Its proponent was my host Professor Glenn D. Paige, global political scientist, innovator, author of his seminal work Nonkilling Global Political Science (2002, 2009), followed by the establishment of a Center for Global Nonkilling in 2008 which was awarded Special Consultative Status with the UN Economic and Social Council in 2014.

As a Canadian peace activist, I discovered the nonkilling paradigm in Hawaii at the First International Leadership Forum of Nonkilling, attended by some 40 wisdom people from around the world.

My own contribution was a paper on Lev N. Tolstoy, the conscience of humanity. Tolstoy absolutely condemned all wars and influenced my ancestors the Spirit Wrestlers / Doukhobors to burn their guns in 1895; he also influenced Gandhi and Martin Luther King Jr. Glenn Paige used these and many other sources in developing a fresh approach to a new world order of loving and caring global citizens with a vision of nonkilling. It is this vision that I brought to Canada.

Nonkilling is the measure of human progress. Killing stops the progress, but when killing is stopped, human progress resumes. Reverence for life is fundamental to survival and continuity of humanity. Without nonkilling, everything else is meaningless whether we are talking about environment, poverty, health or security.

With a scientific bent, Paige sought precise formulations that could be examined, analyzed and tested. For him, peace, nonviolence and nonkilling were not interchangeable, although they were part of the same family. Nonkilling is measurable with zero killing being its ultimate goal. The nonkilling paradigm defines politics in a complete new way from the usual Hobbesian focus of politics on violence and state power.

As the WHO Report on Violence and Health (2002) concluded that 'violence is a preventable disease', so Glenn Paige discovered that 'nonkilling societies are possible'. What we need is new creative alternative institutions with life enhancing mandates and new cooperative ways of problem solving for realizing nonkilling societies. As with the international space station and the Genome successes, this may require a multinational concentrated effort of changing our ways and beliefs from lethality to non-lethality.

Perhaps the UN needs to reinvigorate its Peacekeeping Operations as part of its mandate to show nations how creative peacebuilding policies and programs can be introduced in the 21st century.

Since returning home from Hawaii, my colleagues and I have lobbied the Canadian government to establish a cabinet-level Department of Peace in Parliament. After two private member's bills, no action has followed. However, as the world order is threatened with nuclear suicide, a shift from nation-state to a global society is gradually emerging. There is a growing realization that survival of ourselves and our civilization urgently requires new thinking.

Thanks to my Hawaii trip and meeting wise people, the gift of nonkilling that I brought to Canada is a model for sustainable peace that is urgently needed in our fragile world. Let's hope that more wise people will take up the cause for the creation of a nonkilling society.

Koozma J. Tarasoff, anthropologist, ethnographer, historian, writer and peace activist. (kjtarasoff@gmail.com)

Dolls

A local newspaper article spoke to me. An Ottawa woman was looking for knitters to create small dolls for refugee children. This project was named after a Canadian soldier, Master Cpl. Mark (Izzy) Isfeld, who died in Croatia in 1994. His mother started knitting small dolls for the local children, as a legacy to her son. Once they heard about it, groups of knitters started contributing, as well. As I read about this, I thought to myself, "I can help."

I sent out a request on our condo's internal electronic bulletin board, asking if anyone would be interested in getting together to knit dolls for refugee children.

I was delighted with the enthusiastic response – some wanted to knit, some wanted to donate yarn, some wanted to donate money to buy yarn and stuffing.

An initial group of 10 or so ladies (no men yet) met at my place and I handed out downloaded instructions for Izzie Dolls. We knitted dolls. We drank tea and munched on cookies. Our members ranged in age from 59 to 89. Some of the ladies hadn't knitted in years, some very experienced, some had yet to learn. Others had arthritis in their aged and aching fingers.

No matter, we knitted. And knitted.

At the time, Canada was in the process of inviting as many Syrian refugees as logistically possible. It was the big headline story. For it or against it, everyone was talking about refugees coming. Talk was of finding homes and setting families up. Initially, we thought these toys would go to refugees arriving here in Ottawa and maybe some did.

Last fall, we heard from our Ottawa organizer, who sent us pictures of where our Izzie Dolls have gone, via the Canadian military who pack them with their medical supplies and fly them into hardship areas – pictures of our soldiers handing them out to kids in refugee camps in Afghanistan, in the Philippines, and even one of Prince Harry giving an Izzie Doll to a child in a hospital in Nepal.

For almost two years now, our Izzie Doll Knitters have met every Monday afternoon to knit, stuff, sew and embroider faces – each little doll has its own personality. They are adorable and we love them.

We take turns hosting at each other's apartments. We chat. We visit. We become little girls again, as we admire all our finished and unfinished dollies. We experiment with different hats, faces, scarves, stripes, colours of the season.

Each one a little different.

The face colours vary from white, brown, black and some even with no skin colours.

One person was very ingenious with her dolls, with bibs, aprons and even a made one with a little baby doll of its own. Some had big hats, baseball caps, some with skirts, as I said, each person made them differently.

It was a joy to make these little dolls and we put ourselves into each one. Showing off the completed doll to the group made it sometimes difficult to part with them. They are beautiful and we know each one will bring a smile to the face of a sick or displaced child somewhere in the world.

To date, we have donated more than 350 dolls. We wonder when we will have done enough. As we all continue to pray for peace, we have been assured that there is still great and ongoing need in those war-torn countries.

We'll keep knitting.

By: Patricia Hall and Vera Kielback.

Peacebuilding through Sports
1st All Badakhshan 5km Run Challenge

The use of sport to address social issues, referred to as Sport for Development and Peace (SDP), is becoming widely accepted by actors in the peace and development field as a significant social catalyst – especially in regions affected by poverty, violence and conflict. The 1st All Badakhsan 5km Run Challenge, held in Afghanistan on 3rd April 2015, is a great case in point.

Background: The run was organized by the Aga Khan Foundation (AKF) in Afghanistan, with support from the Maternal and Child Health (MNCH) project funded by the Canadian International Development Agency (CIDA). Because they understood the importance of sports for youth empowerment, and hence for peacebuilding, they willingly invested months of planning and coordination with the Afghan Olympic committee and Civil Society; also, of course, with the Intelligence Department, given the constant danger of violence in the war-torn environment.

Details included route selection, athlete qualification procedures, prizes and equipment, media coverage, logistics, budgeting, dignitaries to be invited and, vitally, security to be provided. Initial confusion coalesced into effective teamwork to avoid prospective complications. For example, at first many families were hesitant, even unhappy, about letting their sons and loved ones participate in such a public event. But soon, with enormous support and tremendous solidarity displayed by the local residents, everyone began to rejoice and welcome the event. Invitees included political and government figures, Mullahs (religious leaders), heads of NGOs, as well as representatives from AKF, the Olympic committee and civil society. Certificates were printed to recognize both participation and achievement and prizes were procured. Arrangements for media coverage, road closure, the deployment of 200 security professionals and refreshments to be distributed, were finalized a week before the race.

The Event: The sun was shining brightly within the picturesque and historic grounds of the Faizabad, Badakhshan. There, more than 2,000 spectators eagerly awaited the start of the 1st All Badakhshan 5 KM Run Challenge. The stage was set with 50 of the best Badakhshan athletes, previously selected through a transparent and a fair process, to compete for the top three spots. The runners set out on the undulating course, commencing from the

Baghish Bridge that followed the quiet Faizabad roads, culminating with a magnificent finish in front of the central roundabout of the city. The runners came from diverse backgrounds, various age groups, and different ethnicities. They were not just there to compete against each other, but also to demonstrate and to spread the message of peaceful coexistence amongst communities; and to show how national unity can be symbolized through sports.

As the athletes set out, there was overwhelming support and cheering by spectators, which echoed and boosted the courage and stamina of the competitors. With all eyes on them, the fastest athletes swarmed to the finishing line right in front of all the seated dignitaries and other VIPs. Spectators of all ages and backgrounds cheered. So successful was the event that the Olympic committee decided to establish the Badakhshan Running Federation to encourage future athletes, and to inculcate international level talent into Afghan athletics.

Conclusion: This was the first ever, large scale, official running event on the streets of Faizabad. Despite security constraints, limited resources and National Government challenges, it showed how sports can build bridges for peace. So much so, that the Olympic Committee, in establishing the Running Federation, is turning this into an annual tradition. Each year, there will be an opportunity to observe the local athletic talent with pride, to ignite the competitive spirit amongst the youth and, ultimately, to contribute to the building of peace in Afghanistan.

By: Ankur Mahajan

How the Philippines Averted Potential Civil War

It is February 7, 1986, the day of the Philippines presidential election. There are two contenders, long-time incumbent Ferdinand Marcos and challenger Cory Aquino, widow of an assassinated opposition leader. Everyone knows that Marcos will not give up power easily.

But if this election is clean, it could be a real contest. Mrs. Aquino's most recent rally, which I attended, drew a reported one million participants. In any event, election monitors are in place throughout the country today, both Filipinos from the group NAMFREL, and international observers.

I am a Canadian election observer, working with NAMFREL in the troubled, newly-created province of Negros del Norte. As Election Day progresses, we encounter increasing intimidation and harassment from pro-Marcos forces. We are forced to stay fifty metres away from the polling stations, so we cannot see the actual voting.

Once voting is over, we try to follow a truck carrying away nine ballot boxes, but are forced off the road by speeding vehicles that pass and cut us off. Finding the school compound where ballots will be counted, we see it is full of heavily armed military personnel. I am allowed into only one school room. In that room, only one person, the counter, is allowed anywhere close to the ballot box.

So the count, which is supposedly going 20-1 for Marcos, cannot be verified by anyone.

Gathering back outside, we are targeted by a car that suddenly roars into the compound, careening very close to us twice. We decide to leave the area for our own safety. But we are followed and stopped by military men, shouting and threatening us with their weapons. Two key NAMFREL leaders are taken to the police station, and the rest of us follow.

There is much questioning, but finally everyone is released, and we drive out of town immediately to find safe places to spend the rest of the night.

According to official results, Marcos wins this election. But everyone—NAMFREL, the international observers and the general population – knows that this is a total fraud.

It takes only two weeks for Filipinos to take matters into their own hands.

Two leading military/defence officials mount a rebellion by barricading their forces into a military camp on a major Manila ring road. They are surrounded by Marcos troops.

But thousands of ordinary Filipinos, prompted by the country's topmost religious leader, insert themselves in the middle, shielding the rebels. The Marcos forces are ordered to fire on these civilians, but no soldier can bring himself to shoot the priests, nuns and lay people protecting the rebels.

The siege continues for three days with no shooting, until a few casualties are reported. By then, more armed forces personnel are joining the rebels, who are fully aligned with Cory Aquino.

By February 25, it is all over. Cory Aquino is inaugurated as the new Philippines president that morning. Marcos flees the country the following day.

And so ordinary Filipinos save their country from a potential massive blood bath, and restore it to a state of peace and democracy.

Power to the People!

By: DJ Kiddo

Development Assistance Programmes...and Peace

How much do the institutions of Development contribute to Peace? Higher GNP means more funds are available for arms: longer life span and lower infant mortality have led to burgeoning populations and bitter, even deadly battles over land and water - and huge economic refugee outflows: empowered women benefitting from microfinance are too often at greater risk of family violence...and so it goes.

Can we create 'global goods' differently in order to avoid 'global bads'? I doubt it. Violence is as old as humanity. When I visit museums around the world looking at what we can find out about antecedent civilizations long past, I am always impressed and depressed with two constants: weapons, and jewelry adornments. This is the way we are: focused on status and on weapons to maintain status - and battle with difference.

And I think that's the clue: - how can we empower people to understand that they have decision power, to understand the difference does not automatically entail strife. Your status does not detract from mine.

Three flashbacks from my days as CIDA President:

A visit to an evening literacy class in West Africa – mostly but not entirely women, all have done a hard day's work. As always, I have huge difficulty controlling tears as I listen to adults go over the basics of alphabet and then talk about WHY they need to know: to market; to read street signs; to know if they are cheated.

What a world that something so basic is not available to all. How can they enter a world of choice, understanding, and empathy for the world around their borders without being able to hear the views of others? Not that illiterate cannot: It's just harder; maybe telephones help.

(I cannot but recall that as I listened and struggled with emotions, the woman behind me was methodically breaking each wing bone of the chicken under her arm to keep it from flying away...paradoxes tumble out. I flinch with each bone break, and gulp with each testimony.)

Lewis Perinbam calls by my office to ask if CIDA could partner with the Agha Khan Foundation and actually support their development efforts. Never been done before: Canadian support to a foreign, religious, Islamic entity run by a multi-millionaire with race horses doing goodness know what in goodness knows where? We did it. The results have been fantastic: schools, hospitals, employment - and a wonderful program to bring nurses out of darkness of 'not nice women' into a whole new world of being independent helpers - and greatly improving the health system. (If Canada has an instinctive reaction to disbelieve the worst of Islam, it is this program, the "Little Mosque", Ismaili-Canadian citizens, and...and...and...I hope it is still going on.)

And finally: in Sri Lanka, beloved country of my first posting, as President I have been helicoptered in to meet with a Canadian engineering firm working to situate and build a dam for dry season irrigation of very poor migrants from the south. The Chief tells me they have used computers, satellites, the best new geological and soil analysis, to decide on the spot. He leans down and pulls out a fragment of a brick, hands it to me and smiles: this spot was chosen 2000 years ago for the first attempt to make a dam for the same purpose. I still have the brick. Humility is perhaps the foundation stone of Peace.

By: Margaret Catley-Carlson; President CIDA 1983-1989; President Population Council 1993 -1999: Deputy DG UNICEF 1981-83; Chair Global Water Partnership 2001-2010

Editors' note: The e-mail accompanying the author's story submission was signed "Maggie (over Greenland)", because it was written and sent en route to a meeting.
A separate message followed: "It is pitch black on the plane – all are asleep. My computer is still awake and a guy walks by – the print is large. He turns around and says, "Excuse me, this is so rude but your print is large and your screen is bright and I saw 'Aga Khan' and 'AKF' and I thought "this cannot be". He's a dentist from Calgary, who is a member of AKF, has organized for them and been a longtime supporter. He was so surprised to see these words on a screen aboard a dark airplane – I was delighted to have one more example of a world that strives together, and in the same direction!"

Easing Up

Twenty years on and we've eased up a tad:
Of occasional leisure I'm heartily glad.
But there are, as you guess, continuous calls
For Penny* to stride out and brave the world's squalls.

For instance:
In an effort to settle a forty-year war
She canoes down the Salwein to old Maniplawr
And charms General Bo Mya, that amiable fart,
And he gives her a pillow, "Till Death Do Us Part".
Next she cans PetroCan, which was drilling in Burma,
Saying oil shouldn't be found in such *terra firma*,
So chairman Bill Hopper just calls it a day
And whistles his rigs home from – yes – Mandalay!

A fair two week's work, as I think you agree,
But she's hardly been home for a nice cup of tea,
When the Commonwealth calls, "We are rather at sea;
"We are worried this polling won't be fair and free."
No problem at all! She takes plane to Nairobi
("Hey, what about Christmas? cry Daniel and Toby),
But she's got more than turkey piled on her platter:
There are Mwai and Odinga – and Moi, for that matter.
She checks out the lions and the cockerels, too.
Feeds my cookies to poll clerks, and learns what is true;
And tells the Observers to stiffen their stays
And write a report that Fleet Street will praise.

Yes, we all need dear Penny, to keep up to scratch.
How fortunate I, to have made such a match!
And, as I have shown, we have eased up a tad.
Of occasional leisure I'm uncommonly glad,
Especially this *braw nicht*, when with Scotch we recline
And I ask, "will ye no' be my fair Valentine?"

By: Clyde Sanger (14 Feb. 1993), international journalist and author.
Penny Sanger dedicated her life to peace – as an activist and
educator – and was awarded the Anne Goodman Award for Peace
Education by Voice of Women (VOW). She passed away in 2017.

Hugh Keenleyside in the Soviet Union, 1954

Hugh Keenleyside didn't like Moscow. Shop prices, he wrote as he visited the Soviet capital in 1954, were outrageous, and there wasn't much on the shelves in any case. He found Moscow's residents were an unattractive lot. True, they were bundled up for a Russian winter.

"But making all allowances, they really did seem to show humanity at its unlovely worst."

At meals, his hosts plied him with unwelcome liquor; in meetings they harangued him about the faults of his employer, the United Nations. Even so, Keenleyside's mission to Moscow, undertaken in his capacity as the first Director-General of the UN Technical Assistance Administration (TAA), was a peacemaking success story.

Keenleyside worked to remove overseas development assistance - foreign aid, in simplified terms - from the realm of superpower confrontation, at a time of escalating Cold War confrontation between rival camps led by the United States and the Soviet Union. Aid, at the time, came mostly in the form of "technical assistance."

The UN and some national governments sent experts, who it called technical assistance advisors, to less developed countries to share their knowledge and skills, while also handing out fellowships to citizens of those poorer counties in the global South to study in the industrialized North. Technical Assistance was colonial, but also promised international cooperation to raise global living standards. The UN established its TAA in 1949 to carry out this work and picked Keenleyside, a top Canadian civil servant and diplomat, to lead it.

But Washington and Moscow were at each other's throats in the decade that followed. The Cold War seemed to engulf everything in global affairs. Aid and the UN were no exceptions. The Soviet Union had originally denounced UN technical assistance as a tool of US imperialism. But in 1953, it offered 4-million roubles, the equivalent of a million American dollars, on certain conditions. Most notably, the currency was to be entirely unconvertible - meaning roubles could not be changed into dollars or any other currency.

For Western powers, the danger was that the Soviets would use Soviet funds to pay Soviet experts and provide Soviet equipment, and thereby create Soviet economic bridgeheads using UN channels. From a Cold Warrior's perspective, this had to be resisted. So the US-dominated UN General Assembly rejected Moscow's money. But Secretary-General Trygve Lie argued that US-Soviet conflict might be lessened if both superpowers channeled their aid through the UN rather than making aid into yet another area for Cold War clashes. He sent Keenleyside to Moscow to work out a deal to let Soviet technical assistance flow through UN channels.

A series of "lurid" Soviet attacks on the UN's technical assistance actually contained some good points, Keenleyside admitted. But he told his hosts that unless they removed their conditions, the UN could not accept their money. In the end, Keenleyside got his way by making concessions in other areas. Compromise did the trick. Keenleyside found ways to work with the "brilliant" Amazasp Arutuinan, who had denounced him repeatedly in UN forums, and got on even better with vice-minister of foreign affairs, Vasili Kuznetsov, whose English bore the marks of his past as a Ford Motors worker in Detroit.

The deal mattered not only for development aid, but also for superpower relations. Canadian Lester Pearson became the first NATO foreign minister to visit Moscow the following year. Gradually, the Cold War confrontation thawed. Keenleyside didn't thaw it alone, of course, but he succeeded against US government wishes in integrating Soviet aid into the UN system, thus removing technical assistance from the arena of superpower competition. From such small steps was rapprochement across Cold War lines made.

By: David Webster, Associate Professor, Department of History, Bishop's University, Sherbrooke, Quebec.

Just Dad

When my father returned from active duty in the Royal Air Force, he was not well at all, as were most aircrew.

Today, the term for his ailment is PTSD. There was very little help for veterans then.

Near the end of the war, the German air force was virtually destroyed so they resorted to firing rockets and flying bombs which were also known as doodlebugs. These rockets were very successful and destroyed a large section of many cities in the U.K. resulting in many civilian casualties. The rocket sites were eventually destroyed and it brought the war to a close soon after.

When the weather conditions were bad, such as heavy fog, it was inevitable that some of the targets were not destroyed and civilian casualties were the result. Many of the German soldiers hid amongst the civilian population just as ISIS and other terrorist groups do today.

At the end of the war, Bomber Common lost 47,000 aircrew and 9,700 were taken prisoners of war. That figure did not include the losses incurred by the army and navy, plus Russian and American casualties.

The Germans also suffered heavy losses. Please remember that most of the aircrew were aged 18 to 23.

Father knew about the casualty figures and this did not help him with the stress and guilt that he felt.

Father was proud to wear the RAF uniform but politely refused to accept the DFC (Distinguished Flying Cross) awarded to a number of aircrew and to be presented by King George on March 21, 1944.

I was very privileged to know one of the recipients named John Patterson who wrote a book called World War II. John was a resident in our apartment building but sadly passed away a few years ago. We had many discussions with regards to his service in the U.K.

Here are a few more tragic numbers regarding casualties in the war of 1939-45:

Military losses: 20 million;

Civilian losses: 40 million.

Father was finally able to help himself by seeking out many parents and young widows of aircrew that he served with.

By spending time consoling them, he himself was able to come to terms with his stress.

He also founded a volunteer group locally where they would help veterans and older people with their daily needs, such as medical appointments, etc.

Father died of cancer in 1954 at the young age of forty-four. He is buried in the military section of the cemetery in my home town of Aberystwyth, Wales, U.K.

He may have been a war hero in our home town but to my sister and me, he was just dad.

By: Ernest G. Stirrup.

White Pine Peace Tree

Centuries before Canada was born, many first nations came together to bury their weapons under what was, thereafter, known as the Peace Tree. It embodied the strong bonds of land and water, as well as an agreement to work towards and maintain peace. From its location in Asinabka, now often referred to as Victoria Island in Ottawa, the original Peace Tree witnessed hundreds of years of change before its passing. As foretold by the Rainbow Warrior, a time would come for pledging once more to build peace, nation to nation.

On June 26, 2015, the original White Pine Peace Tree, was ceremonially welcomed back by the planting of a new young pine - young, yet infused with sacred responsibility. Peace.

The rebirthing once more took place in a Sacred Ceremony with many gathered from Ontario and Quebec to honour the symbol of both the Peace Tree and the Goose. The peace tree symbolizes that we are living as the fruit of the Sacred Tree of Life, to change and to become part of the solution to humanity's pollution. We are all called to work together, thereby also honouring the symbol of the Goose: team work, co-operation, collaborative effort to always put nature first in all our decisions.

Houston, Texas is an example of how replacing farmlands and creeks with cement is now devastating their city and we, in Ottawa/Gatineau, must see this as exactly what the late Grandfather William Commanda could see happening if the land buried under E. B. Eddy cement was not returned to its natural state: with herbs, and trees, and shrubs, and flowing water, to heal this sacred, spiritual meeting place of his ancient peoples.

Green space, returned to these three small islands of the magnificent Chaudière Falls in the heart of Canadian democracy, must now be seen as an urgent call to listen to the voices of wisdom of these ancient Elders.

The "Free the Falls" ad hoc group has been working tirelessly to support free the falls and free ourselves so that, in awakening, humanity will see, as the Dalai Lama said, we are all in the same boat and it is time we explore and work together with the wisdom of the Elders as one human family.

June 20, 2017 brought another ceremonial gathering before the tiny, yet immeasurably vast, Peace Tree. This time, it was to honour the truth that all religious spaces for worship are sacred, including Algonquin spiritual lands. This time, it took the form of a Prayer Circle called by Algonquin Elder Albert Dumont with inter-faith leaders, who had had their sacred space desecrated. Represented were, Iman Samy Metwally, Rev. Barbra Fraught, Elise Mennie of Parkdale United Church representing Rev. Anthony Baily, Daniel Stringer, Maureen Stark and myself, Judith Matheson. It was my privilege to read Rabbi Anna Maranta's profound statement on behalf of herself and Rabbi Bulka.

Yet another tradition, under the banner "Faith in Solidarity is Peace," is a movement of faith leaders, growing every year, who gather on Aboriginal Day, June 23.

Dr. Peter Stockdale, an integral Peace Leader in the National Capital Area, works with me, through Facebook, to have conversations with leaders from all walks of life.

I am also a member of the Monthly Christian Muslim dialogue group. Love and walking in solidarity, shoulder to shoulder in faith, is peace.

This is what growing in real, genuine, authentic, spiritual relationship is all about in these times of awakening. It is the ultimate MEDICINE. We are the ones we have been waiting to meet. In changing ourselves, loving ourselves, we are also as One Universal humanity making a difference by our choices.

It is time now to walk gently with ourselves, each other and especially with Mother Earth herself!

And so I see that faith in love is the real cause of service for us all to make a difference for being here; to walk and to serve in solidarity against any form of hate.

At humanity's greatest time of chaos, this is our opportunity to heal and to work together in one cause. Peace.

By: Judith Anne King Matheson, Director (OWL) Outaouais Wellness Learning Centre, Co-Founder Heart + Soul Light Centre, as told to Evelyn Voigt.

Mes étudiants à Bahati en Zambie

Dans les années 60 et 70, j'ai enseigné puis dirigé une école secondaire de la mission catholique dans la province du Lwapula, dans le nord de la Zambie, un milieu rural. Le pays venait d'accéder à l'indépendance de la Grande Bretagne. Mes étudiants provenaient de milieu pauvre où les habitants pratiquaient l'agriculture de subsistance ou la pêche artisanale. Ils avaient pu bénéficier d'une bonne formation primaire gratuite.

Ces écoles se situaient dans les villages tout près où ils habitaient et se donnait dans la lange locale, le cibemba. La vie au village était dépourvue de tous les avantages de la vie moderne comme l'électricité et l'eau courante. Être sélectionné pour venir étudier à Bahati était un privilège très fortement recherché. Cependant, Bahati était un pensionnat, où ils étaient soumis à une discipline stricte et où l'enseignement se donnait en anglais.

Comme Bahati était une nouvelle institution, nous devions tout créer avec peu de ressources financières. Cela demandait beaucoup de créativité et d'implication de la part du personnel et des étudiants, tous des garçons.

Une des réalisations importantes fut la ferme.

Après quelques années, entreprenant un projet à la fois, nous avons réalisé une porcherie, un poulailler, une bananeraie, un petit troupeau de vaches, un jardin potager et fruitier et enfin une culture de différentes céréales sur un espace de 5 hectares. Comme ces activités étaient nouvelles pour la plupart d'entre eux, il y a eu très souvent des tensions et des conflits que, comme directeur, je me devais de gérer. Si je leur demandais de faire quelque chose qu'ils n'aimaient pas, je m'impliquais moi-même à faire la chose avec eux.

Je me distinguais en ceci des chefs africains. Mon principe était de ne jamais demander à d'autres de faire quelque chose que je n'étais pas prêt à entreprendre moi-même. Le programme du collège était tel qu'ils étaient confrontés à des changements qu'ils n'étaient pas toujours prêts à endosser. Selon eux, il n'était pas digne pour un étudiant au secondaire de se salir les mains sur la ferme. Je m'assurais que toutes nouvelles initiatives leur apporteraient des bénéfices concrets: Tout ce que la ferme produisait allait directement dans leurs assiettes.

En dépit tout, il y eu des conflits. J'avais appris à percevoir les tensions avant qu'une crise ne se déclare et devienne hors de contrôle. Leur moyen préféré de manifester leur frustration et colère était de faire la grève et de s'enfermer dans leurs dortoirs. Ma réaction était également de faire la grève à ma façon en fermant mon bureau et à aller me promener dans la brousse. Cela me permettait de décompresser.

Je revenais quelques heures plus tard et je me dirigeais vers les dortoirs. Je m'assoyais sur un lit en attendant que quelques étudiants viennent me voir et me parler. Je ne faisais qu'écouter puis je commençais à dialoguer. Surtout, j'essayais d'être juste, équitable avec tous et aimant. Puis je leur expliquais ce que je leur avais déjà expliqué mais qu'ils n'étaient alors pas prêts à entendre.

Alors, la situation revenait à la normale. Il fallait leur laisser un espace pour exprimer leur colère. Ces crises permettaient à chacune des parties de faire les ajustements nécessaires. Tout se concluait par un bon repas. C'était comme après un orage. Il fallait qu'ils puissent manifester dans un premier temps leur opposition, pour qu'ensuite ils réalisent les bénéfices de ce qui leur était proposé et acceptent d'y participer volontairement.

J'ai compris que le développement c'est une affaire endogène, ce sont les gens qui doivent travailler ensemble et apprendre à se prendre en main et acquièrent ainsi plus de maturité. À Bahati, je n'ai pas eu peur des crises qui la plupart du temps ont été bénéfiques à nos étudiants.

La paix n'est jamais absence de conflit.

Par: Yves Morneau, Professionnel de la paix,

A Peace Profession in Our Lifetime

"I can't stand this f...g communist country!" – Hardly what you would expect my 'aha!' moment for peace to be.

But there it is. My moment.

It was a few months after 9-11, at a Steering Committee meeting for a project being implemented through international support for Kosovo, in Kosovo, attended by Kosovars and international experts from several countries. In walked a fellow international 'expert' shouting: "I can't stand this f...g communist country!" – followed by a stream of invectives. Like me, he was there to help Kosovo's transition to a peaceful and independent nation.

Shock does not begin to describe my reaction. Add embarrassment. Followed very quickly by disbelief that someone so clearly unsuited for the assignment should have ended up in that position.

'Well,' I thought, 'he's probably here because of his technical know-how. And maybe this is a most unfortunate aberration.'

Turned out, he was neither technically competent nor personally suited.

Another international colleague, though technically competent, was equally out of his depth in terms of personal suitability, endangering not only himself but others in this volatile environment.

It took money and time to remove them both. One returned to Canada. The other was soon hired for duty in another country in conflict - on the basis of his prior experience in Kosovo.

Conversely, I met many people achieving exemplary results without recognition for their peace professionalism.

One thing led to another. And, upon my return home, fellow Canadians and I joined together to found the Civilian Peace Service Canada (CPSC). It focuses on values- and competency-based assessment of peace professionals, for assignments locally or internationally.

Having looked globally, and failed to identify any organization working on this, we set about putting flesh on the concept of "peace professional", a professional that brings both the heart and mind to assignments in areas of conflict, first defined by Dr. Johann Galtung, widely considered the father of peace studies.

Other professions have standards and accreditation, we asserted, so why not the peace profession? Whether doctor or lawyer, architect or accountant, good intentions are not enough for practice in the field. Imagine a world without professional standards and accreditation for dentists.

Conversely, imagine...a world with standards and accreditation for peace workers.

Quality control better protects citizens, screens clients, reassures employers, and takes seriously the goal of achieving peace. Better yet, since recruitment for posting to areas of conflict often happens at very short notice, we added, how about aiming for a standing cadre of pre-assessed and accredited peace professionals that employers and decision makers can draw on at short notice?

Almost ten years later, the Civilian Peace Service Canada, has pioneered – to our knowledge – the first practical, values- and competency-based assessment and accreditation program for peace professionals. We did this through conferences and workshops, with a wide network of NGOs, private sector organizations, academics, and practitioners, including Dr. Galtung.

Our pilot testing has demonstrated its practicality to academic and professional scrutiny. In the process, seven peace professionals have been accredited, with backgrounds as varied as national and international training and intervention in mediation, negotiation, conflict transformation, international development, faith-based training, military and ethics, First Nations communities, strategy and planning, restorative justice, trauma management response, court mediation coaching, and professional ombudsman-ship.

Imagine if we had hundreds – major conflict, including wars, could be prevented. The number of lives that could be saved and property destruction prevented is incalculable. Much clearly remains to be done.

Perhaps this short story can be the 'aha' moment for someone else, someone in a position to help bring our dream of hundreds, even thousands, of practicing peace professionals to fruition?

By: Gord Breedyk, (www.civilianpeaceservice.ca).

My Father was a Peacekeeper

My father has been dead for a long time. We still have his peacekeepers' medal, a medal he cherished above all others. In a photo of him taken in 1963 when he was stationed on the Gaza Strip, the sleeves of his khaki army shirt are rolled up. He's 45 years old, but his biceps are like strong twisted rope. He's standing in front of a plaque with his name on it, shaking hands with the incoming camp sergeant major who would replace him at Rafah Camp.

While he was away, he sent us gifts: speckled sea shells, stuffed camel toys, a prayer book with a rich-grained cover made from the wood of an olive tree. In long letters, he described meeting the king of Jordan, floating in the Dead Sea, visiting the Holy City.

During the day, I was busy with school, but at night I worried about him. I'd sit in the living room watching the snow fall silently under the streetlight outside our Montreal flat. I thought about the desert. The sand. The heat. How far away he was.

Army life took my father from us often, but this year was his longest absence, and a challenge for my mother. She threw up into the toilet bowl every day; she was pregnant with my sister, born months before my father came home. Mom's sisters took care of me and my two older brothers while she was in the hospital. I remember that time as the longest week of my childhood. Both parents gone. And Mom was different when she came home. She talked in a whisper about how my sister had a twin, but this twin was born a gnarled, misshapen corpse. She seemed sad, but didn't stop hugging us close, loving us and our new baby with all her heart.

When my dad finally returned, he was different too. He shivered in a lawn chair on our porch in Montreal. He told us his blood was thin as water from living where it was one hundred degrees in the shade. He waved his arms around, a cigarette cupped in one fist, telling different stories from the ones he'd written to us. Stories about how he and his men got caught in a sandstorm while on patrol. About how camels kicked and spat at him. How the troops he commanded dropped from heatstroke under the boiling sun.

He had taken silent movies of the beauty of Jerusalem and other places he visited in the Middle East. He showed them to us, to our church group, at our school. When everyone grew tired of them, he set up his projector and white screen, pulled the blinds in the living room in the middle of the afternoon, and watched them alone.

He seemed more and more a stranger. We could tell there were things he wasn't telling us. Darker things. He woke up from sleep screaming. He paced the hallway at night, growing more and more distressed.

He orbited our lives after that. He didn't know how to get back into the family circle and we didn't know how to help him cross the lonely divide.

This long-felt absence of my father was probably why, when I married and we had children, my favourite part of the day was the evening, all five of us home and together in our sunroom, the damp Ottawa snow falling softly onto the branches of the tall fir in our neighbour's front yard. I've never experienced war. Or famine. Or homelessness. But still, I recognized the deep peace in those evenings, and am grateful for them still.

By: Theresa Wallace

Ivana

I walked the busy road to Dubrovnik (Croatia) that day, feeling as if the entire Universe was screaming at me to pay attention to the word Ivan. I had become accustomed to listening to intuition on this 5000-km peace pilgrimage that Alberto and I were walking, so when he told me that he was receiving similar messages, we decided to stop and wait.

Across the road, a young woman stepped out of a restaurant and, in English, asked if she could help us. We answered "yes" in unison, and followed her inside. She looked to be in her twenties, with long, flowing auburn hair and a lovely face. Her green eyes struck me not only for their beauty and kindness, but the sadness they conveyed. Handing us our drinks, she asked what we were doing. She listened politely to our story, but her averted gaze and folded arms told me there was something she didn't agree with. We invited her to join us, and introduced ourselves.

"I am Ivana," she said. My heart lurched.

I learned that her family was Bosnian and that the civil war had forced them into refugee camps. Unable to return to their home, they now lived in a land that did not welcome them and that generally regarded them with disdain. Only after years of hard work building their family restaurant, were they finally being accepted in their community.

"I think what you're doing is admirable," she said, smiling sadly, "but I don't think it will change anything. One person can't make a difference."

"Gandhi was one man, and he made a difference," I replied. "He said we must be the change we wish to see in the world. That's all we're trying to do. Every day people stop to speak with us. They honk their horns and wave in support. They offer us food, drink, shelter. For that brief moment, their attention is on peace."

"Most people here only think about surviving," Ivana responded. "They don't have the luxury of thinking about creating peace. They've learned that even when they try to speak about peace, they can be arrested."

"We've met so many people during this walk who are building peace," Alberto added, "but they think they're alone. They're the ordinary people who step out of their daily routines to help us. They're the real heroes of the world. Thanks to them, I believe more than ever in the goodness of people and our power to change the world."

"It's hard to believe I can make a difference by being nice to someone," Ivana contested.

I asked her for a piece of paper and, while she spoke with Alberto, wrote out words immortalized by Nelson Mandela and that I had long ago memorized. They were given me the day I was questioning my audacity to dream of working for peace.

"Our deepest fear is not that we are inadequate. Our deepest fear is that we are powerful beyond measure. It is our light, not our darkness, that most frightens us. We ask ourselves, who am I to be brilliant, gorgeous, talented and fabulous? Actually who are we not to be? You are a child of God. Your playing small doesn't serve the world. There is nothing enlightened about shrinking so that other people won't feel insecure around you. We are all meant to shine as children do. We were born to make manifest the glory of God that is within us. It's not just in some of us, it's in everyone. And when we let our own light shine, we unconsciously give other people permission to do the same. As we are liberated from our own fear, our presence automatically liberates others."

Ivana's lips curved into a smile. It was a smile of hope, of believing in the impossible. I understood then what this journey was truly about: I was giving people back their power. Sitting before Ivana, I couldn't think of a more powerful purpose than to awaken that in each person.

By: Mony Dojeiji, author, pilgrim (http://walkingforpeace.com).

Making Peace with the Ancestors

Two very foreign paradises have helped me to carve out my sense of identity and my understanding of the value of cultural difference. The first was in my wonderful, difficult three years in Zimbabwe. There the logic of mixed opposites, as we philosophers say, came to appear as my initial starry-eyed vision cleared. It was there that I first came to be told that that I was "white".

In Canada, we name ourselves by our countries of origin and not by the colour of our skins. There are English-Canadians (I am one) and Sardinian-Canadians (my hubby), and Jamaican-Canadians, Japanese-Canadians, Polish-Canadians, and so on. But there are not white Canadians and black Canadians. All these hyphenated Canadians, moreover, so-name themselves in this way precisely to show deference to the only true and original Canadians, who do not (with few exceptions) misname themselves Indians, but enjoy the prestigious "First Nations" status.

This generous and honest Canadian self-naming practice is one way that we preserve our awareness and appreciation of the rich diversity that our homeland offers.

Moreover, the naming practice is in moral keeping with our national ethos, symbolized in the metaphor of the mixed salad, so far superior to the national metaphor of the melting pot, held dear by our national neighbour to the south.

Like the beautiful and delicious differences that bring liveliness and flavor to the salad, we Canadians believe that our cultural diversity is our strength and our blessing and not merely some inconvenience to be tolerated.

Learning of my "whiteness" in Zimbabwe has come in handy in my second paradise, as a professor in a historically "Black" university in the Bible Belt of the United States. My white skin colour again identifies me on the wrong side of their history of painful race relations. As an outsider to this way of naming human difference and as an outsider to their troubled history, I do not share either the uncomfortable guilt of the white Americans or the painful shame of the Black Americans, but I can compassionately witness the agonizing results of both these historical woundings, and appreciate the suffering that continues to undermine wellbeing on both sides of the race issue and that endures to drive both groups toward insularity.

We all have hurts and offenses in our distant past, and certainly some peoples have suffered more than others, but we have much to learn and benefit from stepping outside our cultural comfort zone and getting to know those who are different. Moreover, the peace of our democratic societies depends upon it.

I am happy to be a Canadian, and although our history is not free from subgroup suffering, I am proud to know that we have emerged from our difficult histories with an overwhelmingly generous national ethos which celebrates the value of diversity. But this national character does not evolve naturally without an enormous amount of purposeful planning and effort at the systemic level.

We have been intentionally teaching peace in our schools since I was an elementary school teacher in the 1970s. We have a broad open-door policy about immigration and we citizens generally agree that the generous support we extend to newcomers helps to build a more peaceful environment for all of us. We welcome, rather than tolerate, difference, and I believe that I am not at all special, but typical as a Canadian, when I say that I count myself blessed and my life enriched by the rich cultural diversity of my homeland.

When I return to my country, I am deeply struck by the breadth of diversity of our population, and when I return to my temporary home in the long-suffering south, I am convinced that these longstanding, relentless, hate-fostering cultural distinctions endure, not from too much confrontation with "the cultural other," but from not nearly enough!

As important as it is to find solidarity with others who share a common cultural lineage, it is equally important, as Thich Nhat Hahn phrases it, to "make peace with the ancestors in ourselves" and forgive the past, in order to be fully present to reap the fullest possibilities of this moment.

By: Wendy C. Hamblet, Ph.D. (Philosophy) Professor, Department of Liberal Studies, North Carolina A&T State University.

Mother's News

Each day, when I bring her the paper, she tells me
there's no more war. "No more war!"
She's proud of her time carrying those signs
around Parliament Hill month after month.

"No more fighting. The world has come together,"
she says, smoothing the paper face down
on its fold and pushing it aside. "The United Nations
sends food to the starving, drops bags of water
from airplanes whereever there's drought.
I don't contradict her. Television, radio,
don't enter her corner room bright with dahlias,
morning sun, an orange tree in fruit.

She still reads, mysteries, ones with British endings –
we share them back and forth.
But not the front pages. They're blocked
from her view by her own defences:
a censor's black lines in a letter home.

Though something seeps through:
all the children she couldn't save.
Her own kids soon to be left without a shield.

So she's written a better tale. In my lifetime,
she tells me, so much has changed.
At last, we have peace.

"Yes," I answer. "Peace is coming."
Not a lie: in time, we will either save or destroy
this blue haven. Peace of a kind.

I open the paper to the comics page.

By: Susan McMaster, from the book "*Pendle War Poetry Competition: Selected Poems*, 2014". Susan is founding editor of Canada's first feminist magazine, Branching Out, and past president of the League of Canadian Poets.

Murray McCheyne Thomson – Quintessential Man of Peace

"Great idea, both of you!" That's how Murray responds when invited to submit peace stories for this book. "But you make it a challenge: which story for me to choose from the hundreds in which I have had some input or direction." If you don't know Murray, you likely envisage an *éminence grise* - somewhat puffed up and basking in the adulation of his admirers as he flaunts his Pearson Medal of Peace and Order of Canada, among countless other awards. Far from it. He is very present, certainly. And committed. And concerned. But his passion bubbles with irrepressible humour. He loves to play the violin. And, yes, flirt. Above all, he models for us a life lived fully and well in service of peace, embodying the best of what it is to be Canadian: professional, modest, results-oriented, caring and very, very human.

Here's a formidable list from which Murray could choose a story: four years in India, seven in Thailand, seven with **Project Ploughshares**, two with Days of Peace; 15 with **Peacefund Canada** (and its 300 projects in at least 35 countries). **The Canadian Friends of Burma** went on for many years seeking peace and justice in that country. Then, at **Grindstone Island** peace was part of seven conferences for diplomats, seven UNESCO International Seminars, and seven InterFaith Seminars. Not to forget **Peace Brigades International.** Impossible that one man should have participated in all this? There's more: Murray didn't just participate, he's credited with founding the NGOs bolded above.

Into his nineties now, has he slowed down? Not if you count the past eight years of seeking to bring disarmament and peace via Canadians for a Nuclear Weapons Convention. Or his latest book, Minutes to Midnight: Why More Than 800 Order of Canada Recipients Call for Nuclear Disarmament, with 54 mini-bios of eminent Canadians, many of whom sought peace.

"Yet, dammit, despite all that, and everything you and our many friends are doing," Murray e-mails us, "the world is preparing to blow itself into little pieces, maybe very soon, because as Daniel Berrigan said, there is no peace for it is harder to produce and hang on to than war! Sorry; I got carried away. With love from another failure on the rock-strewn road to peace.... mt

Ps: just kidding – peace by Christmas – pass it on!"

And later, in response to my draft story about him: "You are too much and I too little. However, I'll try to live up to the exaggerated picture you paint of little me! Well, it is true that I have had extraordinary opportunities, now that I think of it. And I am certainly thankful for them, though acutely aware of the gap between my "witness" and those who have really suffered (which I have not): Not only the well-known names of Nelson Mandela, Aung San Suu Kyi, etc. but the many with names unknown and unrecorded, caught up in civil conflicts the world over.

Though a second or third-class peace worker by comparison, I'm grateful that I have had a good family and friends (like you), good health, and unlimited opportunities. But I've never been confronted with one wanting to harm or kill me; never faced the pain and humiliation suffered by countless women from violent men; never had to worry about having an income; and, never been in a wartime situation in which I had no control or could not see any way out. (My time in the Air Force was safe, honourable and protected; a bit of a lark, really!)

I seem to have gone on, haven't I? All your fault!"

Evelyn Voigt (volunteer, www.civilianpeaceservice.ca)

Canadian Foreign Minister Joe Clark and the Central American Peace Process

In the late 1970s, civil wars erupted in El Salvador and Guatemala; a 'Sandinista Revolution' gripped Nicaragua. Thousands of Central Americans died; large refugee flows ensued. The Foreign Ministers of Colombia, Mexico, Panama and Venezuela responded in 1983 by creating the Contadora Group. Prime Minister Trudeau's government declared support for that initiative.

Central America had not been prominent in the platform that brought the Mulroney Progressive Conservatives to power in Canada in September, 1984. By contrast, he – and his Foreign Minister Joe Clark – had a clear mandate from Canadians to improve relations with the USA.

Just days after taking office, however, Clark told the UN General Assembly: "Canada rejects the extension to Central America of East/West confrontation." The Reagan Administration did not welcome Canada's position – then, or subsequently.

In 1985, Argentina, Brazil, Peru and Uruguay formed the Contadora Support Group. Clark declared Canada's support, as he did in 1987 when Costa Rican President Arias and other Central American leaders reached the Esquipulas II Accord – a successor to Contadora.

Historically, Canada played a limited role in Central America. Our interests were considered marginal; the 1823 Monroe Doctrine had asserted U.S. regional primacy. Nonetheless, Clark chose to radically 'upscale' Canada's focus on Central America by engaging the peace process, while impressing on his U.S. counterpart (Secretary of State George Shultz) during their many meetings, that Contadora and Esquipulas enhanced regional stability prospects.

Clark believed in fostering public awareness and debate via Parliamentary engagement. He frequently elaborated to the House of Commons on Canadian support for Central American peace. He did likewise in speeches across Canada during the critical 1984-1989 period. Not surprisingly, therefore, the 1986 Special Joint Committee of Parliament's review of Canada's International Relations received more submissions on Central American peace than on any other single issue (including South African Apartheid – another outrage against which Clark was mobilizing Canadian resources simultaneously). In 1988, extraordinarily for a Minister, Clark invited all parties to create a Special Committee on the Peace Process in Central America.

Clark oversaw considerable increases in Canadian aid funding to the region, including significant support for the conduct of elections. He named numerous Canadian observers to those elections. Refusing to endorse the USA's trade embargo of Nicaragua, he approved that country's request to open a Canadian Trade Office, and received Nicaragua's Vice-President in Ottawa (notwithstanding U.S. Assistant Secretary of State for Inter-American Affairs Elliott Abrams' criticism of Canada for "shoring up Nicaragua"). He met with Central American Ambassadors to discuss concrete ways of assisting the process, and corresponded with their Foreign Ministers.

In November 1987, Clark visited Costa Rica, Nicaragua, El Salvador, Guatemala and Honduras. In addition to ministry experts, he took with him senior Canadian military leaders, who thereby became positioned to work with Central American leaders to design a peace-keeping model.

Canada, West Germany and Spain were invited in 1988 to monitor any peace plan – with Canada leading, principally due to our UN peacekeeping expertise. In the end, the structure of ONUCA (the UN Observer Group) closely mirrored Canada's recommendations. We contributed 40 military observers and eight light observation helicopters with crews and maintenance support.

In1989, bolstered by the sense of 'belonging' that flowed from our activist engagement with the Central American peace process, Canada finally joined the Organization of American States. Costa Rican President (and Nobel Peace Prize Laureate) Oscar Arias came to Canada that year, thanking us for our significant contribution to peace in Central America.

By: Roy Norton, Ph.D., Senior Policy Advisor to Foreign Minister Clark from 1984-1989, with responsibilities that included Canada's Central America policy.

Dancing with Elephants – or How to Die Smiling

Life is beautiful, even when it isn't. The following smorgasbord of publications represents my attempt over the years to honour this truth, even as I now live with a fatal disease. It spans my personal bridge to peace. Perhaps there is something in there for you?

"Healing Justice: When There Is No Cure": Before I was on long-term disability for a chronic and fatal disease, I was a professor travelling the world in search of communities and people who are living examples of a healing kind of justice. In this book, I return to those interviews and people, this time searching for any wisdom to walk in a healing way while facing major life challenges.

"Creating Joy Journal: The Interactive Guide to Transforming Fear into Joy": Partnering with my more artistic wife, Rhona, we created this standalone, interactive journal to help people identify and live into those things that give them great joy, while at the same resisting the things that lead to fear. It includes exercises to sit in the fire and not be consumed.

From my "How to Die Smiling" series: Vol #1 "Dancing with Elephants: Mindfulness Training for Those Living with Dementia" and Vol #2 "A More Healing Way: Video Conversations on Disease, Death and the Fullness of Life". They include interviews with Jon Kabat-Zinn, Patch Adams, Lucy Kalanithi, John Paul Lederach and Toni Bernahard.

"Wabi Sabi Lifestyle Experiments: Celebrating The Beauty Of Things, Imperfect, Impermanent And Decaying": We humans have a profound need for the beautiful and radiant. Sometimes, we mistakenly seek this beauty in the perfect, the permanent and everlasting. This book seeks to recover the human acts of recognizing and celebrating the beauty of things that are imperfect, impermanent and decaying. Those who are journeying this path learn to celebrate life's storms while still standing in them. Living life in response to this beauty is a path of awakening.

"Wrestling With Elephants: More Mindfulness Trainings for Those Living With Dementia, Chronic Illness Or An Aging Brain" is the sequel to Sawatsky's "Dancing with Elephants". With wit, style and humor, this book follows my stories as I use myself as a human guinea pig, testing and trying new ways to live in a more healing way.

By: Jarem Sawatsky, author, peacebuilder, researcher and professor.

Becoming Peace

I feel we need outer and inner peace. Inner peace helps us be healthy and happy. This empowers us to contribute to achieving outer peace in our community and, ultimately, in our world. As someone with chronic illness, I struggle with inner peace. Anyone with allergic or autoimmune conditions may wonder why cells in our immune system, our own protective army, would turn on us and cause debilitating symptoms. It's like my inner landscapes harbour needless wars.

Having a chronic illness can also make us feel ashamed. Even though I "know better," I still catch myself wondering if I did something or thought something that causes my symptoms. And since conventional medicine has little to offer me, I have tried almost everything I could find, within my financial limitations, to get better.

This poem reflects on inner peace from my perspective as someone struggling with outer symptoms.

Becoming Peace

Peace.
You elude me.

I am told you are my birthright
That you are in the space between breaths
That I can cultivate you in my inner garden
That you are there in my essence

But my symptoms distract me from you
The turmoil in my guts
The turmoil on my skin
I feel constantly irritated
I can't remember a day without
An open wound

Others seem at peace
And write from that place of knowing

I feel undone and unpeaceful
And write from that place of not knowing
Hoping it is from a place of becoming.

I do believe in you, Peace.

Maybe you really are there
In each of my cells
In the curves of my DNA helices
In the music of my soul
In my sleeping baby's smile

Maybe you are with me always
And I must learn to access
What is already always there

Maybe I am Peace
And just don't know it
In this place of becoming.

By: Dr. Julie Comber, Writer, Songwriter, Researcher
(http://juliecomber.com).

My Peace Story – 72 Years On
The Abridged Edition

I was born in July 1945, steps away from the Manhattan Project in Chicago, and just weeks away from the dropping of atomic bombs on Hiroshima and Nagasaki. The time and place of my birth have informed my entire life.

As a schoolchild, I cowered under my desk during "yellow" and "red" alerts in anticipation of a nuclear attack. On our first TV, I watched terrifying government films of whole families and homes being swept away by the furious winds of mushroom clouds.

As a teenager, my best friend moved to Australia, her parents naively imagining that the distance would keep her out of harm's way. My neighbours dug bomb shelters in their backyards.

At university in Berkeley, I sat-in at the Oakland Induction Center and watched draft cards being set afire and the stunned faces of young men pressed against windows of departing buses for Vietnam.

I marched with thousands in San Francisco against the war in April 1967.

In 1970, I moved to Denman Island, BC, in faint hope of a reprieve from the interventionist policies of the US government and the nuclear madness. I discovered within the first few days of my forest reverie that the US stored Genie air-to-air nuclear rockets at the Canadian Forces Base at Comox, a mere fifteen kilometers to my north. And, sixty kilometres to my south, US nuclear-armed and powered Navy vessels steamed into the Canadian Maritime Base at Nanoose Bay.

In the early 1980s, now a Canadian citizen, I joined with others to form the Denman Island Peace Group. We resisted the testing of cruise missiles at Cold Lake, low-level military flights over Sheshatshiu, Labrador and northern BC, Star Wars, nuclear arsenal buildups, military spending, wars in Iraq, Afghanistan, the Balkans, etc.

We met every issue with letters, artwork, theatre, music, research, civil disobedience, collaboration across Canada and oceans. The number of origami peace cranes we folded and the loaves of banana bread we baked for fundraisers, could reach to the moon and back.

Puzzled by why we humans seem so self-destructive, I decided to study the question by enrolling in a Master's Degree program in Peace Studies. I must admit that even at this late date, I have failed to find a satisfying answer.

Given my long-entrenched activism, my thesis was entitled, "Developing Peace Movement Self Consciousness: Towards an Understanding of Effectiveness." I concentrated on the Nanoose Conversion Campaign as my case study (given that I was associated with the group, the objectivity of the inquiry must be suspect!) In the midst of my graduate work, I became the Resource Coordinator for the Pacific Campaign to Disarm the Seas, a daughter of the Nuclear-Free and Independent movement.

For almost 20 years, I had the privilege of travelling all over the Asia-Pacific region, even to the Demilitarized Zone between North and South Korea, meeting with kindred and dedicated peace activists. Our work to create a Northeast Asia Nuclear-Weapons-Free Zone remains unrealized; however, I learned from my MA study that the results of our peace work are often latent, ambiguous, cumulative, lack causal certainty and are influenced by factors completely external to our efforts.

There is no perfect single solution, path or strategy to be found. The very acknowledgement of this "limitation," contributes to peace movement effectiveness in that it recognizes that effectiveness, or "success," as in natural systems, is associated with diversity, experimentation, innovation, and adaption. Knowing this helps us to redefine how we conceive of our work – to continually, day by day (and every day) reinvent our work for peace.

By: Patti Willis, Peace Activist, including for the Pacific Campaign for Disarmament & Security.

On Constructing a Conscientious Objectors Peace Cairn

Here in southern Manitoba, we have for some years been served by a group known as the Evangelical Fellowship. It consists of a group of persons, pastors and others, who set themselves the goal some years ago of trying to enhance the peacemaking emphasis in existing Mennonite and other churches in the region. They began to publish literature, including a regular newsletter, create videos, give talks, etc., to generate support for greater peacemaking action (not just talk) in their respective congregations. They also encouraged local communities to set up peace cairns in memory of the work done by conscientious objectors of various churches to promote their peace-keeping views and desire for alternative service opportunities in place of induction to render violent and destructive labour in military engagements all over the world.

The Evangelical Fellowship selected three communities, Winkler, Altona and Steinbach, all in southern and south-eastern Manitoba. They hoped these places would lead the cairn construction initiative by raising funds and erecting what they felt would permanently preserve the memory of the beliefs and service of these conscientious objectors. Winkler and Altona committees were the first to achieve this. Each held an unveiling public event to broadcast the commemoration. Sizable groups, a hundred or more persons, found their way to the unveilings. Steinbach took quite a while to mobilize. It did not seem to have the core of a committee or a local vision to make this happen, despite being the largest community of the three involved.

My wife and I lived in Steinbach. I was somewhat familiar with the work of the Evangelical Fellowship and supported its agenda and also had some connection with the Altona committee, where I once lived. I recalled distinctly the soldiers of WWII marching along the streets of the town on their home leave, with public endorsement from the local paper, favoring the war effort. Pacifism lay low in those days. Some veterans returned after the war to finish high school so I thought a working group might be recruited there to build a cairn in Steinbach. Not so. Three of us friends finally agreed to band together, begin the process, and hope that funds would come in once the project caught public attention. We decided that our local museum would be a suitable place for a cairn. The museum informed us that it might be confusing for donors if we proceeded as planned and competed with other projects for scarce funding. Finally, we had to look for ways to downsize our plans, without dropping the project altogether. After prolonged negotiations, our revised plan included getting the project done by 2016, in time to commemorate the 75th anniversary of the beginning of the Conscientious Objectors service program in Canada.

The unveiling ceremony took place on November 12 that year. Announcements brought more than a hundred would-be participants to the gathering. They read the carefully edited commemorative words on a bronze plaque mounted firmly on a large local boulder (geologically explained as likely left in the ground after a huge Ice Age glacier retreated thousands of years ago). The plaque briefly told the story of the emergence of peace teachings among sixteenth century Anabaptist-Mennonites, and recognized their contribution to positive thinking on upholding peace and rejecting war altogether. The biblical base for such thinking appeared clearly in the text as well.

All expenses were met by the time the project was completed. The initial plan which included a large peace memorial, perhaps a small centre on museum grounds, was not forgotten. Several committee members are continuing to develop this concept for construction a while down the road if circumstances permit.

We were thankful to God that a healthy, uniting spirit could prevail in the committee and the museum board. God is good!

By: Lawrence Klippenstein

Creating Invincibility in Nepal's Military

The best way to destroy an enemy is to make them your friend. Crime, terrorism and war in any area of the world are the accumulation of stress and tension of the individuals that make up that society.

Since 1983, it has been demonstrated that when a group of advanced practitioners of the Transcendental Meditation (TM) technique assemble in sufficient number (the square root of 1% of a population), peace begins to break out. The orderliness of individual consciousness of the practitioners spread into the surrounding society. Today, over 23 scientifically validated peer-reviewed research projects in the Middle East, Africa, Southeast Asia, and Latin America have validated consistent positive effects—with nearly immediate reductions in war deaths averaging better than 70%.

The Nepal military, along with other nations including Mozambique, Croatia, Cambodia, Brazil and Ecuador, have implemented the Invincible Defense Technology (IDT) which makes use of the Transcendental Meditation (TM) programme and its advanced practices.

Recently, in Nepal, 300 of the teaching staff and 2700 students at the military schools there began practicing the Transcendental Meditation technique.

Because of the initial success of the implementation of the TM programme, officials in Nepal have decided to implement TM in three of their military schools. The programmes are already underway in Chitwan and Pokhara districts. Based on the extensive scientific evidence of the wholistic benefits of the TM programme, the Veterans Society of Nepal and the Nepal Maharishi Vedic Foundation jointly launched a project to teach the TM program to retired Nepalese army officers and Nepal Army Rehabilitation Center.

Other programmes involving the TM programme are underway in various countries as well. For example, the David Lynch Foundation in the U.S. has implemented its Warrior Wellness Programme, which provides funding to members of the U.S. armed forces who are suffering from Post-Traumatic Stress Syndrome (PTSD) to learn the TM technique. The benefits of the programme include 40-55% reduction in symptoms of PTSD and depression and 42% decrease in insomnia.

Three hundred and fifty peer-reviewed research studies show that TM improves physical and mental health and wellbeing. TM reduces the pathological and physiological results of chronic stress. Clinical trials and meta-analyses show reductions in: anxiety, high blood pressure, smoking, alcohol use, hardening of the arteries, insulin resistance, and, nearly 50% reduction in risk of heart attack, stroke or death.

Invincible Defense Technology is aptly named. For Nepal, the most important benefit to be gained from implementation of IDT is invincibility for the nation of Nepal. Invincible means incapable of being defeated; unconquerable. Defense means to defend and to protect. Technology is applied science. The goal of IDT is to prevent enemies from arising. The military that properly applies IDT can ultimately obtain victory before war. Once this goal is achieved, the military becomes invincible because there are no enemies to fight.

By: Roy Anderson, certified teacher of the Transcendental Meditation Programme.

Escape from Hungary

The Hungarian revolution liberated us on October 26, 1956. Our euphoria was short-lived, however, because on November 4, the Russian army invaded.

At supper on December 1, my parents said: "You must absolutely not tell anyone. We are going to try to escape from this war-torn place. We will try to get to Canada, a much more peaceful country."

To a ten your old this seemed like a fantastic adventure. A guide had to be hired, which was difficult because anyone caught helping people to cross the border illegally was shot on sight. Eventually, we found someone who cost us all our savings and possessions.

We left on December 4th, planning to take a train to Szombathely, about 20 kilometers from the Austrian border; spend the night there; and start hiking on foot at dawn the next morning. We planned to arrive at the border around seven pm when the guards usually retreated into their tents for supper. We reached Szombathely at 10pm, slept a few hours and left again, on foot, at 5am. The day was sunny but cold, about five degrees Centigrade. On we trudged. At dusk, we finally approached the dangerous areas of the border on a dense forest path. Sporadic machine gun fire and the rumble of diesel engines sounded in the distance. Our guide, George, stopped us at the edge of a dirt road.

"Lie down and be quiet!" he whispered. We did so just as three Soviet tanks rolled by. As they passed, they randomly sprayed the forest with machine gun fire. We lay still for ten more minutes, too frightened to make the slightest noise. "Who are they shooting at?" my mother asked. "Not rabbits, I'm sure." The guide answered. Finally, we snuck across the road, back into the forest. It was dark now, but occasionally flares were shot into the air to light up any escapees in the forest. Each time, we fell to the ground and lay still, covered with mud and snow, and shivering. About thirty minutes later we came to a river.

"It is only waist deep," said George, pulling hip waders from his knapsack. We were not as well prepared! George went first. We followed. My father carried me across, but I was soaked up to my waist. "Hurry up," George said. "We must reach the border by seven." We dragged ourselves on, everyone out of energy by now. After about thirty minutes we reached the top of a hill, and could see several miles in each direction. "This is as far as I go," announced our guide. "Are we in Austria?" my father asked. "No, but see that light on the top of the next mountain?" The light was several kilometers away. "That's Austria. Just follow the light. If they catch me, they shoot me on sight." "But you agreed to take us to Austria!" my father pleaded. Then the guide literally vanished into the forest. We were on our own. The light of Austria, seen clearly from the top of the hill, disappeared as we descended into the valley. "I have my boy scout compass!" I proudly announced. My father got down on his hands and knees. We covered him with his trench coat. Under cover, he lit a match. Re-emerging, he pointed. "That way is West."

Two hours later, utterly exhausted and about to collapse, we saw village lights below. "This could be Austria or Hungary." My father said. "In either case, we can go no further." It was two o'clock in the morning. We dragged ourselves to the first house and knocked on the door, conscious of our appearance: drenched, shivering, covered with mud. An elderly matron, her head covered with a shawl appeared. "*Osterreich?*" Austria? My father asked? "*Ja! Willkommen!*" she answered - a toothless smile, arms outstretched to hug me, the smallest.

We spent about four months in Austria, obtaining travel permits, and came to Canada in April 1957. We did indeed find the peace and prosperity that this great country provided.

By: John Rakos

Friendly Influence and Personal Choice

This is a story about learning and how friends can influence our view of the world towards peace. I grew up in a family that was not intellectual. My mother had Grade eight while my father had much less. Dad knew how to calculate grain in a bin and other things useful for farmers. We never had much money, but we always had the Leader-Post.

I must have been in Grade 3 or 4 when I learned about the United Nations and its various agencies. In our family, there was the story that my mother's father came to Canada to get away from war — but I later learned that he was blacklisted as a carpenter fighting for the 10-hour-day in Vienna and ended up becoming a farmer in Saskatchewan. I was ten when President Kennedy was shot and for years I followed the proceedings of the Warren Commission. Around that time I learned about the war in Vietnam and I initially supported the USA's killing machine.

In Grade ten, I met a friend at school and we spent months at his family's farm making a canoe. He helped me understand that I was wrong about Vietnam and that the fight there was not really over democracy, but over resources. My first ever peace action was in school — I participated in fundraising for UNICEF. Later, I joined my friend in efforts to stop the war in Vietnam. We collected signatures on petitions, my friend did some public speaking, and we raised funds for a children's hospital for Vietnam. May 1st 1975, was a very happy day for me because that was the day the USA was forced to leave Vietnam.

By coincidence, I was drawn into all kinds of humanitarian activities because of my friend. If I had not met him, my life would have been entirely different. I was also drawn into learning about social justice and the civil rights movement in the US — the killing of Fred Hampton, for instance, made a big impression on me. Later, I learned how violence was used against the people of Chile to turn back the progressive gains of the Popular Unity government of Salvador Allende. I concluded that progress requires millions of people acting together in one voice — that ideas are stronger than weapons.

Shortly after being introduced to the peace movement, I learned about the great efforts in Canada to ban the bomb after World War II and for nuclear disarmament treaties between the United States and the Soviet Union. I became an advocate for peaceful co-existence and believe that the number one danger today is not global warming, but nuclear war.

I have become a voracious reader of peace literature and am convinced that even though the Cold War is supposed to have been over, the USA, Canada and other allies still believe in fighting a nuclear war with China or Russia or North Korea. If this was not so, Canada today would be embracing a proposal to have a Department of Peace in Parliament and would support some 130 countries of the United Nations to ban the bomb. The announcements by Minister Sajjan and Minister Freeland in early June of this year attest to a hawkishness on Canada's part that is not justified by any events since this federal government took power.

Canada requires peace. The people of the world require peace and the creation of nonkilling societies. The world needs to move the hands of the Doomsday Clock back before it is too late. Although it was a coincidence that led me to the peace movement, it was also my choice that introduced me to wonderful people and fascinating ideas — and this has given meaning to my life as well as hope to the world.

Jed Lehman, Regina, Sask. Worker, educator, peacenik. (edrae1133@gmail.com).

Canada and the Origins of Peacekeeping

When Canada's foreign minister, Lester Pearson, arrived at the United Nations in New York in the midst of the Suez Crisis in 1956, Canadian diplomat John Holmes remembers people rushing up and asking: "What's he got? We hear Mike's got a proposal. It's high time. Can he do it?" And he did, or so the myth of Canadian peacekeeping would have us believe.

For the record, it should be very clear that Pearson did not invent peacekeeping, nor did he single-handedly create the United Nations Emergency Force (UNEF). He would be the first to admit this. The idea of peacekeeping can be traced back to before the 1800s, but in the post-WWII world it was a relatively untried concept. In fact, the word peacekeeping does not even appear in the UN Charter.

However, Canadians in the early 1950s had gained a reputation at the UN for objectivity and consensus building and, with the world's Great Powers flailing in 1956 towards another global conflict -- a potentially nuclear affair -- Pearson knew what to do, whom to talk to, and how to get the ball moving at the UN. Once the General Assembly passed the "Canadian resolution" calling for a peacekeeping force "to secure and supervise the cessation of hostilities" in the Middle East, the speed with which UN Secretary-General Dag Hammarskjöld and his advisors were able to organize the United Nations Emergency Force was nothing short of incredible. In just over two days they sketched out the basics of the mission and a week later, the first troops landed on the ground in Egypt.

For his untiring efforts to bring about a peaceful solution to the Suez Crisis Pearson was awarded the Nobel Peace Prize. Canadians have generally interpreted this accolade as a validation of peacekeeping and their role in it, and of an altruistic foreign policy.

But in reality, it was simply recognition of Pearson's diplomatic abilities on the world stage. Yet peacekeeping gave the world pause in 1956. Britain and France were able to withdraw their troops from Egypt; the Soviet Union did not have to follow through on its threat to rain down nuclear bombs on London and Paris; the British Commonwealth did not split apart along racial lines; the United States and United Kingdom were able to patch over their differences; and the United Nations was able to score a rare success in the arena of global peace and security. Ultimately, preserving peace was very much in Canada's national interest, and the world's.

UNEF was not the first UN peacekeeping operation -- that distinction goes to the much smaller and limited UN Truce Supervision Organization in the Middle East in1948 -- but it was the first major UN force and, at its height, comprised over 6,000 soldiers from ten nations. Previous observation missions had employed no more than a few hundred military and civilian personnel. Canada's contribution of over 1,100 soldiers to UNEF, a reconnaissance squadron, an air transport unit, and headquarters support troops, provided what was considered by many to be the backbone of this peacekeeping force. Though trained for war, Canada's Armed Forces personnel proved themselves very adept at keeping the peace.

Peacekeeping proved popular with the Canadian public. By the mid-1960's, peacekeeping had been enshrined in Canada's national identity and Canada had established itself as the largest UN troop contributor to peacekeeping operations. The value of peacekeeping, and Canada's commitment to it, has subsequently waxed and waned based on the policy decisions of successive governments. However, from its genesis as a Canadian diplomatic solution to its recognition on the world stage, the pride that Canadians feel as a peacekeeping nation remains.

By: Michael K. Carroll, Associate Professor in the Department of Humanities at MacEwan University in Edmonton, Alberta.

From the People United to...the AUM

When I came to Canada, 37 years ago, I was received with the National Anthem and fireworks. Yes, I arrived on Canada Day. My two sons were excited and it took them some time to understand that all the music and celebration wasn't necessarily because of our arrival.

When I look back and see my life in this country, I remember the young woman full of energy and illusions for a better world, walking on the streets of Santiago in Chile, chanting, "The people united will never be defeated." All my being rebelled against children's prostitution, misery, low salaries. "It's not fair to live in poverty" I used to tell my university classmates. We were all looking for an answer and socialism seemed the right path.

Then came September 11, not the Twin Towers but the one in Chile in 1973 when the bombs destroyed the presidential palace, the dreams for a better world and the hopes of too many Chileans.

After all these years in Canada my dream for a better world is still in my heart, only at this time, I'm taking a different path. I want to take responsibility for each one of my actions in a mature way, without blaming my neighbor, the government or the corner store for my failures. Meditation has helped me to calm my mind and it's the silence that guides my action.

Nevertheless, out of habit, many times instead of starting meditating with the Aum, I say: "The people united will never be defeated."

By: Camila Reimers.

Peace Policies and Solutions in International Affairs

For everyone involved in Canadian international affairs, the issue of 'peace' will often arise both as a policy means and an end solution. Following are reflections on 'peace' from a 36-year career in Global Affairs Canada with experience drawn from: diplomatic postings in Chicago, USA, Saudi Arabia, Turkey, Colombia, Iran, Libya, El Salvador, Algeria, Addis African Union; Ottawa assignments in US affairs, arms exports, nuclear non-proliferation/disarmament, Trade and Investment, Middle East, African and European Affairs, NATO Security affairs, Parliament and Cabinet; and involvements in the Liberal Party and NGOs with peace interests i.e. the Peace Festival.

The tools of diplomacy, development assistance, trade facilitation, intelligence, police and legal liaison, consular assistance to Canadians and regulating the flows of people as immigrants, workers and refugees are all essentially 'peaceful' means to achieve solutions that are also 'peaceful' even if forceful, not always successful or conflict free. It is when Defence (or use of military force) enters the policy equation that the likelihood of armed conflict and violence increases. Therefore, getting to 'peace' positions and outcomes is often difficult.

For the most part, in the post-war world, Canadian international affairs practitioners have been able to employ 'peaceful' instruments arising from Canada's role as an international peacemaker and mediator. '9/11' and the 'wars' on terrorism and illicit drugs introduced more militarily oriented action into Canadian international policies. The Canadian decision to intervene militarily in Afghanistan, followed the only time NATO had invoked the collective defence article 5 after the *Al Qaeda* attacks on the US and subject to a UNSC mandate. This was in contrast to Canada's very limited military support for the two US-led military actions in Iraq, but consistent with Canada's role in forceful regime change in Libya and currently, direct military engagement in northern Iraq in support of the Kurds against ISIS.

Although accompanied by massive development and governance efforts, these major military interventions by NATO and willing coalitions, costing hundreds of thousands of lives and billions of dollars, have not brought stability, peace and good governance to Iraq, Afghanistan and Libya, nor won the war on terrorism. These examples, and how the current crises in Syria and North Korea play out, may demonstrate the limits of such interventions.

There are other examples of the role of 'peace' policies. Certain illegal excesses in the war on terror have been met in Canada by more principled positions, as demonstrated in the compensation paid to both Omar Khadar and Mahar Arar, as well as Bill C-51 to better balance security and rights. While Canada has been engaged in solving problems in Africa (AU) and the Americas (OAS), Canada has seemed to back away from its traditional policies for Middle East peace and a two state solution in Israel and Palestine, and has been hesitant to re-establish diplomatic relations with Iran. It has struggled to balance trade, commercial resource and human rights interests (LAVs and human rights in Saudi Arabia).

Canada's intention to legalize 'marijuana' may bring greater sanity to the US-led war on drugs, although it may further complicate Canada-USA relations just as sensitive NAFTA negotiations are set to start. The greatest 'peace' challenge going forward is how the projected considerable increase in Canadian defence spending can be balanced against the resources needed to combat serious non-military threats such as climate change, refugee and irregular migration flows, human and natural disasters, infrastructure needs, cyber conflict, etc. A current dilemma is how can Canada (as a non-nuclear weapons state party to the NPT) resolve its historic active commitment to nuclear disarmament with its membership in NATO, whose strategic doctrine allows for the use of nuclear weapons, in such a way so as to become a member of the new UN Nuclear Weapons Ban Treaty?

Hopefully, practitioners in Canadian global affairs will find the most 'peaceful' policies to maximize effective 'peaceful' solutions, while holding military means in last ditch reserve. Such a positive approach to 'peace' in international relations will help Canada set a good example and return to its rightful place as an elected member of the United Nations Security Council.

By: George Jacobi

Boy with Umbrella

"Not only have people been forced to flee...they are now facing new challenges in the camps for displaced people." MSF 2008 website posting.

The stutter of gunfire and vibrato of overhead drones
as his family gathered up their few clothes and sandals
to track along eroded trails and gutted roads
of their valleys, past shattered towns
littered with rounds of spent cartridges
charred hulks of cars, ruined homes and shops.

He stands on a worn path. On one side the tents
are like foam washed up on the sands of this plateau,
are tethered by a cross-stitch of jute.
On the other, despite the invasion of heat and flies
in a makeshift hospital, doctors
knot sutures, that zigzag, truss trauma wounds.

An umbrella, striped in rainbow colours, shadows
blisters on his face and wiry russet hair,
but cannot eclipse his impish grin.
I raise my camera to shoot. He runs away.
The umbrella leaps into the air, descends,
spins, a top orbiting on its axis across the dust.

By: Blaine Marchand, Award winning poet, author and program manager. 'Boy with Umbrella' is from his 2015 book: My Head, Filled With Pakistan, based on his international development experience in Pakistan.

Hockey and Peacebuilding

It was the last game that I would play in our over- 40, competitive men's hockey league. It had been a long time coming. I had played in the league for many years and had long ago passed the age of 40. I have played competitive sports long enough to know that at some point you can stay around too long and outlive your welcome.

So, at the end of the previous season, I had announced that the upcoming season would be my last. If the organizers wanted me back for one final season, they could include me in the annual summer draft, but this way the awkward phone call informing me that I should think about moving on, would be avoided.

It had been a pretty good season. I had scored a couple of goals and, while missing some games due to the assorted ailments suffered when trying to play at a higher level than your body will allow, I had enjoyed myself and also satisfied a personal goal of playing the game through to a milestone birthday year.

Now the game, and my unremarkable hockey career, were both winding down. We had made it to the consolation game and I had even scored a goal to contribute to our comfortable two goal lead.

With a few minutes left I was handed a goal when the puck unexpectedly squirted out from under the goaltender's pads. I just had to tap it into an empty net. Two goals! Wow. The cry from my teammates went up: "Let's get him the hat trick".

The boys started to feed me the puck. I received a beautiful pass and got off a good clear shot only to see the goalie's glove come out to rob me. The boys on the bench were standing and cheering in anticipation, and then groaned in disappointment, as the puck disappeared into the goalie's glove.

With only seconds remaining, I was given another golden opportunity when, left all alone in front of the net, beat the goalie only to see my shot ring off the cross bar. Again, more groans of disappointment from our bench.

The whistle blew and the game was over.

I was skating back to our end of the rink for the customary team handshakes when something strange happened. Players from both teams skated to the sides of the ice forming two lines. The opposing goaltender stayed in his net. The referee put the puck at center ice and pointed to me. My friends were giving me a chance to finish this part of my journey with a hat trick.

Time slowed down as I skated in on my penalty shot, looking for an opening. I saw one – low on the glove side. I let off a decent shot and thought for a moment that the hat trick was mine. At the last minute, the goalie's left pad flicked out and the puck was kicked away.

I maintain to this day that, had I not been distracted by the tears in my eyes, I would have scored.

What has this story got to do with building peace? I'm not sure. I have spent 40 years trying to help people out of difficult conflicted situations as an advisor and as a mediator. I have spent a good part of my life studying conflict, thinking about how to be an effective peace builder, and training others in the art of doing so. Yet

I'm still not sure that I can define what the essence of peacebuilding is, or, at the end of many of my work days, say that any particular action of mine has helped build peace.

What I do know is that small simple gestures of appreciation and kindness, like giving me my chance to go out with a hat trick, are never forgotten. They enrich lives, connect us more closely to each other, and help build community. They inspire us to be better peace builders, whatever that is.

Richard Moore, MDR Associates Conflict Resolution Inc.

Peace in a Time of Net Curtains

It was a warm, bright July morning and I was in a good mood. The previous day, London had won its bid to host the 2012 Olympic Games. There were celebrations throughout the city. My husband and I were overjoyed as the Olympic site would be within walking distance of our East End home. Exciting stuff!

I set off for work - boarding the Jubilee Line at Canning Town heading for Green Park. At the time, I was working for the Commonwealth Foundation, an international organisation providing an invaluable link - a safe space - between Commonwealth governments and civil society. It was committed to working towards a peaceful and equitable society. Located in Marlborough House on Pall Mall - the Foundation was a short walk from the station. However, as the train approached Westminster, passengers were instructed to alight and leave the station ASAP due to 'a problem with the power supply'. There was nothing particularly out of the ordinary in this request - 'problems' on the underground were not uncommon. I continued my journey on foot.

I arrived at Marlborough House and headed directly to my office. As I walked down the corridor, I noticed windows had been left open overnight. The net curtains were pulled back and billowing in the breeze. Although the building was undeniably majestic, it could become unbearably hot and stuffy in the summer. Every office I passed was empty. I reached my office, turned on the computer and checked the phone for messages. There were over a dozen. As I was listening to apologies from staff encountering difficulties getting in, a colleague burst through.

"There's been an explosion on the underground! Check your computer!"

Three bombs had exploded in quick succession. News was sketchy. The underground was completely shut down. And then, the fourth bomb went off on a bus in Tavistock Square. It felt like we were under siege. The phone rang - another colleague.

"I'm sorry I'm late. My tube station's closed. I'll try to get a bus."

"Don't," I said. "Turn back. There are bombs. The city centre is closed. It's not safe."

I fielded more calls from colleagues and instructed everyone to return home. My husband phoned to make sure I was okay. And then, silence. The phone system was overloaded. Unable to leave, I went through the building closing windows and making sure the net curtains were closed and weighted down. Better safe than sorry. I remembered this routine from decades before. Net curtains - it took me back.

When I first visited London, I noticed many old buildings had net curtains in the windows. I thought it odd. I associated net curtains with little old ladies - not public buildings. It was explained to me that the curtains provided protection for those inside. The sheers - thick, overly long and sagging at the bottom - were held in place by weights sewn into the hems. In the event of an explosion (World War II or IRA bombs), the nets would catch the flying glass from the shattering windows.

During my subsequent career in London, I worked in several buildings that had these sheers. I'd secured them on a number of occasions during IRA attacks. However, after the truce in Northern Ireland, there no longer seemed a need for net curtains.

On 7 July 2005, as I closed and adjusted the sheers to protect colleagues from possible imploding glass; as I felt my earlier optimism disappear; as my body tensed and a long-forgotten edginess returned - I realised that a precious thing had been lost - peace.

It's startling how you don't realise you are living in a time of peace - until that peace is broken.

By: Patricia Mahoney (www.patriciamahoney.com).

Peace Leadership – an Idea with Canadian Roots

There is an emerging discipline, peace leadership, thus far specifically addressed by few published scholarly books and journal articles. How did it get started and why is it related to Canada?

Within the leadership community, peace leadership was identified as a new leadership field during the Annual Conference of the International Leadership Association in Prague in 2009. The initiative came from and is still strongly supported by Jean Lipman-Blumen (author of Connective Leadership. Managing in a Changing World) and Erich Schellhammer, then an associate professor at Royal Roads University in Victoria, B.C.

Erich lives in Canada and is now a Canadian citizen. He greatly appreciates the country's multiculturalism and international reputation for peacekeeping. He grew up in Germany and came to Canada as a young student. He brought with him a personal and family history with many connections to the Czech Republic. His mother grew up there and his father served in Prague as a German soldier during World War II. As a child, Erich experienced Czech citizens all excited about new freedoms during a visit with his parents in the summer of 1968, just two days before Russian tanks moved into the country. He visited Prague in 1985, witnessed the despair of a stalemated society, and again in 1989, when the city was transformed by hope displaying streets full of music, joy and life.

In 2009, outside the conference location, an exhibition commemorated the suffering of Czech people during the many conflicts endured in the 20th century. The city displayed deportation trains and camps from World War II. There were also strong reminders of the Prague Spring of 1968 and it being crushed by force.

Vaclav Havel, the successful leader of the Velvet Revolution, a novel and successful peaceful political transformation, gave the key note address of the conference. He alluded to peace leadership skills allowing for a social transformation that stands in stark contrast to previous political conflict resolutions that hampered the richness of the country based on its traditional multiculturalism. His speech was inspiring and compelling.

Like Erich, others felt the need for peace leadership, often also with reference points in personal and family history such as having Czech roots or a Jewish background. There was a space to meet and an opportunity was seized. The memory of human failure towards the other and his or her human rights gave birth to a discipline that can facilitate peaceful transformations towards a culture of peace.

Soon afterwards, a development started within the International Leadership Association towards establishing a separate community specifically addressing peace leadership. This got formalized through a Peace Leadership Affinity Group that allowed members to engage in and network in the field of peace leadership. This forum generated many discussions, collaborations, proposals for journals and books as well as published works. One of these initiatives came from Stan Amaladas and Sean Byrne from the Arthur V. Mauro Centre for Peace and Justice in Winnipeg who worked with authors and Routledge to produce "Peace Leadership, The Quest for Connectedness (2017)" which promises to become the first textbook of the new discipline.

By: Erich Schellhammer, Ph.D., Board member of Civilian Peace Service of Canada, Board member of the Canadian Association of Peace and Conflict Studies.

Canadian Co-operators Take a Stand for Peace against Apartheid

I first visited South Africa in 1974 following a UN assignment in Tanzania. My visit was personal--I wanted to see what apartheid looked like.

What I saw was a country whose different races, categorized as white, colored, Indian and black, were kept entirely apart from each other except when business required interaction. Each race had its own communities, schools, beaches, airport waiting rooms, etc. White people lived in mansions, while the others lived in townships, often in poor and squalid conditions.

When I tried to speak with black people, they backed away, saying little. Not surprising—such interaction could have led to their arrest. What a shocking change from 1974 Tanzania where people of all races mixed together freely; even while future South African President, Nelson Mandela, and future credit union leader, Kwedi Mkalipi, languished in prison on Robben Island, near Capetown.

My second visit to South Africa was in the late 1980's, when I was working for the Canadian Cooperative Association (CCA). I had heard about a fledgling multi-racial credit union movement based in Capetown, known as the Cape Credit Union League (CCUL). It was supported by the Catholic Welfare Bureau who gave me the name of a white Catholic nun to contact if I wanted to visit CCUL. I did so, and she met me at the Capetown airport. In order to get my South African visa, I had to identify her as my girlfriend. I could not mention CCUL.

This nun took me to the office of the CCUL General Secretary, Kwedi Mkalipi, who had recently been released from prison. He was a small, jovial black man, who I soon realized carried a lot of charisma. He was an excellent leader for CCUL, gaining the immediate respect of township dwellers as a person who had stood up to apartheid at the cost of his own freedom. I met his multi-racial staff, visited some CCUL member credit unions, and returned to Ottawa sufficiently impressed to develop a first small CCA-CCUL project.

This project progressed well, and gave me the foundation to propose a much larger CCA-CCUL program. But this time I needed CCA Board approval. Would the Board agree, I wondered, considering CCA's long-standing requirement for host government endorsement?

I told the Board frankly that, in this case, there was no support from the South African Government, nor could we even inform them about the CCA-CCUL relationship.

Despite this, the Board, chaired by Dr. Ian MacPherson, approved the program without question or qualification. So we were able to proceed with this CCA-CCUL partnership even as South Africa evolved into an independent, multi-racial, democratic society following the release of Nelson Mandela in 1990.

With this transformation, the armed struggle that had been going on in South Africa for decades came to an end, proving that the peace solution in that country was simple and obvious: i.e., the abolition of apartheid.

CCA also helped CCUL lay the foundation for its evolution into a much broader-based credit union movement known as the Savings and Credit Co-operative League of South Africa.

All this was in the best tradition of the co-operative movement's millions of Canadian members.

By: Jim Carmichael

Opening Doors for Survival during the Cold War

The Cold War in the 1980s was very scary with some Westerners calling for 'Better Dead Than Red'. Something had to be done to counter the Big Lie of fake news that 'we' Westerners could not live together in peace with 'they' the Soviet Union. The threat of nuclear war was imminent.

I immediately wondered how bridge-building, peace-making, and friendship arrangements could help get to know the stranger. My friends and I approached the Canadian External Affairs and other departments to see if we can use their reception rooms to host Soviet champion skaters and scientists.

'This was never done', they said, 'We can't set a precedent.' What then were we to do to facilitate learning and help change public opinion as with the Hundredth Monkey phenomenon?

My home was a friendly place and could accommodate up to 60 people. So in 1984, I opened the doors for Living Room Discussions on Saturday afternoons from 2pm to 5pm, with 17 sessions ending in April 1985 with an Adventure Peace Tour to the Soviet Union.

Speakers came from the Soviet Embassy, the Consulate and the Press Office, with open invitations to over 60 groups in the Ottawa area. Themes included: semantics, education, constitution and political system, women, the arts (culture, theatre, cinema and ballet), environment, social services, family structure, east-west trade, defence and military policy, foreign policy, literature, agriculture, religion, media, longevity and health, and a general review. As an anthropologist, I used the metaphor of stepping into the shoes of the other as well as going on an exotic journey into a strange land, with weekly stops along the way.

For many participants, this was the first time to personally meet Soviets on a person-to-person basis, thereby helping to dispel many misconceptions about our northern Soviet neighbour.

For some of those who came one or two times, they came away with little change in their perspectives — their readings and lectures at the university did not fit the findings of the direct experience and so they went along with their professors' views. Whom was one to believe?

While CBC TV did a good job in reporting on one of the sessions, a competitor CJOR-TV sent a reporter one day before the next session and came out with a sensational story targeting us with being a training ground for spies. As a sensational Big Lie, the report discredited us as a bona fide friendship project and had an effect in disrupting the discussion sessions.

The adverse publicity had little effect in dampening interest for the Peace Tour. We got a full house with 33 Canadians and one American joining the tour of some of the most exciting cities of Leningrad, Moscow, Volgograd, Tbilisi, Baku, Tashkent, Samarkand, and Sochi. Participants ranged in age from the mid-20s to 82, and came from a cross-section of major peace movements, religious groups, ethnic organizations, as well as civil servants and those in private business.

What united us was a common concern for the survival of our civilization on planet earth and the hope of giving our children an opportunity of growing up in a world without wars. In practical terms, this meant No First Use, the Freeze (to stop the arms race), and genuine efforts towards disarmament and peace. That to me is the real meaning of peace.

With fake news in today's Cold War world, are we not repeating again the dangerous lies about our northern Russian neighbours and others?

When will we ever learn?

By: Koozma J. Tarasoff, anthropologist, ethnographer, historian, writer and peace activist. (kjtarasoff@gmail.com).

It wasn't War and it wasn't Peace

It was Balochistan and the North West Frontier in the early 1990s. The USSR war in Afghanistan had sputtered to a halt. One and a half million Afghani refugees and *mujahideen* families were living in camps the size of cities all along the frontier. Hardly a tree was left standing. Roads were destroyed by overuse and lack of repair. Irrigation canals were crumbling and blocked. Peasant farmers had left the land for the riches of war, ironically creating the poverty of war at home.

In this havoc, a World Bank team of which I was a member was preparing the way for a large, multi-phase infrastructure repair loan. Our boardroom was a campfire at each location along the borderlands. Tribal leaders and our team of consultants sat around fires, as the sun lowered itself behind the hills, and discussed the land's future and regeneration.

As I replay these scenes, I see our team as the only people without weapons. The tribal leaders' bodyguards kept their Kalashnikovs on their knees as they ate and watched. Our UN-provided guards stood off on higher ground with their ancient bolt-action rifles. Every boy over 14 carried a rifle.

What appeared on paper and in speeches in Washington to be an action for peace and reconstruction, was in fact, on the ground, a hard fought business negotiation. Who would control the money? Who would approve the projects? How would my area of control benefit? What if we don't trust the politicians and bureaucrats? It was just everyday business for the tribal leaders, but 'please point that gun the other way' nerves for the team.

On reflection, this peace story isn't much of a story, and isn't really about peace, but about the fact that in the absence of direct conflict, yet in unstable conditions, people behave in very normal and understandable ways.

So how does that help anything? Well, suppose I took the kernel of that idea, and instead of viewing its message from the remote, top-down or institutional approach of nations and governments and tribes and politics, I looked at it from the people point of view.

Because I'm people too.

This realization is embarrassing, as it turns the microscope from the UN, the government and all the other organizational bogeymen in the world scheme of things onto me. But what good is that? I'm not an actor on the world stage. No, but I am an actor on my local stage. And presumably my actions mean something or have some cause and effect.

Wracking my mind, I can come up with only a few instances in which my actions could be classified as promoting peace on a personal or immediate surroundings level. Which is, after all, perhaps one of our main responsibilities in life.

Picture this. I arrive at a downtown Ottawa bus stop with two of my young sons, to find a drunken bruiser of a man menacing a smaller, older Asian-looking man waiting for a bus. The bruiser is shouting and spitting, waving his arms and threatening violence on the old man. Shamefully, I wait until no one else is going to act, then I stand between the old man and the thug. The surprised drunk shouts 'who the hell are you?' No response as I stare off into the distance; except, my two sons sidle up and stand next to me. This new wall of flesh switches on some rational part of the drunk's brain, and he eventually wanders off shouting belligerently.

Years later, one of my boys told me how proud they were to stand there with me. I have no doubt they will, in their turn, stand between an innocent victim and an aggressor.

What if a million people just stood between two armies?

By: Harry Monaghan

James S. Woodsworth — Conscience of Canada

The search for peace, equality and social justice was a lifetime effort of James S. Woodsworth (1874-1942), a Methodist minister, social worker, politician.

While observing the grim results of industrial capitalism in Canada and Britain, Woodsworth concluded that his church's stress upon personal salvation was wrong. At the All People's Mission in Winnipeg, Manitoba, he worked with immigrant slum dwellers 1904-13, when he wrote extensively on expounding the 'social gospel' - a creedless movement calling for the establishment of the Kingdom of God 'here and now'.

By 1914, he became a supporter of the trade-union collective bargaining and an ardent democratic socialist. He was also a principled pacifist who identified capitalism/imperialism as a factor in promoting war. He was fired from a government social-research position in 1917 for openly opposing conscription.

In 1918 he resigned the ministry in protest against church support of the war. He left the church in opposition to the war, saying 'I thought as a Christian minister, I was a messenger of the Prince of Peace.' To support his young family, he joined the longshoremen's union and worked for a year on the Vancouver docks.

Woodsworth returned to Winnipeg and with zeal organized the Manitoba Independent Party (ILP) where he succeeded in being elected to the House of Commons in 1921 for Winnipeg North Centre, with the slogan 'Human Needs before Property Rights'. He held this position until his death in 1942.

When the Depression struck, he joined with various labour and socialist groups to found a new party. At Regina in 1933, the new party adopted a democratic socialist manifesto and chose Woodsworth as its leader under the banner of the Co-operative Commonwealth Federation (CCF).

Rejecting violent revolution, in the House of Commons, Woodsworth mastered the rules of parliamentary debate and used the public platform of the need for socialism, free speech and pacifism. Throughout the 1920s and 1930s, he forced the Commons to debate Canada's military and foreign policy. He led a long assault on military estimates, cadet training, war memorials, and the militia owed much to his understanding of Hobbesian analysis of imperialism and capitalism.

At each session of parliament, Woodsworth called for the replacement of capitalism's competitive profit motive with public and cooperative ownership of the means of production and distribution. In 1927, Woodsworth was able to persuade the Liberal government to enact an old age pension plan, the cornerstone of Canada's social security system.

In his focus on the war-peace issue, Woodsworth concluded that capitalism, in league with militarism and imperialism, caused war. His eloquent final statement in parliament was his opposition to Canada joining World War II. In a speech to Parliament, he said in September 1939:

'I have sons of my own, and I hope they are not cowards. But if any of these boys, not through cowardice but through belief, is willing to take his stand on this matter and if necessary to face a concentration camp or a firing squad, I shall be more proud of that boy than if he had enlisted for the war.'

In response, PM Mackenzie King said: "There are few men in this Parliament for whom I have greater respect than the leader of the Co-operative Commonwealth Federation. I admire him in my heart, because time and time again he had the courage to say what lays on his conscience, regardless of what the world might think of him. A man of that calibre is an ornament to any Parliament."

By: Koozma J. Tarasoff, anthropologist, ethnographer, historian, writer and peace activist. (kjtarasoff@gmail.com)

Peaceweaving

I recall one case I mediated that seemed at first to be a rather straightforward two-party dispute over a parcel of land. A farmer wished to have some of his land rezoned to extend his pasture. Approval had to be granted by the local municipality. Both sides agreed to mediation without much ado. The Mayor and head of the planning department represented the Municipality; across the table sat the farmer with his teenage son at his side.

We followed the classic mediation model and as I was trying to get the Mayor, who was doing all the talking for her side, and the farmer to come to what should have been a relatively simple arrangement that would meet both sides' expressed interests; it was obvious they would not agree. We began to repeat what had already been said, and it really was a case of both people 'talking past the other'. Neither was prepared to acknowledge anything positive that the other put on the table, as though neither had even heard what was offered.

While this was taking place, another kind of energy crept into the 'exchange', a negative undercurrent that I could not understand. Previously courteous behaviour turned hostile, and blood pressures were visibly going up faces turned red. Even though they had each offered and conceded enough to be able to reach an agreement, this had turned personal. The department head had now withdrawn from the table and was visibly embarrassed by the Mayor's behaviour. The farmer, a large and physically strong man, had taken on a fighting stance, aggressively leaning forward and into the Mayer's face. His son sat passively with his head drooped.

I broke in. I took command and, like a primary school teacher, I stood and said this had gone far enough, that I wanted to see both of them in private. I stood up, turned and walked towards the small room in the back that had been set aside for private caucuses. As I entered the room, my body language clearly ordering them to join me, now, I could see they were shocked. But they were getting up as a great silence filled the room. The department head and the farmer's son just watched in amazement.

I closed the door behind them and told them that I could not believe their behaviour; that they were acting like children when they were obviously adults and leaders in their community who should be showing respect for one another. I told them I was not willing to waste any more of their or my time and needed to know whether or not they wished to reach an agreement, which I said was obviously possible.

This was when I began to learn what was really driving them. Their relationship went back decades. The farmer's family, fiercely independent, had been fighting 'city hall' for years and the Mayor represented everything he detested. For her part, the Mayor had been offended years ago by the farmer's father and she thought the farmer was 'cut from the same cloth', rough and ignorant. The negative energy I was dealing with here involved rivalry, injury, and suspicion associated with an ancestor who was not at the table.

We spent quite some time in the private meeting and I am sure the others left outside must have wondered what was going on. But I was not going to lose this opportunity for people, who lived as neighbours in a small community. In the process of telling each other what they really thought of one another, more constructively now with my strong yet calming presence, something shifted. The latent hostility that had surfaced at the mediation table dissipated and they began to listen and to hear one another. They stopped trying to bully each other, and while they didn't get to warm and fuzzy feelings or an apology, they did reach a level where they could cooperate.

I sensed that and suggested we go back to the table and settle the re-zoning issue. The head of department and the farmer's son were waiting expectantly and were relieved to see everyone still in one piece. It did not take very long at all to reach an agreement.

By: Dr. Ben Hoffman, from "Peaceweaving: Shamanistic Insights Into Mediating the Transformation of Power".

Reflections

Being a Canadian 'post-war baby boomer' means that I've lived a fortunately 'peace-full' existence, without the test of major political conflict. But unlike most of my age-mates here, I have experienced war and its corrosive aftermath elsewhere.

As a CUSO cooperant, I happened to go to teach literature at the University of Lagos while the Nigerian/Biafran civil war was dragging on. Then in January 1970, the surrender of secessionist Biafra was announced. Everyone on campus was overjoyed, and classes were cancelled in that celebratory atmosphere. One group of students created huge peace banners behind which they marched around, singing "All we are saying is give peace a chance". Another group crowded into a large transport truck and drove to the barracks to congratulate General Gowon, then the head of the federal government as well as the military. But they soon returned in disarray, after being sprayed with tear gas! On a more positive note, in the following days, returning former faculty and students were welcomed back to Unilag.

A few months later, I was approached by Tai Solarin, founder of the Mayflower School and human rights activist, to accompany him (and others) to what had been Biafra, to check on continuing needs for private relief supplies that he was sending there. In a Land Rover for four days, we jounced around tank traps and over roads slashed repeatedly by retreating troops, to visit with survivors still caught in deprived conditions. We camped where we could, including in a deserted Nsukka University building pock-marked by bullets. It was a harrowing experience. Back home, this was the era of FLQ separatist violence, and although I had little information on such events while abroad, the issue of 'reconciliation' after such a level of conflict impressed itself on me, and has remained a matter of personal consideration as a Canadian ever since.

I might say (as background) that I was taught in graduate school by renowned Renaissance scholar Rosalie Colie, herself a student of famed art historian E. H. Gombrich. Colie emphasized THE critical question always posed by Gombrich, who apparently lisped: "What are the pothible alternativeth?" This continues to be a touchstone for me. For example, what might Nigerian decision-makers have done to prevent civil war in the first place, or to assuage its destruction of lives and resources?

But sometimes I apply this question in a lighter vein -- for instance, when thinking of the arts as well as of typical news coverage. Conflict, it is said, is the essence of drama -- and as for television news, well: "If it bleeds, it leads."

Recently, Ottawa was visited by 'La Machine', performance art consisting of giant mechanical beasts, the dragon-horse Long Ma and spider Kumo, who undertook activities around the city. I couldn't help noticing that these were mainly macho fights between Long Ma and Kumo. So I fancifully imagined some 'possible alternatives' for Long Ma and Kumo here, featuring feminist and peace themes. They could have:

- Visited the Peacekeeping Monument with the Minister of Defence, along with veteran peacekeepers receiving appreciation awards
- Held a tea party at the Women are Persons Monument with gender equality activists
- Convened a seminar about maternal health and reproductive rights with Kumo's cousin Maman, the giant spider sculpture, in front of the National Gallery of Art
- Taken flowers for a photo op with the Chief Justice & the statue of Justice at the Supreme Court.

A world with peace and no war? What a 'possible alternative' that would be.

By: Wendy Lawrence, Gender Equality Specialist

Canadian Support for American Resisters of the Vietnam War

One way many Americans demonstrated their opposition to the Vietnam War was to refuse to fight in it. Tens of thousands of these war resisters fled to Canada where they were accepted as landed immigrants. Many stayed on and, eventually, became Canadian citizens.

The Canadian Government had a mixed record on Vietnam. We were never a war belligerent. Our official position was one of neutrality. But many Canadians perceived our government as being pro-France and pro-USA in the two Vietnam wars, and even complicit with the USA in the latter. This gave rise to the emergence of a broad Canadian war opposition, whose activities ranged from protests to support for American war resisters.

One of the Canadian faith groups that became part of the anti-war movement was the Board of Evangelism and Social Service of the United Church of Canada. This group was new to social activism, and in fact, Ray Hord, its anti-war Secretary as of 1963, was often on (and sometimes beyond) the outer fringes of United Church policy. Hord was a moral dynamo, attuned to and passionately involved with the major world issues of the day.

I first saw the Reverend Ray Hord in the early 1950's, through the eyes of a child, when he was the minister at Lakeview United Church in Regina. My parents took me to his services from time to time. As a restless pre-teen with a limited attention span, I always breathed a sigh of relief when his sermons were over. But I was struck by his solemn and earnest demeanor, and eventually realized that many adults in the congregation listened to his stirring sermons, transfixed.

He left Regina in1959 and moved to Toronto. It was only after he assumed his new Board Secretary position that I happened to meet him once. By that time, he was a strong opponent of the Vietnam War, and I can remember him speaking of the underground railway that was bringing American war resisters to Canada.

Hord rose to national prominence when, in 1967, he described Canada's prime minister as a "puppy-dog on LBJ's leash". He stated that "Canadians should not support Americans who are bombing the hell out of those poor people", adding that a God who is on the side of the hurt, the maimed, and the defenseless, must be on the side of the Vietnamese.

His next move was even more controversial. After contacting the Toronto Anti-Draft Program, he persuaded his Board to offer financial grants to congregations and groups who wished to provide American war resisters with temporary residence in Canadian homes.

This decision was quickly overturned by the United Church's Moderator, and a few months later Hord died of a sudden heart attack.

But his stand was applauded by many other ministers, peace activists and even the future United Church Moderator, N. Bruce McLeod. His Church then went on to take much bolder action against the Vietnam War, working in conjunction with the Canadian Council of Churches and the Toronto Anti-Draft Program to aid American resisters in Canada.

Thus did Ray Hord leave his mark as a Canadian proponent of peace-building and non-killing.

By: D. J. Kiddo

Choosing Peace

Approximately five years ago, my husband was diagnosed with Dissociative Identity Disorder (DID). DID is a disorder caused by severe childhood trauma and results in multiple personalities who dissociate their actions from the host's memory. In childhood, this protects the host from the experience of the abuse. In adulthood, this creates chaos.

When I married my husband, I married the host of his DID system. Through the years, as his other personalities (called alters) made choices and engaged in behaviours that harmed our relationship, I many times pushed back in anger and frustration. I did not understand that my husband had a disability. It was invisible to us both and, having a lack of knowledge, led to a lack of compassion.

As my husband and I have learned more about his condition and journeyed together towards healing, we have had to commit to seeking peace in our relationship. This is not an easy commitment to fulfill when parts of my husband rage against the injustice of a world where predators can thrive; the predators command silence through violence and threats of further harm.

My husband's system must learn, one part at a time, what it means to truly forgive and have inner peace. This is not to suggest that his abusers should go without consequence for their actions but rather to accept the reality that even if that consequence should be visited upon them, continued anger, hate, and fear will only serve to damage my husband further and impede his ability to become whole.

Together, we chose to share our story and encourage others like us who are struggling to extend grace and kindness to those who do not understand. To those who would first judge and condemn, perpetuate the violence that is the origin of this disorder.

We share our story for those who have hurt us and for those we have hurt; we forgive and we seek forgiveness.

We choose peace.

By: Charmaine Panko, Wife and Mother,
https://mymanyhusbands.wordpress.com.

Rising

The rapping on our apartment door woke me. I didn't hear my parents in the next room moving to answer it so I got up and opened the door. Mr. Dthemedsis from the top floor stood in the hall in his pyjamas and said, "Get your father." They spoke quickly in Greek and my father told me to go back to bed. The two men hurried upstairs to listen to Mr. Dthemedsis' radio.

In the morning, only minutes into school, the Principal made an announcement beyond my new-to-Greek comprehension, but I followed the other kids out onto our buses to be driven back home. To keep me out of my mother's hair, my father took me with him downtown for some forms we needed signed by the police. If he had known what was going to happen, we certainly wouldn't have gone.

Police dashed everywhere in and around the headquarters. The officer behind the desk spoke to my father; I couldn't understand the rapid foreign words, but his volume and gestures made the message clear, "Not today! Get out of here and come back some other time! Go!" Leaving, I held my father's hand for reassurance as we weaved our way through rows and rows of towering policemen now formed up in ranks.

At the bus stop, the ground rumbled and I clutched my dad's hand tighter. Half a dozen dinosaur-sized tanks rolled past us—I could have reached out my short six-year-old arm and touched one, but didn't dare under the firm stare of the tanned taut face of a soldier riding on top.

At night, we watched the flickering black and white images on the Dthemedsis' television to learn that the army and police had stormed Athena Polytechneion, where students had barricaded themselves in a strike against the Junta. My mother explained that they were students at school like me; the army and police had killed them. I felt sick and scared, and knew that this was wrong—my six-year-old sense of justice was offended. My parents could not answer "why?" in a way that I could understand.

We soon returned to Canada. The image of the soldier on the tank, and what he may have done, continued to haunt me. I never wanted something like this to happen in my country.

By: Nicholas Curcumelli-Rodostamo, Lieutenant Colonel (Retired).

Saskatchewan Leads the Way to Canadian Medicare

Peace of mind can be sought by individuals in numerous ways, including meditation, yoga, religious worship, nature exploration, and physical exercise. But sometimes, when factors blocking personal peace are external rather than internal, this quest cannot be satisfied by individual endeavor alone.

A case in point is access to medical care. Should it be based on need, or ability to pay? If the latter, those without sufficient income to cover essential medical expenses will never enjoy peace of mind. Yet, that is how Canada was before 1962, when North America's first universal, comprehensive medical insurance program came into effect in Saskatchewan.

The idea of Medicare had been present in Saskatchewan since the Depression, when Reeve Matthew Anderson introduced a municipal medical care program in the rural municipality of McKilop in 1939. Five years later, the province elected a new CCF Government, led by Tommy Douglas. He soon showed his passionate commitment to easing the burden of medical costs by introducing a universal hospitalization insurance program in 1947. But it was not until the 1960's that his government felt ready to bring in a full-fledged Medicare program.

I was a high school student in Regina in the early 1960's, and can well remember the fierce acrimony of the Medicare debate. Tommy Douglas was Medicare's champion during Saskatchewan's 1960 election, making it his central campaign pledge. With its victory in that election, the CCF had the people's mandate to proceed with the Medicare act. Douglas steered the legislation through the Saskatchewan legislature until it was adopted in late 1961. Responsibility for putting it into effect (in mid-1962) was then passed to the new premier, Woodrow Lloyd.

Lloyd faced a phalanx of vitriolic opposition from the College of Physicians and Surgeons, the Canadian and American Medical Associations, provincial media, business interests, the provincial Liberal Party and pressure groups such as the Keep Our Doctors Committee. All were claiming that this "socialized medicine" would destroy the doctor-patient relationship, drive most of our doctors out of the province, and create a woefully inferior standard of medical care.

My mother discussed the issue with our family doctor who opposed Medicare, while she supported it. They agreed to disagree, although this became increasingly difficult when Saskatchewan's doctors went on strike for three weeks in July 1962. British and other European doctors came in to fill the gap, and finally an end to the strike was mediated. Medicare was then free to operate across the province.

Amazingly, all the supposed issues disappeared almost immediately. There was no government interference in the doctor-patient relationship. Doctors were paid by the government at the going rate, sometimes more quickly than before. Efficiently run, the program became so popular that other provinces soon followed suit.

Then in1966, the Canadian Parliament adopted the National Medical Care Insurance Act, providing for federal-provincial cost-sharing. By 1971, all provinces had Medicare in place, and access to medical care had become a basic right for all Canadians.

For this, a tip of the peace-building hat should go to Matthew Anderson, Tommy Douglas, Woodrow Lloyd, and the people of Saskatchewan who refused to bow to Medicare's fierce opponents in 1962.

By: D.J. Kiddo

How an Aid Worker Gained the Respect of Torturers

"I could see Marcella, still blindfolded, handcuffed, standing against a wall. She looked like a still photograph – objectified, dehumanized. It was then I knew I couldn't leave her. Not a big courageous decision; (it was) just the right thing to do."

With quiet intensity, 28 year-old Winnipegger Karen Ridd recently mesmerized audiences across southern Ontario, recounting her experiences in El Salvador. A clown-worker with autistic children, Ridd now belongs to Quaker-oriented Peace Brigades International which keeps spaces open in Central America for organizations committed to peaceful change. In November, with Colombian co-worker Marcella Diaz, she was assigned to a church sanctuary for refugees fleeing bombers over the inner city where they lived.

Suddenly, soldiers arrived. Church workers were seized, removed and not seen again for six weeks: Karen and Marcella, blindfolded and shackled, were hustled to the death squad torture centre. Separated, they were beaten, threatened, and interrogated for seven hours. The blindfold, Karen says, performs three functions: "You can't see your interrogator; you don't know where anything is coming from; you become faceless, and the unspeakable can be done."

After intervention from Ottawa, orders came for Ridd's release. Unexpectedly glimpsing Marcella, she refused to leave without her. "You wouldn't abandon your *campagnero*," she told her astonished captors.

Amazingly, behind the uniforms and rituals of terror they understood. Off came the wrist-locks and blindfolds. "They put me with Marcella; we could reach out and grab hands. For the next two hours, men came and stared; not in mockery, but with respect, and even a little bit of awe.

"I know those men were torturers," says Ridd. "But there in the heart of darkness, a spark of human caring bound us all." The experience confirmed her faith in "the god-presence in everyone". Also her confidence in non-violence "as a way of overturning the rules, breaking open a violent dynamic and changing it to something else."

Karen's Winnipeg family was never wealthy. Growing up she realized, however, that "as white North American, middle class, educated, I will always have access to power that most of the world's people do not..."

In El Salvador, "it's not communism versus democracy; it's a struggle of abject poverty versus opulence." The struggle has lasted centuries; 14 families still control the wealth. "When you talk to people living in cardboard houses, they don't spout Marxist theory. They talk of not having food for their children, fear that someone will bang on the door at midnight and take one of them away."

How do people go on in the face of that? A Salvadoran friend tells Ridd, "Despair is a first-world luxury. Those living in the issues of life and death don't indulge themselves by giving up."

Jubilant Eastern Europeans and Nelson Mandela, free at last in South Africa, are witness to that. Canadian support for people struggling for freedom, says Karen Ridd, means that "when they finally celebrate, we can be present with them, while they are dancing in the street."

By: Bruce McLeod, former Moderator of the United Church, written while Minister at Toronto's Bellefair United Church. Toronto Star, 1989

(Karen Ridd, winner of a Governor-General's Gold Medal, has since attained an M.A. in Peace and Justice, practiced as a mediator, facilitator, teacher and public speaker around the world, as well as teaching in the Conflict Resolution Studies programme at Menno Simons College.)

Lewis Perinbam

Lewis was Canada's most preeminent innovator in and champion of international development and cooperation, as Vice President of the Canadian International Development Agency (CIDA) in charge of voluntary sector (NGO) programs for nearly two decades. Born in Malaya in 1925 to Indian parents, he left as a child to be educated in Scotland, where he earned a degree in engineering.

The execution of his father at the hands of Japanese soldiers during World War II profoundly influenced Lewis to seek peaceful resolutions to global issues. In 1953, it also led him to Canada, a country he claimed embraced values and principles which did not prompt domination of others. He joined one of Canada's first NGOs, World University Service Canada (WUSC) who continues to honor his contributions through an annual award in his name. Lewis also co-founded Canadian University Service Overseas, Canada's equivalent of the Peace Corps. It sent young Canadians abroad as partners in development. Through both NGOs, he did much to shape the way that thousands of young Canadians came to view the world and their role in it.

After brief stints at UNESCO and the World Bank, Lewis joined CIDA in 1969 to head its fledgling NGO Programs Division, and stayed until his retirement in 1991 as Vice President of the Special Programs Branch (SPB). Under his leadership, SPB launched numerous initiatives to involve the private, NGO and institutional sectors in international development. Many were the first of their kind in the world.

This heightened Canada and CIDA's reputation as practising humane international development due to the premium they placed on policies and programs that were ethical, cooperative, and non-coercive. Colleagues in and out of government (and he built extensive and impressive net-works) remembered Lewis as a dynamic leader, an "anti-bureaucrat" who made things happen, and did not simply administer the status quo. His work was driven by a belief that the chief enemies of humankind were poverty, disease and illiteracy, which could only be defeated through international cooperation on many fronts.

Canada's growing stature among the nations of the world in the second half of the twentieth century, he often claimed, was not due to force of arms, but a commitment to peace. NGOs, he reminded Canadians, played a central role in creating Canada's international image as a compassionate and generous nation. Equally, they were often at the vanguard of great social justice and human rights struggles. Lewis used his power in and out of Ottawa to facilitate timely, consistent, and at times generous assistance to Canada's NGOs. While praising NGOs to his final days, he also warned that modern humanitarianism could lead to a new imperialism dominated by "donors" and "recipients;" and advocated for North-South relations based on partnership, not patronage.

Retirement from CIDA did not end his career in humanitarianism or commitment to justice and equality. As chief advisor to the president of the Commonwealth of Learning (COL), a Vancouver-based NGO, he helped improve access to education through distance learning resources, knowledge and technology. He chaired its Board of Governors until his death in 2007 and in 2000 led the landmark Canadian Government Task Force on the Participation of Visible Minorities in the Federal Public Service to make the public service more representative of Canadian society. Known for his leadership in "affirmative action", Lewis helped colleagues from disadvantaged communities chart new paths in much less inhospitable environments.

Lewis's tireless, if not relentless, devotion to the dream of international cooperation based on a truly equal partnership of service and learning were widely recognized with honorary doctorates (Calgary, York, Quebec, Brock, St Mary's and Victoria); the Sir Edmund Hillary Humanitarian Award, the Queen's Golden Jubilee Medal and the Order of Canada.

By: Kevin Brushett Ph.D., Assistant Professor/Professeur adjoint, Chair Military & Strategic Studies Program, Royal Military College of Canada/Collège Militaire Royale du Canada.

Making Peace between Two Families

In the mid 1980's, I was responsible for introducing a Canadian and Bangladesh government sponsored road repair program in 400 'Unions' around the Bay of Bengal. The objective in each 'Union' was to repair and maintain 15 of the most important miles of dirt roads, engaging 15 destitute women in each 'Union', either widowed, divorced or abandoned, usually a single parent, to do this road work on a year around basis. Altogether, 39 young Assistant Field Engineers (AFEs) were hired to introduce and implement the program.

In teams, they met each union chairman who identified 15 miles of the most important roads to be repaired and 15 'destitute' women for them to work with. The AFEs then trained each group of women to fix and maintain the roads and also monitored them regularly for two years. Among the AFEs was Rahim from Noakali District. From the other AFEs I learned that his young wife Rosina had been 'abducted' by her father because she was not being allowed to finish her secondary schooling, as agreed to in the marriage arrangements. Neither had the family bought her the promised clothing. Rahim, extremely distressed about the abduction, was only prevented from several suicide attempts by his fellow AFEs. They finally asked for my help.

I initially refused, since I was non-Bangladeshi and non-Muslim, and therefore did not feel qualified. But they continued to badger me until I finally agreed. Kamal, a very socially skilled AFE, agreed to help me. Getting involved in this family problem required careful planning, including meetings with Noakali government officials, the couple's match-maker, each family, as well as Rahim and Rosina - separately of course. Meeting Rosina at her father's home was emotional. Rosina was deeply unhappy and when asked if she wanted to go back to Rahim and his family said that, according to her understanding of her faith, there should only be one husband and wife and they should be together. Her obvious wish to be reunited with her husband and to live with his family, spurred me on to try my/our very best for her.

In the meantime, we learned that her father also had some financial motives for this abduction.

Finally, after months of heart wrenching efforts, I managed to arrange an official meeting - as was traditional, made up only of male members from both families, the match maker and a government official. Surprisingly, Rahim was also allowed to attend, and of course I was expected to be there. When asked why I had called the meeting, I explained that according to my understanding of Islam all efforts should be made to keep a husband and wife together and not separate them without justification, which seemed to be the case here.

The animated, frequently tense discussions took several hours. In the end, it was concluded that, while Rosina's father had some justification, he had acted wrongly. He was, consequently, to return his daughter to her husband's family. They, in turn, had to allow Rosina to attend school and have new saris. While Rosina's father was not happy with the overall outcome, he accepted the decision - including that he was to organize a meal for everyone to compensate for the abduction, with me as the guest of honour because of my effort to help make peace.

The next evening a fancy meal awaited us, and as so often was the case, I was the only woman among men. Following the meal, I was asked to go to the women's section to see if the new saris met with my approval. After checking with Rosina, I approved the selection. I was then asked to take Rosina and Rahim back to his family compound – directly to the mother-in-law's home. Why me? Because I had the only vehicle!!

After tear-filled and affectionate good-byes, I took Rahim and Rosina to Rahim's family who welcomed her with open arms. While it obviously took more time and effort to ensure long term peace between the families, Rahim and Rosina's reunion was the beginning of that peace. The following year, a child was born to Rosina and Rahim.

By: Ute Gerbrandt

Make Room for Peace at the Canadian War Museum

In 2005, as a panellist speaking at a local peace-related event in Ottawa, I was asked to reflect on what an "inclusive vision of peace" meant. At that time, about a kilometre away, a new building to house the Canadian War Museum was being built at the cost of about $137 million. I explained that the construction of a new museum building dedicated to war was interfering with my vision of peace.

As a result of that evening, a group of individuals began meeting to talk about what the new museum should include. The museum was not being called the Museum of Canadian Military History and therefore, to be true to its name as a war museum, why would it not also reflect Canadian efforts to oppose war and work for peace.

We did not question the need to honour the sacrifices and contributions made by thousands of Canadians in times of war, but felt that the new museum, with such potential to educate and inform, should also reflect Canadians' efforts to prevent wars and to promote disarmament and peace. It was always our concern that working for peace not be depicted as only a protest movement but reflect also peace literacy and the growing body of scholarly knowledge being generated through peace studies.

While we acknowledged the value of preserving and studying Canada's military history, increasingly, our small but determined group (including Penny Sanger, Murray Thomson and several other local activists) began to discuss if and how the new museum would address issues related to Canadians' involvement in war prevention, disarmament and peace. Would the thousands of visiting school children gain a broader understanding of conflict resolution and peacemaking and, for example, the role of diplomacy, international law and treaties in preventing and ending wars?

The group became known as "Make Room for Peace Committee" (MRFP) and met regularly. We sought and obtained the endorsement of our activism from more than 1000 Canadians from across the country. We met several times with senior officials at the Museum to gain a greater understanding of their plans. We requested and were given a tour of the partially constructed museum to get a feel for the building.

Not long after the War Museum opened, MRFP held a community consultation to discuss early impressions. One speaker who had come to Canada from Vietnam said of the museum "It failed to create an understanding of war, of how to deal with conflicts among groups and nations without using force. It also does not help me reflect on how we can live our life to promote peace and avoid war....How can we know about war if we don't learn about peace?"

The public meeting also focussed on the museum's displays and whether or not the CWM's mandate was fully reflected. Ideas for museum exhibits that teach about war prevention, disarmament and peacebuilding were also presented. The meeting was well attended by the public and, to the War Museum's credit, several senior officials accepted our invitation and were seen taking notes.

After many stops and starts, the CWM did go on to develop and mount an eight month exhibit "Peace - the Exhibition" in 2013, with plans to have a smaller version go on tour. While we can't be sure, the "Make Room for Peace Committee" likes to think that we had some (very) small influence in helping make room for peace at the new Canadian War Museum.

By: Debbie Grisdale

Faith is Peace: A Walk to Save our Sacred Site
Akikodjiwan

A special moment in my life occurred on June 23rd, 2017, when Algonquin elders led the Faith is Peace walk (Victoria Island to Parliament Hill, Ottawa). What made this walk so profoundly memorable for me is the fact that many of the region's faith leaders walked with us in support of our struggle for sacred *Akikodjiwan* (Chaudière Falls and nearby islands), a place of peace and harmony for Anishinabe since time immemorial. Together we stood as one. Indigenous roots intertwined with settler roots. The faith leaders, no doubt realizing that spiritual solidarity with us is surely something in line with Creator's plan for great Turtle Island!

The walk became a moving, breathing statement to Canada. First Nations spirituality is a faith. And as a faith with its own unique foundation and creation story, the First Peoples' places of worship must be protected with the same force and vigour Canadians would put into motion to protect a synagogue, a temple, a mosque, a church, or any house of worship, if a holy site came under attack by people who had absolutely no respect for it. Are we not duty-bound by Canada's constitution to do so?

It was with humility in my heart that I heard faith leaders eloquently express their support for our cause. Words from Archbishop Prendergast, Rabbi Bulka, Imam Samy Metwally, the Very Reverend Shane Parker and many others gave us renewed hope that *Akikodjiwan* will be saved.

First Nations spirituality was outlawed until almost 1960. This terrible act of oppression was, in my opinion, the worst of the many outrageous actions Canada took in her efforts to destroy the culture and identity of the First Nations Peoples. Today we often see media-produced photos or film footage of politicians partaking in a smudging ceremony. For most of the politicians who do so, smudging is nothing more than a photo op. Anyone who really respects the sacred medicines would never vote to allow a developer to defile and destroy *Akikodjiwan*. Yet that is what Ottawa City Council did when they allowed *Akikodjiwan* to be rezoned for the proposed "Zibi" condo development.

Terrorism and catastrophes are taking place in all areas of the planet. The world does not need more condos! We need more sacred sites, not less of them. It is not too late, we can still save

Akikodjiwan from destruction. The Faith is Peace walk reassured us of this!

As difficult as it might be for the good people of this country to emotionally digest, the truth is that the First Peoples are still fighting every day against oppression. We fight to regain our languages. We fight for resource sharing so that our impoverished communities can grow an economy and build schools.

But it is the struggle to revive our ancient spirituality which is of greatest concern for me and many, many more Algonquins and their supporters. Our spirituality was our way of life! Is it too much to ask to have it present once again for those of us who respect and honour it?

To my knowledge, the Faith is Peace walk was the first of its kind: interfaith groups rallied to support Indigenous spirituality. Let us hope it is not the last! Let us work together to save *Akikodjiwan* from the proposed "Zibi" development, and any other desecration.

Let us reclaim *Akikodjiwan* as a sacred place for peace and fellowship, not just for the First Peoples but for all Canadians. Canada will be greater because of it!

By: Keep the Circle Strong, South Wind (Albert Dumont)
Spiritual Advisor, Traditional Teacher, Mediation Facilitator

Toutes les Cossettes du monde

Un soir, à Montréal, je retrouvais mon auto dans la petite rue De Bullion, après être allé au Théâtre. Comme je m'apprêtais à monter à bord, tout près de moi, à une fenêtre, une jeune femme est soudainement apparue. Comme s'il s'était agi de Cosette, l'héroïne des « Misérables » de Victor Hugo. Dans son maigre visage, tous les signes de la pauvreté pouvaient s'y lire. Je ne l'ai jamais oubliée. Pourquoi était-elle pauvre quand beaucoup de ceux et celles que j'avais côtoyés ce soir-là étaient relativement à l'aise? Du point de vue de la justice sociale que pouvons faire pour combattre les inégalités et sortir toutes ces jeunes femmes de la pauvreté condition essentielle pour la paix?

Partout à travers le monde, les mesures d'austérité affectent davantage les femmes. Elles gagnent moins en salaire, dépendent davantage des bénéfices sociaux et se retrouvent souvent mères célibataires. Leur chance de vivre dans la pauvreté suite aux coupures budgétaires en sont multipliées.

Une solution pour réduire la pauvreté des femmes serait, comme l'a fait cette fois-ci notre gouvernement, d'élaborer des budgets qui tiennent compte de la situation particulière des femmes. Pour ce faire, les politiques de dépenses devraient être planifiées, élaborées et évaluées de façon à connaître quels seront les impacts pour les hommes et pour les femmes, grâce à une analyse différenciée selon les sexes. Ceci permettrait d'éviter des politiques qui créent de graves inégalités et de déterminer des opportunités d'appliquer des fonds pour aider des femmes. Ces mesures pourraient avoir un plus haut taux de retour sur investissement. Tous en bénéficieraient.

Par mon action à l'ACDI, J'ai fait en sorte qu'en investissant en eau, en électricité, on a pu réduire le travail domestique afin de permettre aux filles d'aller à l'école et de terminer leurs études et aux femmes de gagner de l'argent dans des activités lucratives. En Afrique, le travail agricole est en grande partie dévolu aux femmes. On a investi dans leur travail en leur procurant de meilleures technologies, meilleurs accès aux marchés ce qui a augmenté la production agricole et réduit la rareté des aliments, un bénéfice pour tous.

Ici-même au Canada, dans certains domaines, à travail égal, les femmes gagnent moins que les hommes. En gagnant moins, elles peuvent moins bien nourrir leur famille et risquent d'être en moins bonne santé. Tout ceci a un coût économique pour notre société. C'est très inefficace. Pourquoi le travail des femmes n'est-il pas autant valorisé que celui des hommes? La femme a pourtant une plus lourde charge au sein du foyer d'où l'importance de lui donner tous les moyens financiers pour bien remplir ses tâches et se sortir de la pauvreté.

Combien de petites Cosettes de la rue De Bullion y a-t-il au milieu de nous ? Elles aussi ont le droit d'aspirer à une vie meilleure. Je voudrais suggérer qu'il est de notre devoir de nous assurer que les jeunes filles et les femmes autour de nous acquièrent une pleine confiance en elles-mêmes. Faisons en sorte qu'elles ne soient pas dans la pauvreté et l'ignorance et qu'elles puissent assurer, par leurs propres efforts, leurs droits à travers une solide éducation.

Voilà une façon d'œuvrer pour la paix.

Par: Yves Morneau, Professionnel de la paix, CPSC, (www.civilianpeaceservice.ca).

An Objective Technology to Create World Peace

June 8, 1974 was a life-changing day for me. It was the day I learned the Transcendental Meditation (TM) technique. It quickly became my most powerful intervention for personal development and my greatest business tool. The Transcendental Meditation technique is also a technology that can create world peace. Prior to June 8, 1974, at the tender age of 21, I had little hope for the future of mankind. But on that auspicious day, after transcending for the first time, my view of the world changed permanently.

Fast forward to December 1983, in Fairfield, Iowa, USA, the home of Maharishi University of Management, I had the opportunity to participate in an extraordinary research project. Maharishi Mahesh Yogi, the founder of the Transcendental Meditation programme, brought together a group of 8000 advanced practitioners of TM from around the world to demonstrate the use of this technology to create world peace.

The actual number of practitioners required was only 7000. This was the square root of 1% of the population of the planet at that time. This number was calculated by the application of principles in modern physics and it was hypothesized to be the number required to create coherence in collective consciousness of the world, creating world peace.

We were watching world events very closely during this two-week experiment for signs of rising coherence in the collective consciousness of the world, as evidenced by reduced negativity and increased positivity. Most notably, we saw major conflicts in the world come to an end – including the Soviet invasion of Afghanistan, a seven-year war between Iran and Iraq that had killed millions, and, most notably and unexpectedly, the Soviet-American Cold War that had threatened the world with nuclear annihilation for forty years.

In 1993 the TM creating coherence experiment was replicated in Washington, DC. Government leaders and police were advised of the effects this large group was to have on the city and surrounding area. During this time, violent crime rate was down 16%. The maximum decrease was 23.3% when the size of the group was largest during the final week of the project.

When the prestigious Journal of Conflict Resolution was presented with the data, they were not satisfied and asked that the data be rerun with more rigorous criteria before they would publish the results. To the chagrin of the Journal of Conflict Resolution, the results were even better.

Since 1993, large TM peace-creating groups have participated in over 23 scientifically validated peer-reviewed research projects in the Middle East, Africa, Southeast Asia, and Latin America. The results produced by temporary TM peace-creating groups (lasting weeks or months) have been consistently positive—with nearly immediate reductions in war deaths averaging better than 70%.

With only a small group of people creating coherence in their own consciousness through the TM technique, practitioners can affect the collective consciousness of the region thereby reducing negative tendencies and increasing positive tendencies in the area.

One day this technology will be implemented on a large scale and permanent TM peace-creating groups will be resident and every nation – or at least a couple of large groups with a capacity to create world peace.

By: Roy Anderson is a certified teacher of the Transcendental Meditation Programme (randerson@tm.org).

Buddy

In my late 40s, I said goodbye to my partner and grown daughters, and took to the road on a peace mission. I walked from town to town, talking to church groups and kindergarten classes, camping outside military bases, sharing my concerns and hopes.

In 1988/89, I was crossing Canada. The scenery was truly awe-inspiring, every day revealing beauty—sailboats bobbing like white corks on a lake; Aurora Borealis dancing across a midnight sky; a lone crocus in a prairie meadow.

I often walked alone and usually relished the freedom. But one day in Northern Ontario, having trekked through long stretches of tree after tree after tree, it hit me how vast and unpopulated Canada was and how bored and lonely I felt. I longed for a bit of comfort and conversation, or at least something novel.

Suddenly I spied another solitary figure on the distant horizon. Oh great—someone to talk to! I thought at first, but my enthusiasm waned as I began to wonder why someone was out there all alone. I didn't clue in to what an equally unusual sight I must have been.

I could tell the shape was a man. He stood still, which struck me as peculiar. Maybe he's waiting for a bus, I proposed, soon realizing how irrational that was considering our remoteness. Frightening thoughts then filled my mind. Is he a serial killer? Nowhere to run.... No witnesses.... My dread grew with each slowing step I took towards him. Then I noticed the backpack slung on his shoulder, the tan, the beard, and travel-worn expression. It was like looking in a mirror. As I reached his side, I smiled and nodded. He smiled and nodded. Next, I swear, we exclaimed in unison, "What the heck are you doing out here in the middle of nowhere?" Laughing, we sat down at the side of the road, letting our stories unravel.

Buddy was hitchhiking to Edmonton to visit his sister. He shared sad tales of relationships gone bad, jobs lost, alcoholism, and even time served at the Kingston Penitentiary. I didn't want to know about his criminal record, as that serial killer image still lurked in the back of my mind. He went on though, desperate to talk to this captive audience. His tragic tale revealed one wrong turn after another, but he was looking on the bright side, sincerely willing to change his life.

Eventually I shared my mission, to which Buddy exclaimed, "Get outta here, you're pulling my leg! All the way across the country? That's so cool. And for peace? Right on!" He must have quizzed me for a good half hour; it was as if he'd met an alien and wanted to know all about life on Mars. Soon, I heard the familiar roar of an oncoming semi and I turned to face it. The driver was slowing down so I stuck out my thumb for once instead of two fingers in a "V" for peace.

The semi stopped, and my new friend picked up his backpack. "Are you coming?" he asked. I reminded him I was relying on my feet. He laughed, shaking his head, and then dug down into his dirty blue jeans to pull out a fistful of change. "It's all I have, but it's yours."

"Thanks, friend, but you'd better keep those coins," I said. "You've got a long haul ahead."

"No way, man," he replied. "I need to do something for peace too. Take it, bro, please."

I couldn't insult him, so I held out my hand and his offerings—including a sticky fuzz-coated piece of candy—tumbled into my palm. I grimaced at the sight of the gooey gumball. "The money's for peace, but the candy's for being so sweet to listen to my gripes," he said with a laugh. He gave me the peace sign and climbed into the cab of the truck. I watched the semi roll away into the distance. Alone again, I walked on, grinning.

By Carolyn Affleck Youngs, Victoria Written by her late husband, Derek Youngs

Power of Listening and Being Heard

A family was caught in a dilemma. The parents were in agreement that their teenage son should attend a faith-based school with great teachers, an excellent reputation, and a record of instilling solid moral values in its students. Their son, on the other hand, passionately wanted to attend the same school his friends would be attending. This would mean that he would have to get up much earlier than if he chose the school his parents preferred. However, he would be with his friends, and this meant the world to him.

This was no small matter – the young fellow was so distraught he cried every night, getting very little sleep and had lost all interest in anything but his future school. He wouldn't talk to his family, refused to attend any social functions and was just miserable and angry all the time. His parents were very concerned, felt they were "losing" him, and ultimately sought help. It was agreed, with their son, that they would attend a mediation session.

The "normal", traditional arrangements were made, i.e., agreeing with the mediator on the approach (in writing), "rules" of behaviour for all parties (e.g., respectful listening), what form any agreement would take (e.g., no agreement would be concluded until all elements were agreed to), etc. Regardless, the early stages of the discussion were difficult, very tenuous, with both parents and son very emotional and, at times, a lot of walking on eggshells.

Opportunities were provided for both parents and their son to express their views from their unique perspectives, making sure that:

- Both the son and the parents were listened to and understood (by one another),
- Equal opportunities were provided to express feelings/emotions as well as concerns,
- Both parents understood and accepted that their son, too, was concerned about growing up with solid moral values and a good education.

Gradually, the elements of a potential solution began to emerge. Ultimately it was agreed that the son would go to the school he had chosen so that he could be with his friends, even though this meant getting up every day significantly earlier to catch the school bus. It was difficult for the parents, but they acknowledged, they agreed, that this was best for their son. Contingency plans were also developed, i.e., the son made commitments whereby, if he did not keep them, he agreed to transfer to the parent's choice of school. Everything was documented in writing and a third party identified to arbitrate any resulting issues or disagreements related to implementation.

Several days after the mediation session, the mediator received a call from one of the parents. The parent said "You won't believe what has happened. Our son has changed his mind - he wants to go the school we suggested he go to before the mediation session."

According to the son, the key reasons for his change of heart were a) he could get up later every day, if he went to his parent's choice of school, and b) they had listened to him...really listened to him, and he felt heard.

As a result, he could relax and think the situation through logically...and he decided that what they proposed was the best option for him.

By: Gord Breedyk, (www.civilianpeaceservice.ca).

2014 Ukraine Presidential Elections Support Mission

I was part of the OSCE 2014 Ukraine presidential elections support mission. I felt the trip would change anyone's perspective about the need to reflect on the ethic of care for others.

I think this experience was not so much about the technical or observing side of elections, or even the security issues, the police, the war, military presence, checkpoints or roadblocks, the political problems, but about the people living there. People seemed either caught in the middle of all this, living every day with anxiety, uncertainty or fear; living away from the conflict in big cities like Kiev, in lives quite normal and happy.

My team was sent to an area next to Donetsk on the Asov Sea, a Russian speaking area.

I guess it was the emotional context that struck me the most. Once we were in a remote village in a Russian speaking area and stopped to get directions. Unfortunately, we were driving in a big black Jeep Grand Cherokee with tinted windows. My driver and interpreter, both Russian speaking, were assumed to be separatists or gangsters and were asked if we were here to kill anyone. Is this what some live with when strangers show up here?

In another village, they obviously had never seen international observers before. After being denied access to a polling station, we had a long discussion with the police, even attracting the attention of a very suspicious district police Colonel who allowed us access under strict police escort and presence.

At another polling station, the Colonel showed up again and, as it was closed, called the polling station committee member, an old lady with a headscarf. With some concern for her, my interpreter told me the Colonel told her not to be afraid of these people and just answer their questions. There were two police there, one a quite watchful policewoman with the most wooden, unemotional look I have ever seen, almost as if helpless to prevent anything I could do to upset the old woman or make her afraid.

No response when I said hello to her. I was sure she was figuring where she would like to shoot me if she could.

Since everyone was so tense, I decided to put the checklist aside and just sat beside the old woman and talked about Canada, and why we were here, and how she was doing, and her views on the election and life in the village. I had her show me how people would vote here and I commented on how ready she was, and the good she was doing for the village and country.

After a while she really brightened up and became quite animated and my translator could not keep up.

When I got up to leave she took my hand in both of hers and would not let go for a while, wanting us to come back on election day to be with them. I put my arm around her for a moment. I then did the rounds of everyone there saying *spasibo* and *das vidanya* and shaking hands and began to leave.

As I stepped through the door to leave to building, I turned and the police woman was there behind me. She looked at me and simply and firmly said "Good Bye" in what sounded like the only English words she knew, and gave me a smile that I do not think I will ever forget for the rest of my life.

Sometimes life has a way of working out.

All this was in my head for quite a while. Seemed to me that the peacemaker thing of "presence, impartiality, values and communication" really counts. The value of heart-level relational talk before mind-level checklist stuff. Just being with people in their lives and times of crisis. Anyway, a tiring but rewarding mission. A beautiful country with many good people. I have hope for them but know it will not be easy.

Paul Maillet, Colonel (retired), pmaillet@magma.ca, PAUL MAILLET CENTER FOR ETHICS (http://paulmailletethics.wordpress.com), ACCREDITED PEACE PROFESSIONAL Civilian Peace Service Canada, (http://paulmailletpeacemaker.wordpress.com).

Faithfully Yours

In a situation when our land Sri Lanka,
With its bells and clocks and flowers gone to dogs
And it with its triple gems gone to rocks
Due to civil war,
In a situation when Sinhala, Tamil and Muslim communities
struggled to survive so far,
In a situation when peace and co-existence was at peril
It was Canadian High Commission and other INGOs came forward
In 1998
For us to emerge as a Consortium headed and guided by
Mr. Senthurajah in the district of Ampara
With Community mobilization,
Engaging in community development activities, facing risks and
Challenges.
The lives of civilians had become sentences without a subject and a
predicate
in our district and ended with a comma or question mark due to civil
war
and ethnic conflict as a result,
Yet, our Consortium had and has been playing its role to help
civil societies in their needs
through its member organizations, as a strong networking body in
the district
till today.
Hats off to all including Canadian High Commission supported
Our Consortium to go ahead with its vision and mission till today.

From the Heart of a Civilian in Ampara District, Eastern Province, Sri
Lanka

By: V. Paramasingam, Vice Chairman

Making the World a Better Place, One Person at a Time

Prologue: A few weeks ago, I – Evelyn – was copied on the e-mail below. Earlier that day Diane had been called away urgently from our meeting. Her explanatory message that evening touched me so deeply that I urged her to submit it as a peace story. Diane was reluctant to do so - partly because she felt it might sound too self-serving. I can testify that self-serving is not in Diane's DNA and that this was not penned for promotional purposes. After much arm-twisting, I was permitted to submit her story.)

"My ex-husband had a stroke this morning. It was his day off. When he got out of bed to go to the bathroom, his hands were numb. And when he called to his dog, his speech was slurred. His wife was already at work. But he managed to reach 911 on his own.

I spent a large part of the afternoon at the hospital and was there when they did some neurological tests on him. His cognitive function is fine (no idea of his long-term memory yet) but he did remember meeting my daughter's boyfriend last night! And he did crack a couple of jokes, but his speech is slurred. His right arm and right leg are weak but not paralyzed. He is very, very lucky! They won't know long term effects until 24 hours after the stroke as his body has to go through the whole stroke process. I was glad I went and it was his current wife, my daughter and myself who spent a couple of hours by his bed, turning him, propping him up, etc. I am very fortunate that we all have a very good and supportive relationship.

When I left my husband, in 1993, I left for the kids. We were more friends than partners and I wanted the kids to know what a loving relationship could be (in marriage). But we remained friends and became a "parental unit" with Paul, my second husband. I remember telling the kids that family consists of those people that love you. It's not defined by birth or by marriage but by love and support and that they had many people, many grandparents and parents that loved them.

My daughter saw that again today, when I was there for Sandy (my ex-husband) and for Francoise (his wife). We just are there for each other. That is my way of making a difference in this world.

What I forgot to say in my introduction this morning is that my mission in life is to make the world a better place, one person at a time. And that is why I do the work that I do, which is that I facilitate, train and coach in the space of relationship system intelligence. I work in the interpersonal relations area and help to surface what is going on at a subconscious level to help people understand themselves and others better. The more I can normalize someone's experience, the easier it becomes for them to understand where they or someone else may be coming from."

Epilogue: Within 24 hours of being admitted, he was fully paralyzed and breathing with a respirator. After almost three weeks, the doctors finally figured out that he had suffered a bilateral brain stem stroke. Almost two months later, he is still in ICU, quadriplegic, has a tracheostomy and is fully conscious, the stroke having avoided the brain but rather hit the brain stem and motor functions. He has a wide circle of family and friends who continue to be by his side to keep his spirits up. Our daughter has found a way for him to communicate using an alphabet board. Aimee shared with me that she was so grateful that we all get along and especially that Francoise and I get along so well. It has made it easier for her as she can be open with all of her emotions and concerns. She is grateful that she was brought up that way and can see other options than relationships falling apart and people hating each other. It makes her sad that others don't see that too.

By: Diane Brochu-King (as e-mailed to friends by Diane after the hospital visit, and submitted in this form by Evelyn Voigt, after much brow-beating for permission to do so!)

Canada and the Founding of the United Nations

"The new organization must come to think and act less and less in terms of force and more and more in terms of forces – the forces that create and destroy international unity and goodwill; the forces that create poverty and promote well-being." – Lester Pearson, April 1945.

The Canadian delegation to the founding conference of the United Nations arrived in San Francisco in late April 1945 in poor spirits. Their American hosts' assurances notwithstanding, the Canadians found themselves without office space and typewriters. To compound matters, one of Canada's chief negotiators, Ambassador Lester Pearson, had shared a train from Washington with Herbert Evatt, Australia's chatty minister of external affairs. Evatt's non-stop waxing about Australia's emergence as a rising power had left Pearson with a terrible head-ache. Making matters worse, the train had lost his luggage.

Nonetheless, the 22-member Canadian contingent quickly got down to business. The San Francisco conference had been called to create a new international centre for global governance. The negotiators' text had been drafted largely by the United States and the United Kingdom, and their plan already had the general approval of the Soviet Union, China, and France. Together, these five countries were set to become Great Powers: the only permanent members of the United Nations executive body, the Security Council, and the only ones with veto power over international responses to global crises. The latter was a touchy subject. How could a purportedly inclusive organization – one that committed to recognizing the equality of sovereign states – grant special powers to five of its members? To many, Evatt included, the veto undermined the spirit of the United Nations before the project had even gotten underway.

The Canadians shared Evatt's concerns, but not his attitude. They, too, recognized that the future world organization would be judged in large part on the sincere commitment of its founding members to equality and peace. But they also understood that successful international diplomacy sometimes required compromise. The Americans and Soviets had been clear for months: if the new world body did not grant them the right to veto United Nations Security Council decisions, they would walk away from the negotiations and never return. With memories of the failed League of Nations fresh on their mind, Prime Minister William Lyon Mackenzie

King, his ministerial colleagues, and his government officials responded accordingly.

At first, the Canadian delegation sought to modify the scope of the Great Powers' privileged position. Perhaps the veto could be limited to specific cases of international conflict, for example. Their suggestions were poorly received. The Soviets reiterated that any modifications of the power of the UN Security Council's permanent members would lead to their immediate departure from San Francisco. Evatt refused to back down, and New Zealand's Prime Minister, Peter Fraser, publicly declared the veto "an evil thing." The Canadians responded differently. Having secured confirmation from both Washington and Moscow that there would be no United Nations without the Great Power veto; Ottawa took a public stand in its favour. The need for an inclusive world organization dedicated to the promotion of international peace and security was too critical to be risked for the sake of abstract principles.

The New York Times announced the Canadian decision to back the veto on its front page, and a number of the smaller powers accepted Ottawa's argument. An Australian amendment to limit the veto failed, and the organization launched successfully at the end of June.

The experience was a lesson for Canada's diplomatic community. Peace at any costs was no peace at all. The United Nations was never meant to achieve nirvana; rather it was designed to prevent catastrophic failure. Keeping the Great Powers involved was a positive step in that direction.

By: Adam Chapnick, Professor, Deputy Director, Education, Directorate of Academics, Canadian Forces College, National Defence.

Peace – The Way of the Horse

Peace has many different meanings - Peace from war, violence or hostility, Inner Peace, Nature's Peace. I want to tell you about the "horse" peace and how it can teach us humans about true peacefulness, about being in a true state of serenity and calmness.

Our horses at Unbridled Coaching - People Whispering™ - show our clients how presence = peace of mind. You see, horses are prey animals who have survived on the planet for more than 50 million years. They are completely attuned with their environment. So completely that they can detect your heart rate from 200+ feet away. And they know how to detect danger in the split of a second. In a wild herd, the lead mare simply needs to caulk her ear and the whole herd will look up. If she says there is true danger, they all run; if she said there is no danger, they go back to eating the grass.

Horses are a flight animal so their first instinct is to run. Funny, though, once they have run far enough away to feel safe and the so called "danger" has not followed them, they will turn back around and look and slowly and cautiously approach whatever it was that was so scary. Once the "danger" has dissipated, they will come back to the present moment. Ah, the present moment! Yes, that moment when there is no future to be anxious about and no past to be sad or feel regret about. That moment when all is right in the world.

Horses are connected to their natural intelligence. Something that humans seem to have lost over the years. What do I mean by natural intelligence? I mean our intuition, our ability to read and listen to our bodies. In our societies and fast-paced world we have come to learn to disconnect from our bodies, to override them and to spend most of our time in our heads, telling stories about what is going on in our life — most of them untrue and most of them exaggerated.

Horses are spiritual beings who reach us to the depths of our soul. Once you have seen yourself through the eyes and soul of the horse, you will find that inner peace you so sought after. You will see yourself as completely perfect in your imperfection. You will find that serenity, that calmness that we all long for. Living in their presence is a gift that I am eternally grateful for.

By: Marlene Armstrong, Co-founder, Unbridled Coaching www.unbridlecoaching.com

My Friend's Greatest Gift

From my earliest years, my family filled me with the belief that there is a God that, above all things, is love. This belief in a Supreme Intelligence who loved me beyond conception made me feel safe, happy and at peace.

I stood out for my natural ability in the arts, encouraged by a father who also loved to draw. But it never entered my mind to become an artist. "It's a nice hobby, but not practical, and will never give you enough money to feed a family," my loved ones would say whenever anyone commented on my abilities. And I believed them.

My self-esteem was abysmal, compounded by the importance my family placed on humility. To aspire to anything greater in life was to presume to be more than others. "Who am I to dream such an impossible dream?" I concluded.

After high school, I worked in jobs that didn't require much skill until, to my surprise, I was contracted to work fulltime at a respected insurance firm. Everyone was thrilled to see me become a tie-and-jacket office man.

But my happiness didn't last long. Between resolving customer claims and complaints, to filling out endless, redundant administrative forms, I had little time for anything else, including my creativity. I began to glimpse a very dark road ahead. Was this all that the future held for me?

"Work is not meant to make you happy," my family would say. "Work gives you dignity. It is a great honour to put bread on the table with the sweat of your brow."

But all that changed in an instant when Javi died.

Javi was my best friend. We grew up together. We lived in the same neighborhood, went to the same school and were in the same classes together. We were twenty-four when he died.

They told me it was an accident, that the guard-rail upon which he leaned at the construction site did not support his weight. After a week in a coma, he was gone.

In the days that followed, I moved like a zombie, blinded by feelings of impotence and rage. And a burning question: "why?" One fact was indisputable: It could have been me lying in that coffin. All my sacrifice, all my hard work, and for what? To live a life that, sooner or later, would take me to that same place?

I remember lying in bed one night and – was it a dream? – watching him appear, a smile on his lips, and sit by my side. He held my trembling hand in his, in the same way he used to every time we saw each other. A torrent of emotions flooded me and, in a loud voice, I promised:

"Javi, I will live the life that you couldn't. My life will have meaning. I will do the things that truly make me happy; that would have made us both happy. I will never again live in fear. I promise you."

When, two months later, my firm informed me that they would not renew my contract, I saw it as an opportunity to fulfill my promise. It was at this time that the seed of trying to live from my artwork was planted. And the day would eventually come when I would leave everything behind to make that promise a reality.

Javi's passing was a wake-up call for me, the point at which how I saw the world and how I made decisions would be forever changed. It was a fundamental step in what would later become the most precious gift that his friendship would grant me: a powerful awakening. It would lead me to connect once again with divinity – the great lost Love of my childhood – and to experience an unshakeable peace that would accompany the next steps of my life's journey.

By: Alberto Agraso, Intuitive Artist, Peace Pilgrim
(http://walkingforpeace.com).

Music – My Conduit to a Place of Peace

I have always loved to sing. From the time I first learned to speak I was probably already singing and making up songs. Sometimes to the chagrin of my siblings, who would beg me to stop singing the same song over and over again. Music also made me feel good and gave me a sense of purpose.

Over the years I honed this craft and became a professional singer.

It was not always an easy career choice and it did come with a lot of setbacks. Disappointments, long and late hours and loneliness too. There is a lot to give up in order to gain in this industry and I soon felt I had to make a choice.

In the end I chose to have a marriage and a family, with a career in music as a part of my life and not my whole life.

Why did I make the choice to keep music in my life?

Singing and performing is a communication that can break down barriers. Sometimes I feel anger about things. Whether it be a personal disagreement, receiving bad news or generally finding that the world is not an easy place to live in. But once I start to sing and perform I feel transformed. It's as though my songs act as a conduit to a quieter more peaceful place. A place that I can carry my listeners to.

Every December for the last 5 years, I have been putting on a small seasonal performance. Most of the audience are friends and sometimes new faces show up. There is always a deliberate sentiment to these performances. A mixture of playfulness and melancholy. An opportunity to reach out and touch the hearts of my audience and to connect at a time of year when so many of us are coming together to celebrate. That time where we collectively gather our thoughts on the year that is leaving us and the year that is ahead.

To be able to make people feel emotions, cry, laugh and, hopefully, enlightened is a gift that I am pleased to share. A gift that others, like myself, can use to make a difference. To help open up those dark places and let out the demons. A place that is filled with a myriad of colour and sound that all humankind can relate to.

By: Geri Childs. Her two CDs are "Intimate States of Mind" (1994) and "More than Magic" (2014). (www.gerichilds.com).

Peace, Please

I haven't been touched by war. I'm one of the lucky ones. My first father-in-law served with Royal Canadian Air Force during the Second World War. He lost an eye and the use of two fingers, shot by the enemy while he was in his tail gunner position in a Lancaster Bomber.

He seldom talked about it.

My current father-in-law, whom I never met – he died before my husband and I got together – served with the Canadian Army as a truck driver in France during the Second World War. Back home, his hair went white prematurely, and he jumped nervously at any unexpected noises.

Family said he seldom talked about it.

My father was a Captain in the Canadian Army and served in Korea and Japan. My mother said he was gone for 11 months, 10 days and 9 hours, approximately. I was a baby; my younger brother was born while Dad was away.

Dad seldom talked about it.

My step-son served with the PPCLI, Princess Patricia's Canadian Light Infantry, as a peacekeeper in Bosnia, then as a soldier with the first contingent of Canadians who went to Afghanistan in 2003. He was right there when our first four soldiers were killed - in a "Friendly Fire" accident, by Americans. When he phoned home to tell us that he was not among the dead, we heaved a huge sigh of relief – and cried. I understand that PTSD also affects the survivors.

He seldom talks about it.

I am richly endowed with good friends, many of whom are immigrants. Some come from war-battered countries. They don't talk about it much, they are here to start over and give their families a better opportunity to succeed and prosper. In my previous career, I was an ESL teacher. English as a Second Language. Several keen learners came from war-torn countries.

They didn't want to talk about it, but I heard stories now and then of the difficulties they and their families endured when they came to Canada as immigrants or refugees. One newly-arrived mother told me how her children were terrified by the sound of thunder – they were used to hearing bombs dropping nearby.

We lost our innocence and naivety when the New York Twin Towers went down. Had war come to our continent? Surely not to Canada. We boast of our clean, safe country. We can toss a soccer ball or enjoy Yoga Wednesdays right on the front lawn of our Parliament Buildings, the seat of government. What other country in the world can say that?

But wait, what happened when a home-grown Canadian lad crept up and killed our War Memorial guard, then managed to try again right inside the Centre Block?

Are we safe?

Are we secure?

Have we become suspicious of every stranger we meet?

When the Tomb of the Unknown Soldier was inaugurated in 2000 by Governor General Adrienne Clarkson, my husband and I stood in Confederation Park with thousands and thousands of others. The entire downtown was eerily silent, we heard only the occasional bird call or baby cry. Emotions welling, I listened to the GG's eloquent speech about that boy, that 19-year old Canadian WWI soldier whose bones represented all soldiers who had been killed in war, and had been brought back to Ottawa to rest in that beautiful granite tomb on the site of the War Memorial.

I looked around at my fellow observers. Many like me, were choked up, tears running down their faces, pulling Kleenexes from their pockets. I thought to myself, 'That anonymous young man, it could have been my grandfather, my father, my brothers, my sons – but it wasn't.' I was one of the lucky ones.

No one close to me has been killed in a recent conflict; but in thinking about all the sacrifices of so many, I can't say that I haven't been touched by war.

By: Pat Hall

Canada and the UN: Building Bridges to Overcome HIV/AIDS, 1994

What was the greatest threat to societal peace in 1994? The rapidly spreading HIV/AIDS epidemic was surely a contender for this dubious distinction. By the mid-1990's, AIDS had killed 6 million people worldwide, some 21 million people were living with HIV, and in five different countries of hardest-hit Africa, more than one in ten adults were HIV-infected.

The UN system, particularly WHO, had begun developing programs to help affected countries. But these programs were uncoordinated, narrowly-based, and devoid of any inter-agency focus.

Recognizing this, two WHO staff members approached Canadian UN delegates, asking us to take the lead in creating a joint and co-sponsored UN program, later to be known as UNAIDS. We accepted this challenge, and set our sights on getting a UNAIDS resolution adopted by the UN Economic and Social Council (ECOSOC).

This was no easy task. Traditionally UN economic and social resolutions are formulated through bargaining sessions between donor and recipient countries, with the former wanting to do less and the latter wanting to have more. This is often a debilitating process, more conducive to erecting walls than building international bridges.

So we decided to dispense with this usual procedure in favor of reaching out to the most affected regions right from the outset. We established a small core group, initially including Canada, Uganda (with one of the highest HIV infection rates in the world) and India (with the highest absolute number of HIV/AIDS cases).

Ugandan and Indian delegates then gathered support from other African and Asian governments, while we expanded our core group to Sweden to get the Europeans on board; and, Argentina to gather support from the Americas region. We also worked closely with Australia, whose delegation would chair all 1994 ECOSOC meetings on this subject.

We asked the UN development system to put together an outline describing what UNAIDS would look like, but they were not yet able to do so. So we developed this outline ourselves, and attached it to the draft UNAIDS resolution we had already crafted.

This two-part document then became the focus of ECOSOC negotiations.

In the end, negotiations were a breeze. With our united inter-regional front, our resolution gained the sponsorship of 50 countries, and was adopted, without opposition, during ECOSOC's 1994 summer session. Congratulating Canada on its leadership, Sweden called it "probably the most significant single decision" of the session.

And so UNAIDS was created, with an initial membership of UNDP, UNICEF, WHO, UNFPA, UNESCO and the World Bank. Later five other organizations joined, for a total of eleven. To this day, the UNAIDS family remains the focal point for UN advocacy and programming aimed at overcoming the global HIV/AIDS epidemic.

DJ Kiddo

A Brave Step for Peace

In the early post-war days of 1999, tensions remained high in Kosovo, wounds were raw, suspicion permeated daily transactions and boundaries were deeply drawn between Albanian, Serb and Roma. I ran the Training Unit for the Organization for Security and Cooperation in Europe (OSCE).

A and L were two young men hired as Training Assistants. A came from Pec/Peje, deep in Kosovo Liberation Army heartland, close on the border with Albania and devastated by the war. The fires still smouldered amidst ruined walls scrawled in defiant Serbian graffiti by departing troops, the market reduced to charred rubble and ruin. The Pej monastery was the core of Serbian Orthodoxy in the old lands of Kosove/Metohija and a source of Albanian resentment.

A's father was well-known and respected, the family name a pillar of Albanian culture. A, his education interrupted by the war, came to Pristina where he impressed with his enthusiasm, knowledge of computers and wonderfully warm, cheerful personality. He was hired to teach computing skills to eager colleagues, until so recently deprived of such opportunities.

L came from a long-established Pristina family that spoke Albanian, Serbian and Turkish. His grandmother was Turkish, and his parents had helped a Jewish family emigrate to Palestine after WW2. The family had fled to Macedonia with thousands of others during the height of the fighting in Kosovo. They later re-established themselves in their former home. L had worked with the earlier OSCE Verification Mission in Kosovo, knew his way around and was a born politician.

Early in 2000, the Training Unit was mandated to provide "Land Mine Awareness Training" to all OSCE field offices throughout the territory. This included the Serbian enclaves where much of the remaining Serbian population had retreated. We had held such sessions occasionally on request, in partnership with the Swedish De-mining Company attached to the NATO forces. This was different.

Above having the Swedish soldiers give information and do the demonstration, it required A and L, representing the OSCE, to give both Albanian and Serbian translation to ensure that all the staff, national and international were made aware of the continuing risk from land-mines, many poorly or not mapped. It felt irresponsible to require these two young men to take such a risk but lacking a Serbian staff member, we felt we had no choice. Still we debated. The Swedes already had a good working relationship with A and L.

Yet there was hesitancy on their part, given the intensity of feeling between the two ethnic groups, with language paramount in the mutual distrust and animosity. An international OSCE staff member had been killed on Pristina's main street for using the wrong language. Serbian homes were still sometimes set alight, an old woman killed in her bath-tub, a funeral attacked. Reconciliation was still a dirty word on both sides. The decision was A and L's.

So it happened. Two bright young men would stand up in front of Albanian and Serbian audiences together. They claimed to feel safe with the military, that they loved each other as brothers and that the job had to be done. This was not a huge gesture of peace, it lacked glamour and public attention. Small by the measure of diplomatic efforts, it brought no awards or clever papers, it was not publicly blessed by our head of mission.

We do not know if lives were saved because of the mine awareness training. For all that, it was a grand gesture of courage and peace. In their way A and L signalled the steps to be taken to create a future of acceptance and inclusion for their families and ultimately, their country. I see them still, courtesy of the wonders of social media, with growing families and flourishing careers.

Their brave step for peace remains unforgettable.

By: Angela Mackay

A Child, a Donkey and Peace

My inauspicious beginnings were behind barbed wire as Enemy Alien baby #1098. The British locked up my parents because they were farming in a British territory at the outbreak of World War II. Dad (#235) was sent to South Africa. Mum (#514) and toddler son (#515) to Southern Rhodesia, a few countries away, with all the other German women and children (including boys under 16).

The women immediately made life as normal as possible for their kids, despite roll calls, barbed wire, and war. Nothing mattered but protecting their children. Teachers taught. Mothers set up a kindergarten. There were games and songs and bedtime stories.

One day, my mother took the little ones for a walk. As usual they could go no further than the barbed wire. There, grazing on the other side, was a donkey. One of the little girls burst into tears. When asked why she was crying, she said: "Look at that poor donkey. He's locked up!"

What a tribute to those mothers and how well they, later with their husbands, shielded their youngest from the horrors of confinement... for eight long years, until their release in 1948, well beyond the war. (Scarce transportation was first used to reunite Allied families and, significantly, the British were not sure what to do with the Germans. During the war, German farms and businesses were overseen by British caretakers, who had in good faith eventually invested their own resources and could not now easily be removed. Especially in favour of ex-Enemy Aliens).

My parents were finally allowed to return to the farm they had never sold, on condition they buy it back. Running free with my little friends in the African bush, I had no idea that I was white and they were black. Nor that I did not see other white kids, besides my siblings, because their parents were victorious British Allies, not defeated ex-Enemy Aliens.

The word 'war' meant nothing to me until one dark day in a distant classroom. My parents had no choice but to send us to boarding school, hundreds of miles away. There were none close by.

I was six. So, in my diminutive khaki uniform, I entered the bus and a world in which people spoke a strange language, English. Not the familiar German, Swahili or Kihehe. As children do, I picked up English quickly. But there were always new words to learn. For example, 'war'. I first heard it one Monday morning, two days after a film was shown about people shooting each other. My classmates came in, ringed my chair and, pointing their fingers at me, jeered: "Yah! Yah! You lost the war! Yah! Yah! You lost the war." I was stunned and, as of that moment, determined to find the 'war' so that we could all be friends again.

Soon I spoke English like any other. Which meant that English folks would forget I was there and ridicule Germans in front of me. They might say, "The Germans always ...?" Germans meanwhile, might equally say, "The English always ...". Often, they accused each other of exactly the same things. Very confusing.

Equally confusing was a new label: colonialist. Wasn't I actually just African? No wonder then that I dreamed of a UN passport and being done with labels. I found my UN passport one Canada Day, not far from the Peace Tower, while watching dances from as far afield as Afghanistan and Nigeria, Russia and China, Thailand and Australia. The dancers, although so different, were equally celebrating their ethnic and Canadian selves. 'At last!' I thought.

I am a global citizen who chose to be Canadian. Why? In celebration of diversity. Why? Because I believe celebrating diversity is a powerful tool for peace.

Evelyn Voigt, penning for peace, (www.civilianpeaceservice.ca)

Remembering a Soldier of Peace:
Dr. Lotta Hitschmanova

Dr. Lotta Hitschmanova (1909-1990) was a World War II refugee who made a lasting impact on her adopted country and acted as a Canadian ambassador for peace around the world. From the 1940s to the 1980s, Dr. Lotta helped educate and mobilize Canadians from coast to coast, putting Ottawa on the map – not just as a seat of government and political debate, but as a center for Canadian caring and concern for the rest of the world.

Hers is one of Canada's most tragic and compelling refugee stories. She was a journalist by profession, an outspoken critic of the Nazis, and had to flee her native Czechoslovakia in 1938. For four years she was forced to wander about Europe, eventually finding her way to Marseilles, where she worked with refugee support groups.

She lost both parents in the Holocaust, and in 1942, after a 46-day voyage on a converted banana boat, she arrived penniless in Montreal – "with an unpronounceable name," feeling "completely lost." Yet just three years later she became the founder of an organization to whose humanitarian mission she would dedicate the rest of her life: the Unitarian Service Committee (USC Canada).

Her work took her to post-war Europe, Africa and Asia, to conflict zones and newly-independent nations, to people in need. Long before the age of 24-hour newscasts, she urged Canadians to become aware of people's living conditions far away, to take action and help: "Charity begins at home...and then it goes on to embrace next door neighbours and all those who need help."

Thousands of Canadians from all faiths and walks of life responded to the sincerity of her message, and became lifelong supporters. Who can forget her distinctive Czech accent (and her unique uniform) during those TV and radio ads in the 50s, 60s, 70s and 80s? For many, USC's address – "56 Sparks Street, Ottawa 4" – became the most recognizable address in the country.

Dr. Lotta's influence went well beyond her work with USC Canada. Thanks to her tireless educational efforts over four decades, a solid foundation was laid for the Canadian public's ongoing support for international humanitarian and development assistance. As Nova Scotia author Joan Baxter put it: "It was Lotta Hitschmanova who shaped my values as a Canadian, and the type of Canada I believe in. She helped give us our identity."

Dr. Lotta received countless awards and honours on four continents, and became a Companion of the Order of Canada in 1980. In 2007, the Canadian Museum of History included her as one of our "founders" in its Canadian Personalities Hall. And in 2016, Dr. Lotta was honoured to be amongst the twelve women nominated to appear on a Canadian banknote.

Seldom has a refugee had such an impact on Canadian society, and indeed around the world. A reminder that those we help today will be enriching our society, and helping many others tomorrow. The next Lotta Hitschmanova may soon be arriving in Canada. Let's welcome them.

By: David Rain, who worked for USC Canada from 1993 to 2015, and in 2016 he created a website/blog in honour of Dr. Lotta: www.lotta56sparks.ca. In 1988, Peter Lockyer produced "Soldier of Peace", a video on Lotta: http://lotta56sparks.ca/resources/videos.

Silent Woman

Woman, bearer of mankind,
silent as general cry death
to her children,
suffers unspeaking
the loss of her sons
fighting in wars
with no meaning or end.

Woman, mother of mankind,
tranquil, unseeing
as predators hunt daughters,
passive, unfeeling the
pain of the helpless
crying in streets, alone and afraid.

Sanction of freedom denied
to her young ones,
unheeded questions of
her right to decide
to allow the destruction of
humans, children
she'd pained giving birth to
their life.

Woman, silent woman
bare me your soul,
share with me your identity,
but above all tell me
why you allow such atrocities.
The silence was broken, she said,
an unborn child, God created a miracle
whispered His love
breathed soul in a body,

Listen, look around you,
can't you see it, hear it
the spirit of life,
no colour, hatred or pain,
strong as infinity reigns

beautiful as heaven's glow
joins together, mankind to woman.

Her voice echoed 'cross lands declaring,
'no more will I give you my children
daughters, sons to destroy,
away your guns and violence,
enough bloodshed, stealing of souls.

I've waited, watched for a glimmer
soon peace would be part of life,
yet soldiers lay dying
these children of mine,
they can't see, they don't know
it's their time.'

Children huddled in fear
'round the woman
whose silence had smouldered too long,
then listened in joy, tears dry forever
as the sound of her promise
came clear.

'Worlds of this universe
hear me, listen so well
for I am woman
the giver of life,
He is God, giver of soul,
these are our children, together
we stand for the right to live,
remember, this hour has beckoned
I am woman, silent no more.'

By: Virginia Svetlikov.

Being a Mensch – Bob Bossin

If there's someone who can connect with an audience, it's Bob Bossin. He is a writer, folksinger and founder of the group Stringband. For decades he has touched the hearts, minds and funnybones of Canadians. His songs range from those like Pete Seeger's to satires reminiscent of Tom Lehrer.

When I came to Toronto in 1968, he had just graduated from the University of Toronto. When Stringband was founded in 1971, it soon became my band. It was actually OUR band: all my friends flocked to his concerts. He and Marie-Lynn Hammond sang about our generation, about politics, distant places, surprising events in Canadian history and even sex. His song, "Show us the Length," described a young girl's creative revenge on macho men: it always got laughter from the audience.

At one concert in Toronto in the 1970s, Bob announced that he had been paid way more than he expected for a gig for CBC, so he was giving a piece of cake to everyone in the audience after the show. Toronto writer Doug Fetherling once said that Bob may have created the "Canadian sound" that was in the air in the 1970s and 1980s. Well, I think Buffy Sainte-Marie, Gordon Lightfoot, Joni Mitchell, Leonard Cohen, Stompin' Tom Connors and Stan Rogers had something to do with it, too. But Bob wrote the history and the feeling of Canada in those years into his songs as surely as The Group of Seven painted the Canadian landscape of the decades before then. He also brought Canada to the world: in the 15 years when Stringband was touring, they performed in the US, the UK, the Soviet Union, France, Mexico and Japan.

As an active supporter of peace and disarmament, he titled his 1987 album "Bossin's Home Remedy for Nuclear War". No event of the peace movement of the 1980s in Toronto would be complete without some songs by Bob Bossin. After he moved to enchanting Gabriola Island off the coast of Vancouver Island in the early 1980s, he released his 1984 album, "Gabriola V0R 1X0". A brilliant stroke in the days of snail mail: you could send a postcard to Bob with just that as an address and it would quickly arrive, no problem.

But danger was lurking in paradise: logging had increased in the virgin forests of Clayoquot Sound on Vancouver Island where First Nations people lived. Along with environmentalists, university students and others, they joined forces to win a victory against clear-cutting. They carried out the largest nonviolent civil disobedience action to that day. Bob wove the story of that movement into his award-winning song and film, Sulphur Passage (*No pasaran*) in 1994. The film included the cream of the crop of folk singers and songwriters in BC. Singing their hearts out in the film were Stephen Fearing, Roy Forbe, Veda Hille, Ann Mortifee, Raffi, Rick Scott, Valdy and Jennifer West.

To tell the story of his father, David Bossin, Bob wrote the book Davy the Punk, in which he documented his father's early career in Toronto's gambling underworld in the 1930s. He turned it into a one-person musical that he performed coast to coast. In 2017, there was another danger out west: the Kinder-Morgan pipeline. Bossin released a video showing the chances - and the effects - that a fire would have at the proposed pipeline's terminus just downhill from Simon Fraser University in Vancouver. He titled the film "Only one bear in a hundred bites", but they don't come in order. He posted the video on YouTube, as he did with Sulphur Passage. Only one bear went viral but she didn't turn on the environmentalists. Instead, that bear played a role in defeating the province's right-wing BC Liberal government, which was going to help the Kinder-Morgan pipeline get built.

Among the dozen or so Yiddish words most common in the English language is *mensch*: it means a good person. That's Bob without a doubt.

By: Carl Stieren

White Owl

In sharing my story as a Peace Ambassador, Advocate and Activist for Earth, I am a 73 year-old Universalist Grandmother with life experience in six cultures. My husband Bob and I have two children and two Grandchildren after fifty-one years of marriage as a Foreign Service Couple beginning in Tanzania, East Africa 1967.

The Aboriginal Grandmothers, my wisest teachers, tell me we must care for ourselves to stay alive a long time! We are ancestors showing younger people wisdom to see that what we are doing to the Earth is not natural. They also tell me we are here to remember the reason we came, to live joy and protect water, that we are all creators of a new life on Earth.

Trained in listening presence in hospital spiritual/palliative care ministry and, as a Spiritual Director in 1998 under the auspices of the Upper Room of Prayer, I co-founded the Heart + Soul Light Centre, a spiritual growth centre embracing Aboriginal understanding, creating sharing spiritual circles to share the vision of the late Algonquin Spiritual Leader Grandfather William Commanda, founder of the "Circle of All Nations and a Culture of Peace."

On radio CHIN sharing this visionary voice that attracted leaders to hear his wisdom from all over the planet and inspired hearts with the seed to see the returning of this sacred land and waterway back to his people, to restore it to its original magnificence as, once again, an ancient Spiritual Mecca meeting place for all to visit and give thanks. He saw the need due to pollution and Climate Change to build an "International Indigenous Peace Healing Centre" so wise voices of Elders would be heard teaching us how to work with nature, not against her.

My life is blessed to live and learn the spiritual ways of sharing in mutual, equal, respect and trust without which there cannot be peace. Here are some highlights: 1995-Attending the Sacred Assembly in Hull called by the late MP Elder Elijah Harper was life changing!

2009: Honoured with the Peace Ambassador award from Universal Peace Federation.

2011-2012- Trained as Agent of Conscious Evolution with Barbra Marx Hubbard, the Shift network and as Project Co-ordinator of "Birth 2012 and Beyond" celebration of the Canadian Museum of Civilization worldwide celebrating the Mayan Calendar and indigenous Algonquin peoples. See www.birthottawagatineau.com for ongoing multi-media interviews.

2012–2015-Recognised as a Grandmother with spiritual name White Owl invited as Peace Ambassador to attend the "2013 World Summit on Peace, Security, and Development" in Seoul, South Korea.

2015- Helped organise the burying "Earth Treasure Vase" tradition from Tibet protecting and healing Earth and all beings. Following this, at Truth + Reconciliation Process, was gifted with a Golden Eagle Feather by an Inuit Elder from the Crow Family.

2016- Speaker at 41st Annual International SSF-IIHS Conference. "Becoming One with Universal Consciousness and the Significance of the Ottawa River Watershed to Planetary Healing." Serving with cause of ad hoc free the falls group, I became one of four Directors of OWL Outaouais Wellness Learning Centre for wisdom.

2017- As Faith Peace Leader, witnessed solidarity with Algonquin Elder Albert Dumont and many faith leaders that all religious space is sacred.

I believe all citizens can create a new unity of consciousness where ecology is our new economy; using less, we can put nature first in our new synergistic democracy. My faith, life journey has led to the heart of The Medicine Wheel and the Holistic four directions that call us all to seek to live from peace inside in ever stronger, spiritually, moral ways as our legacy as Earth star people for Canada's next 150 years.

By: Judith Anne King Matheson, Director (OWL) Outaouais Wellness Learning Centre, Co-Founder Heart + Soul Light Centre.

Building Multi-national Cooperation

The creation and use of multi-national institutions and various forms of international cooperation and joint action since the end of World War II, for which Canada was an early and committed supporter, had a number of objectives. For Canada, it has been partly one of acting in our national interest, to leverage our influence and provide economic and political benefits.

But Canada was a significant player in the formation of the modern United Nations and the Bretton Woods institutions (the World Bank and IMF), and regional institutions designed on those models, as well as a principal instigator for the formation of NATO, and a supporter of the progress European nations have made in building, piece by piece, a conflict-resistant integrative structure culminating in the formation of the European Union. The list of multi-national institutions in which Canada has been a player, sometimes a major player, is a very long one.

Many, almost innumerable, Canadians have played a role in this long story, which has become part of our national character and identity. Not just the best known such as Lester Pearson, Dana Wilgress, Escott Reid or David Hopper.

But many others at the government official level and, of course, Lewis Perinbam and those who were inspired by and worked with him, have contributed so much as voluntary and non-governmental participants in developing the fabric of international and humanitarian cooperation. All of this was aimed at building a peaceful and cooperative world – even if we are continually reminded of the sometimes horrific challenges that the international community still faces.

In my own case, I had the privilege, as a young government officer in the Department of Finance, to be a part of this Canadian story. I had the good fortune to be able to play a role in the formation of three multilateral development institutions. Working from a Canadian base and later internationally, I was involved in the policy development and programs of these and other multilateral agencies. I was part of the governance structure of one of them, as well as providing input and advice on the governance of others, and a role in leading a particular international initiative to strengthen multilateral cooperation and joint action in development assistance.

There was also a role, on one posting, in designing the international response to a flood of several million refugees from a particularly miserable war. There was a sense of mission and commitment amongst those who worked together on these challenges and, in many cases, Canadian influence was extremely important.

In my case, I once represented, for several years, a number of different governments, including Canada, on the Board of the Asian Development Bank, with the then third largest voting strength after two major world powers - deployed, I hope, to good effect.

There were rewards, of course, in a sense of accomplishment, in expanded horizons and a wide circle of colleagues and friends. There were postings in different countries in Asia and Europe, and assignments that took me to many places in Asia, the Caribbean, sub-Saharan Africa and the Middle East. And, like others, I have since had opportunities to build on that experience in different and continuing roles.

Circumstances change, and Canadians in 2017 play a different role from that in 1967 and earlier years. But the challenges remain, the diagnosis and prescription continue to be highly relevant, and hopefully Canada's role and that of individual Canadians will continue to evolve and contribute to the fabric of international, peaceful and humanitarian solutions.

By: Allan Barry

The Battle of Two Wolves inside us All

This is a gesture of appreciation from the heart and head to James Miller, local editor and Master of Ceremonies at a recent political debate I attended. His use of words, especially his no-tolerance attitude towards bullies and booing was rare, refreshing and needed.

Miller brings to mind the story of a Cherokee grandfather that I knew telling his son about a battle that goes on inside people. He said, "my son, the battle is between two wolves inside us all. One is NEGATIVE with qualities of anger, envy, jealousy, greed, arrogance, self-pity, resentment, lies, false pride, and superiority.

The other is POSITIVE with feelings of peace, love, hope, serenity, humility, kindness, benevolence, empathy, generosity, compassion, and faith." The grandson thought about it and then asked his grandfather "Which wolf wins"? The wise Cherokee replied: "The one you feed."

And feed we must if we are to have the wisdom and the energy to achieve our highest life goals. Whether we are on a quest for peace at home or abroad, or whether we are trying to find solutions to bullies in our society, our words do matter. As Dr. Gwen Randall-Young once wrote: "Words are not just words. They are the way in which we connect to others and make meaning in our lives."

Or, as Siddhartha Gautama-Buddha reminded us: "Whatever words we utter should be chosen with care for people will hear them and be influenced by them for good or for ill."

We are also reminded that Rudyard Kipling, years back, said: "Words are, of course, the most powerful drug used by mankind." Many years earlier, King Solomon is recorded as having said: "Life and death are in the power of the tongue."

More recently, Eleanor Roosevelt shared a related wisdom: "Great minds discuss ideas; average minds discuss events; small minds discuss people."

So let us choose our words carefully and wisely. Negative words create a 'me' versus 'you' mentality. Positive words create the qualities that we urgently need on our Planet: cooperation, community, reconciliation, and forgiveness. These are the ingredients that ultimately make peace possible.

But much more is needed to nurture good words and values. An important source of wisdom comes from the Bella Bella Natives on the west coast of British Columbia where I once taught. This was an exquisitely beautiful community on the mainland, with an abundance of sensations: the scent of fish being smoked, the sounds of music flowing from open windows and children playing, the sight of eagles soaring above the trees. Their customs were elegant, and culture was teeming with magic. The warmth and hospitality of its people was indeed a place to celebrate living and loving.

Here in Bella Bella, my special teacher and friend, Don Wilson, reminded me to find love in my own consciousness and the time to appreciate the beauty of life around me. He encouraged me to use my subconscious mind — which he described as the all-knowing Universal Mind with the God Within — as my best friend in the search for happiness, health, prosperity and peace. He said it was like having your own Aladdin's Lamp — and you are the Genie!

So, my friends, readers of this book, go inside and search deeply for those inner truths of love joy, and peace. Let the good wolf within us win. You have the capacity to create a better world. You are the Genie!

By: Jon-Lee Kootnekoff, Penticton, BC www.jlkootnekoff.com

The Existential Challenge of our Time

It is both tragic and astounding that 71 years after atomic horror was visited upon the people of Hiroshima and Nagasaki, killing hundreds of thousands of people, the world has still not yet eliminated the most deadly weapon of mass destruction ever conceived. Although events of the past year have moved the global campaign to rid the world of nuclear weapons incrementally forward, success is far from assured and failure could result in the end of the world as we know it.

Nine of the world's 195 states retain more than 15,000 thermo-nuclear weapons, many with multiple warheads hundreds of times more powerful than the atomic bombs dropped on Japan in 1945. Further, they've embarked upon a new nuclear arms race, precipitated by the United States budgeting one trillion dollars to 'modernize' its nuclear arsenal over the next 30 years.

The NATO Secretary General warns that 30 countries have, or are developing, ballistic missile systems capable of carrying nuclear warheads, and there is enough weapons grade fissile material in the world to produce 200,000 nuclear weapons. Add to this deadly mix, terrorist organizations such as *Daesch* (ISIS) have pledged to acquire nuclear capability and will almost surely use it, if they do.

With expanding nuclear arsenals and increasing world tension, there is a corresponding increase in the risk of accident or human miscalculation. After in-depth study of the near misses over the decades, former Australian Foreign Minister, Gareth Evans, stated that: "It has not been a result of good policy or good management that the world has avoided a nuclear weapons catastrophe for 70 years: Rather it has been sheer dumb luck."

Most of the world's nations have concluded that humanity's best and perhaps only hope of avoiding nuclear catastrophe - possibly on a global scale - is to outlaw and eventually eliminate all nuclear weapons. To this end, they sought and won a mandate from the UN General Assembly in 2016 to negotiate a nuclear weapons treaty. Negotiations concluded on July 7, 2017, with 120 of 122 participating states endorsing the Treaty on the Prohibition of Nuclear Weapons that, among other things, imposes a total ban on nuclear weapons and an obligation on States Party to encourage all other states to join the Treaty.

At the behest of the United States, all 28 NATO states except the Netherlands - and including Canada - boycotted the negotiations, clinging to the dangerously misguided notion that nuclear weapons contribute to, rather than detract from, international peace and security.

Canada has an opportunity to show leadership by challenging the nuclear security policy in NATO and becoming a champion for nuclear disarmament throughout the world. The lives of our children and future generations could literally depend upon it.

By: Earl Turcotte, former Canadian and UN disarmament diplomat, on the Steering Committee of the Canadian Network to Abolish Nuclear Weapons, a member of the Canadian Pugwash Group and a member of the Board of the Group of 78.

Les Barabaigs

En 1988, alors que j'étais en poste avec l'Agence canadienne de développement international (ACDI) en Tanzanie, je reçu un message d'un anthropologue britannique, Charles Lane. Il me demandait de l'accompagner à une rencontre avec les anciens des Barabaigs, à Hanang, dans le nord de la Tanzanie.

Une des mes responsabilités était la supervision d'un projet de 7 fermes de blé situé au pied du mont Hanang. Quant aux Barabaigs, ils étaient des nomades, avec de larges troupeaux et constituaient une nuisance pour les gestionnaires des fermes de blé. Connaissant peu sur la relation entre les Barabaigs et les fermes, je décidais d'aller voir ce qui en était. Après avoir conduit au milieu des grands acacias rabougris où il n'y avait aucun sentier dans le »bundu », nous sommes arrivés à l'endroit où les représentants des Barabaigs nous avaient donné rendez-vous, un endroit sacré où les palabres du groupe s'y tenaient.

Ils étaient vêtus de peau de vache, tout de brun. Ils étaient là, grands, élancés, en silence. Après les présentations d'usage, chacun des chefs nous expliqua ce qui rendait leur vie difficile et comment les fermiers "bantu" avaient pris leurs terres pour y faire pousser du blé. Elles constituaient traditionnellement les lieux de pâturage pour leurs troupeaux de vaches. Surtout, ils n'avaient plus accès aux points d'eau. On rapportait même des actes de violence où des membres de leur groupe avaient été attaqués par les fermiers. Même des cas de viol étaient mentionnés. Je me trouvais directement au cœur d'un des conflits qui a marqué et qui marque encore les relations entre les fermiers sédentaires et les populations non sédentarisées, qui sont obligés selon les saisons de migrer d'un région à l'autre afin de trouver la nourriture pour leurs troupeaux.

L'ACDI, qui finançait depuis au moins une dizaine d'année les fermes de blé de Hanang qui accaparaient 40 000 hectares de terre occupée traditionnellement par les Barabaigs, avait choisi d'ignorer les conflits que ce projet avait suscités. Il revenait au gouvernement de la Tanzanie de statuer sur le sort des populations nomades dont les sépultures avaient été violées et détruites sans aucune compensation. Un juge tanzanien avait déclaré que si les Barabaigs lui avaient démontré (avec documents à l'appui) qu'ils avaient des droits sur les fermes de Hanang, ils auraient pu être dédommagés. Comme tous les nomades analphabètes à travers le monde, ils n'avaient aucun document définissant leurs droits sur des terres qu'ils avaient ainsi utilisées durant des centaines d'années, sauf quelques lieux de sépultures qui avaient déjà été profanées et détruites.

J'ai été frappé par la dignité des notables. Ils demandaient qu'on puisse leur permettre de se rendre avec leurs troupeaux à des points d'eau. Et surtout que cessent les violences à leur égard.

J'avais bien lu différents documents sur les fermes de blé. Nul part on n'y faisait mention des populations nomades qui avaient de tout temps utilisé ces terres pour y faire paître leurs troupeaux. Se pouvait-il que l'ACDI ait contribué à une grave injustice en permettant grâce à son financement au développement de ces sept fermes de blé?

En dépit de l'opposition des mes supérieurs, je décidais d'agir avec les quelques moyens mis à ma disposition par ces derniers pour entreprendre quelques gestes concrèts: En premier lieu, je fis faire le cadastre des fermes afin d'en limiter l'extension au dépend des Barabaigs.

Ensuite, j'amenais l'ACDI à planifier un projet en vue de permettre une certaine sédentarisation des populations nomades. Enfin, un projet d'adduction qui visait à aller chercher l'eau sur les flancs du mont Hanang fut initié afin d'approvisionner les 7 fermes d'eau potable. Des points d'eau furent prévus pour permettre aux Barabaigs d'y puiser l'eau pour eux et leurs troupeaux.

Lors de la rencontre, les chefs avaient admis qu'ils ne pourraient continuer indéfiniment leur nomadisme. Ils avaient besoin d'aide pour changer leur coutume de vie. Je crois y avoir contribué quelque peu.

Par: Yves Morneau, professionnel de la paix

Education for Peace in Bosnia and Herzegovina
A project aiming to transform an entire society (Dr. H. B. Danesh)

In mid-2000, the International Education for Peace Institute, started by Dr. H. B. Danesh, launched a two-year pilot Education for Peace project in three primary and three secondary schools in Bosnia and Herzegovina. It involved approximately 400 teachers and school staff and 6,000 students, plus 10,000 parents and guardians (1).

"The aim and challenge of the project 'was' to educate every new generation of students to become peacemakers and to devote their talents, capacities and energies towards the creation of a civilization of peace based upon the pillars of a culture of peace, a culture of healing and a culture of excellence."

In light of the project's success in its early years, Education for Peace was ultimately invited by the Ministry of Civil Affairs, the 13 Ministries of Education and the nine Pedagogical Institutes to introduce its program into all primary and secondary schools in Bosnia and Herzegovina – a mammoth undertaking. These schools have over 1 million students, 110,000 teachers and staff, and 1.5 million parents.

Personally, I am not aware of another project of this kind anywhere in the world...that is, an attempt to transform an entire society from the "ground up" through the education of primary and secondary school children in peace principles and practices. And yet, it seems to make so much sense!

I am reminded of hearing about an early meeting where parents and community leaders were discussing whether or not to accept the Education for Peace program into the initial six schools. When the discussion amongst (mostly) men grew heated and descended into threats and anger, a lady, a mother, stood and shouted,

"For years we have sent our sons off to fight and die – for what? Here we have a possible solution to this foolish conflict. I say we try it." (Note: Approximate wording). This was a turning point and the Education for Peace-Balkans program was born.

In addition to the education and training in peace principles and practices, a main component of the Education for Peace program is the holding of peace events in schools and communities. This involves the sharing of student's perspectives on the application of the peace principles being taught. Presentations are made to teachers, friends and family, the media, officials and the public. Some of these are huge events, with students from 100 or more schools gathering together for conferences and events.

Over the years I have lost touch with the long term, sustainable results, and outcomes, of the Education for Peace-Balkans program; however, I heard and experienced the impact the program had on some of the teachers and students. It is personal, emotional and life-changing. One huge measure of success is that ,"In 2012, all pedagogical Institutes in Bosnia and Herzegovina, under the direction of their respective Ministries of Education, assumed the implementation of the Education for Peace programs into schools in Bosnia and Herzegovina."

I believe the Education for Peace-Balkans program is a fascinating, challenging example of an initiative that offers huge promise for changing individuals and entire societies that are mired in conflict.

By: Gord Breedyk, Civilian Peace Service Canada,
www.civilianpeaceservice.ca.

(1) EFP – A Country-Wide Peace Education program in Bosnia and Herzegovina (HDIM.NGO/241/08, 3 October 2008)

From Guns to Flowers

One hundred years ago, in 1917, my father lied about his age and signed up with the German Army in the little town of Tilsit. The phrase "*Dulce et decorum est pro patria mori*"- "It is sweet and honourable to die for your country" - was carved into a plaque at his high school. Hans-Georg Stieren fought in those horrible trenches in World War I and won the Iron Cross. As I was growing up in the suburbs of Chicago, he told me that no one gained from that war at all - except the arms makers.

In 1963, I was an undergraduate at Swarthmore College just outside of Philadelphia. To do something nonviolently for justice, I participated in a sit-in in Cambridge, Maryland. I was arrested along with seventeen Swarthmore classmates and others protesting the segregation of African-Americans. Later, when I was back in Illinois during the Vietnam War, my mother and I both joined the Quaker Meeting in Downers Grove. In 1967, I carried up donations to Toronto for the Canadian Friends Service Committee, the Quaker agency sending medical relief to all sides in the Vietnam War. When my local draft board denied me conscientious objector status because I had only been a Quaker for a year, my pacifist options were just two. I could go to jail rather than serve in the US Army, or go to Canada. I chose Canada. There was a moment of shock when I unexpectedly failed my physical exam for the Army. I was free! I could go anywhere. I went to Toronto in the spring of 1968.

After I finished my BA in History at York University, I became a reporter and then news editor for a local community newspaper from 1974 to 1977. My next job for three years was planning and organizing the summer school on Grindstone Island known as the Grindstone School for Peace Research, Education and Action. I was then hired as the coordinator of Canadian Friends Service Committee, where I worked from 1982 to 1987. My first marriage, to Pat Newcombe in 1992, did not last: we separated in 1995 and then divorced.

Reinventing myself as a technical writer in Ottawa, I worked for two software firms, from 1992 to 2001. During that time, I met David Hartsough at a peace conference in New Jersey where I was hosting a workshop. I was inspired by the vision and the work that he and Mel Duncan had done toward creating a nonviolent peace force. My friends and I hosted two meetings of their international steering committee – in Wakefield and Gracefield, Quebec – in the early 2000s. I went to New Delhi in 2002 where I was one of the 140 delegates from around the world founding the Nonviolent Peaceforce.

At the Friends General Conference Gathering in Wisconsin in 2007, I met a woman named Isabelle Yingling. We were married in the Ann Arbor Quaker Meeting House in 2009 and she moved up to join me in Canada in 2010.

In 2013, I created the board game, It Happened in The 60s. In it, I sought to show the successes and the failures, the joys and the sorrows of the peace and civil rights movements. With 328 question cards, I could reflect the incredible creative energy of the 1960s. Those years were fuelled by a fire that burned brightly but also destroyed some of its finest singers, songwriters, poets and organizers.

For the 50th anniversary of the March on the Pentagon on October 21, 1967, I wrote a song about my experiences there and those of others who even put flowers into the barrels of guns.

By: Carl Stieren

One Family

Peace was a cruel mirage in Vietnam a couple of generations ago. A seemingly endless war ultimately killed nearly 60,000 Americans and perhaps thirty to fifty times that many Vietnamese - children, women and men. After the war hundreds of thousands fled, many by boat, under appalling conditions and with huge loss of life. By June 1979, some 350,000 were in refugee camps across Southeast Asia.

In Ottawa, Mayor Marion Dewar launched the unprecedented Project 4000, a community drive to welcome that number to the city, and the federal government, led by Joe Clark, raised the refugee quota from 8,000 to 50,000. Volunteer groups formed quickly, including one in our east Ottawa neighbourhood, raising funds and collecting clothing, furniture and supplies. A local landlord donated a row house, free for a year, and soon 'our' family arrived — a very practical man, a gracious woman, and their two small daughters.

They settled in well though the woman, who fell unconscious on the crowded boat and barely survived, worried about her young brother, a soldier in the South Vietnamese army, and their mother, still in Vietnam. The girls started school while their parents began language lessons — where, in a school hallway, the woman found her brother. He had lain among bodies in a ditch to survive a firefight, and had later found his way to a camp in a different country — then had been accepted by Canada.

The family adapted to their new, different, cold homeland. They moved to Toronto and opened a clothing store. The brother managed to sponsor his mother, making a compelling argument (in his third language) to an immigration appeal judge. He also learned how to make the special cheesecake of a trendy Byward Market cafe, ran a restaurant in Nova Scotia (learning some words in Mi'kmaq to welcome First Nations customers), and finally settled and raised a family in Niagara Falls. The whole experience was good. For the volunteers, spin-offs included new friendships, the opening of a small business that continues to serve the neighbourhood, and a contact that led to a career for an unemployed teenager. For the sponsored family, Canada meant freedom, opportunity, and above all peace.

By: Allan Thornley

One Independent Mom, Four Independent Sons

My husband and I are both retired engineers, out living the dream. We live on a pristine lake in cottage country with towering pine trees. We love to spend time with our four sons, two grandchildren, extended family and close friends. We travel the world, play bridge, eat healthy and keep fit.

Recently, we have found purpose in helping parents who have adult children who are stuck. We have knowledge and experience to offer because not long ago, one of our sons was dangerously close to living on the street, after five years of being on his own. The situation was causing severe stress and discord in our otherwise loving and peaceful family. This is the story of how we found a path to harmony and joy.

We decided to invite him back home to help him figure out what was going on. For over a year, we were guided by experts, finally finding a diagnosis and then, gratefully, a solution. He agreed to enroll in a five week residential program that combined healthy practices and holistic treatments with discipline to enhance self-awareness and empathy for others, leading to full independence.

Personally, the thought of letting go was terrifying; yet I knew it was the best for him and I chose love over fear. I was able to find peace with our decision because of work that I had been doing with several coaches and healers.

The most impactful experience happened while he was living at the retreat centre. Friends were visiting us at home and I shared my difficulty of letting go. They led me through an exercise of imagining the chords that connect me with each of my sons. One by one they walked me through a process of cutting those maternal cords that connected me with my sons.

One by one, four times, I recited "I LOVE you, and, I release you to be an independent adult." Hundreds of miles away, on the same day, staff noticed a shift in my son's appearance, attitude, and behaviour. I knew that cutting the invisible cord had a profound impact on both of us, all five of us actually. We were all released that day to thrive as independent adults.

My newfound independence enabled me to fully participate in a family intervention, during his stay at the centre. Our family was guided through a loving, peaceful and profoundly powerful exercise that was life-changing for all of us. We shared truthfully, deeply and emotionally. At the conclusion, we lovingly offered him a "Gift of

Independence", which included keys to a modest room and cash for groceries for two months, with guidelines for his behaviour that came with tough consequences. He chose to accept our gift, for which we are forever grateful. There have been hiccups in the last year and a half, of course, testing me. I learned that to maintain my independence and respect theirs, I need to treat my adult sons like close friends. I love them, I am there for them and I let them live their own lives.

It's been over a year now. Our family is more harmonious, loving and connected than I could ever have imagined. All four of our sons have bonded closer than ever before and all of them celebrate their successes without concern for shaming anyone. Rob and I have more energy to spend on us, with time together to travel, play bridge, visit friends and work on our business, to give back.

As an independent Mom, I am now free to see and embrace the possibilities that life has to offer and so do my independent sons.

By: Cille Harris offers Real Alternatives for Out Living the Dream, with her husband in Ompah, Ontario, Canada. Visit www.ra.ca.

Peace

A single word with thousands of meanings, however, the primary one in most dictionaries reads as follows and I quote, "the state of existence during the absence of war" or "period of time in which there is no war or violence" or "freedom from war and violence." However, there is one dictionary that gives a slightly different meaning. Merriam Webster Dictionary's version is "a state of tranquility or quiet," but then is followed by this example, "peace of 50 years before the war broke out again."

I find it disturbing that peace is portrayed as an abnormal state that finds itself present when the natural state of war is absent. I was raised a pacifist. I believe that 'peace' is a right, a human right, and not a privilege to be enjoyed when the powers of the world decide to allow you to enjoy it.

I believe that murder committed on the streets of our cities is no different than the killing of humans on the fields of war. Just because a president, or the ruling power of a country, has the unqualified power to send our children to kill others, does not make it right. It is still murder in my eyes and the murderer is that person that sent your child or mine to die for a cause that makes no sense.

The belief that war is a natural state is wrong and we need to start to change the way we raise our children. Many countries teach children, from the day they are born, that to die for one's country is honourable. It is not. There is no honour in going into a strange country, where you have no right to be, pointing a weapon at another human, whom you've never met, and killing him.

I used to think that if women ruled the world we would have no wars, but I was wrong. Many women that have held that kind of power have created wars and sent our children to die on their behalf.

If peace is to be attained on this planet, we need to stop the insanity. Women, we need to change the thinking of everyone around us. We need to instill into our children's minds and hearts that killing, regardless of its form, is wrong and has no place in mankind's society. Our children are being brain-washed that war is honourable, that being a soldier is glorious, that killing the enemy is the right thing to do. But we have no natural enemies. The powers of the world create our enemies and we allow them to do so.

Women, step forward, stop the insanity and let's start teaching our children, our friends, our neighbours, anyone that will listen, that we have to stop the powers of the world from killing humanity.

It starts with us, one person at a time.

Talk to your teachers, your school boards, any place where your children spend time, that you do not want them to be taught that war and killing for your country is acceptable.

Social media has taken over our minds and our hearts and we need to stop the unknown outsiders, who create this media, from being the ones that teach our children the values of life.

We as parents need to step up, we need to be involved every second of the day, we need to teach the upcoming generation that peace is not the absence of war, but that peace is a natural state of tranquility and quiet, it is contentment, serenity, lack of ego, compassion and harmony. Women, mothers, we have a voice; we can no longer be silent.

Peace. Peace for me is when I walk down the street and fear nothing; when I smile at someone of a different colour and they smile back; when I go to sleep at night and know that all of mankind feels safe.

My word for that feeling is 'freedom.'

By: Virginia Svetlikov.

If my Life as a Child Soldier could be Told

I met him on a sunny afternoon, in our bright living room overlooking the tranquil Ottawa River. A world away from one of his most brutal memories. Searing. Not referred to that day in conversation, but read about previously in his book, "If My Life As A Child Soldier Could Be Told":

'As for my comrade, when the driver started, he was still on the ground, holding the side panel of the vehicle with both hands in order to get on board. And as the vehicle was already moving, I tried to hold both his hands to pull him up to us. The rebels, who could see us, shot a rocket that unfortunately hit his hip and tore his body in two. On board the vehicle, I was left with the upper part of his body – the head, hands, and torso...I was just thirteen.'

Kadogo is now a grown man. Robbed of his own childhood, he devotes himself to protect those of others, mainly through Paix Pour L'Enfance (Peace for Childhood), an NGO he founded and now runs.

As I said, that sunny afternoon in Ottawa, we never spoke of this particular memory. We touched generally on peace, on kinship. But most of all we spoke about his passion for his work, about generating funds for healing, about his reason for writing his autobiography.

"This book is a cry from the heart that I would like to send as far as it may resound," he says in its preface, "so that the message in it shall succeed in changing the state of things in the lives of many a child who was a victim of political violence, and of many other cases of violations of the rights of children.

What is told here is the true story of what I actually went through, and when you read through it,

I would like you to do so with a mind open to understanding the great suffering that many child soldiers have been subjected to and are still being subjected to when snatched away from childhood; and for not receiving appropriate treatment after being demobilized, if they were lucky enough to survive this human adventure, which has not yet dared to say its last word...".

The sun is now moving lower on the horizon beyond our living room window. And still we chat. He has brought with him fellow Canadians, like me, originally from Africa.

Continental kinship forms an instant bond.

No longer strangers, after so short a time.

And still, with every sip and every word and, yes, joke, the unspoken spectre of kidnapped children with guns hovers. Try as I might I cannot lift the cloud and marvel at Kadogo's apparent serenity.

Why am I, who has not suffered his indignities and horrors, so fraught? Perhaps because hope seems elusive.

But is it really?

As Lucilie Grétry writes in the afterword of Kadogo's autobiography, "...Beyond the cold reality of a violent enrollment and of a distressing military life, a warm message of hope can be read between the lines: to entertain love rather than hatred and to keep up the struggle until one succeeds."

By: Evelyn Voigt, on meeting Junior Nzita Nsuami – Kadogo, founder of Paix Pour L'Enfance (PPE)

paixpourlenfance.wordpress.com/author/paixpourlenfance/

Canada says "No" to Star Wars

It was in late 1984 that President Ronald Reagan invited western allies including Canada and the UK to join a futuristic research programme formally known as the Strategic Defence Initiative, and popularly called "Star Wars".

I was an international security policy advisor to Canada's foreign Minister, the Right Honourable Joe Clark, in the newly elected Mulroney government. We immediately set about trying to learn as much as we could about the project which was controversial from its inception. It envisaged striking down incoming intercontinental ballistic missiles (ICBMs) in one of three phases – shortly after take-off in the boost phase, during their mid-course in outer space and upon re-entry into the atmosphere before reaching the target – in the terminal phase.

Canada examined the arguments (including possible lucrative research contracts for Canadian industry) and decided that the negative impact on strategic stability outweighed any possible benefits.

While research was technically legal under the 1972 ABM Treaty, development of strategic defences was not. The rationale behind this enlightened arms control agreement between the Soviet Union and the USA was that any attempt to develop "defensive" missiles capable of shooting down incoming ICBMs would inevitably set off an offensive nuclear arms race, to ensure that the defensive missiles would be overwhelmed.

It is infinitely cheaper and easier to build offensive missiles than defensive ones. And the latter have to work 100% of the time whereas only one offensive missiles needs to get through for horrendous damage to be inflicted. So the two adversaries agreed that any increased defensive capacity would be dwarfed by the threat from new offensive missiles.

To put this another way, the implications of SDI ran directly counter to the prevailing nuclear orthodoxy of "nuclear deterrence" through "mutually assured destruction" (MAD). Only if each side had sufficient nuclear weapons to survive a first strike and be able to launch a devastating retaliatory blow would each side thereby be "deterred" from launching a nuclear first strike.

So how was it then that a newly elected Progressive Conservative government, anxious above all to get along with the

USA, said "thanks but no thanks" to this very high profile, high stakes invitation?

With Canada hosting the "Shamrock Summit" of NATO leaders in Quebec City in March 1985, our Ambassador to the USA, the almost legendarily-powerful Alan Gotlieb, forecast utter disaster if Canada did not sign on to SDI.

Mr. Clark did not buckle but summoned the Director of the Arms Control Division and the Director General of the International Security Bureau in Foreign Affairs. Both had huge expertise and an equal determination that Canada make the right decision. They offered their best judgment that, despite Gotlieb's dark warnings, the Americans had not "dug in their heels" and would likely agree to a Summit Statement referencing respect for the ABM Treaty. Mr. Clark, in turn, was able to secure the Prime Minister's agreement to this approach.

So the Shamrock Summit, rather than endorsing SDI, instead highlighted the importance to international peace and security of limiting the deployment of strategic defences.

Canada gave its formal, very diplomatic, response to the American invitation in September, 1985:

"The Canadian government has reached the conclusion that the policies and priorities of Canada do not justify a government to government effort in support of SDI research."

This story is a testament to what Canada can achieve with a principled, determined Foreign Minister backed up by equally fearless Canadian diplomats.

By: Peggy Mason, President of the Rideau Institute. The author wishes to note that nuclear deterrence is a deeply problematic concept but any move to make a first strike more likely is a move in the wrong direction. Private companies were still technically free to pursue contracts although there was little hope of attaining them without government backing.

Canada's First High School Peer Mediation Program

"If we wish to have peace in our world, we must begin with our children."

So replied Charlotte Lemieux, Ottawa Board of Education Director, in 1987 when approached about introducing a Student Peer Mediation Program into Ottawa high schools.

In my heart I knew we had to work with students to give the next generation knowledge of the choices they have to prevent, manage and resolve conflict. I had left a lucrative 10-year practice as an Ontario barrister and solicitor and was working with a group who shared an interest in alternative dispute resolution (ADR). We believed ADR was a trend, not a fad. We set up the Dispute Resolution Center of Ottawa-Carleton.

Our early ADR research revealed that a U.S. organization, the National Association for Mediation in Education, was introducing mediation skills to U.S. schools. Our goal was to establish a similar program in Ottawa. School peer mediation programs did not exist in Canada. So, selling our vision would be an uphill challenge. Director Lemieux notified me that only one Principal Christine Hubbard at Woodroffe high school was interested. A small beginning!

That fall, conflict resolution trainer Cheryl Picard and I met with Principal Hubbard and two Vice Principals (VP). Ivan Roy, one VP, was a skeptic. He feared a student peer mediation program could erode the school's authority to discipline. Principal Hubbard accepted that students needed exposure to alternative ways to resolve conflict.

After a series of presentations to teachers and students, we reached an agreement. Sixteen students were selected for three days of training that winter. We launched Canada's first Student Peer Mediation Program in March 1988, at Woodroffe High School.

In early 1989, Cole Harbour District High School in Dartmouth, Nova Scotia, gained national media attention after some 50 students were involved in a major brawl requiring police intervention. Soon after, Woodroffe administrators braced for a similar situation upon learning students from another school were on their way over for a fight.

About 40 students met in confrontation in the schoolyard. The older brother of one student arrived carrying a baseball bat.

Police arrived. One Woodroffe administrator proposed peer mediation to the combatant students. They agreed. The dispute settled peacefully. Police did not get involved.

In another student conflict, peer mediation achieved remarkable results. The conflict began between two students in elementary school, escalating in high school with an argument over a girlfriend. Several peer mediation sessions ensued--tensions were defused and friendships restored.

Inspired by the students and the accomplishments, I contacted several national media outlets to share how the Program had prevented such violence and arrests as had resulted in Nova Scotia. Alas, stories without conflict or visuals were not of interest. Students asked me why they had to do bad things to get in the news. The saying goes, "if it bleeds, it leads". Only two local news organizations reported: Ottawa Citizen's Dave Brown and CBC Ottawa. Student mediators experienced the power of mediation and peer interventions continued.

From an Acorn does an Oak Tree grow! Ivan Roy, the skeptic VP who initially questioned the program, was so convinced by his experience that he left his job to dedicate himself to teaching mediation and conflict resolution in other Canadian schools, including Ridgemont High School in Ottawa.

We are indebted to the late Charlotte Lemieux for her vision and her wise words which bear repeating: "If we wish to have peace in our world, we must begin with our children.

By: Ernest G. Tannis, President, Global ADR Strategies (GADRS), with Ivan Roy. Editor: Doreen Kahalé.

Ladle Power Diplomat: Peter T. Oglow (1913-2004)

Can gifts of wooden spoons bring understanding and peace? As a crusader for world peace, whose Russian parents burnt their guns in 1895, Doukhobor wood carver Peter T. Oglow (1913-2004) of the interior of British Columbia made this happen.

His most famous symbolic offer was to 12 world religious leaders who in 1986 attended the Summit for Peace in Assisi in honour of their rocky road to peace. He carved 12 ladles (with 12 peace doves circling its rim and globe in its centre), one each to the leaders, plus one for Mother Teresa for her contribution to world peace, and sent them off by diplomatic pouches and personal couriers. The Pope replied, as did Emilio Castro of the World Council of Churches, the Dalai Lama, Mother Teresa, the Archbishop of Canterbury and Metropolitan Filaret of Russia. Peter and the community were delighted!

At the First Global Conference on Tourism in Vancouver, without formalities, Peter walked up on stage with a brown bag of ordinary ladles and politely asked to say a few words. He then proceeded to invite select guests to come up and receive their gifts. This was a spectacle to behold as a peasant-looking Doukhobor with Russian roots made a friendly gesture that few would ever dare to, let alone by publicly cutting through formalities.

He carved hundreds of ladles from the size of small necktie holders to six foot long ones, some of which he donated in 1984 to departing Katimavik students who had completed a museum work project in Castlegar, BC.

In practicing his philosophy of cutting across boundaries, Peter was a member of several diverse Doukhobor societies. At the close of the International Doukhobor Intergroup Symposium, 28th June 1982, in Castlegar, BC, Peter, with the skill of a diplomat, diffused a potentially disruptive terrorist situation at an outdoor Peace Day gathering with hundreds watching.

When a zealot woman stripped naked, chairman Peter Oglow borrowed an idea from the nonviolent movement which at that very moment, a million strong, was in front of the United Nations urging world leaders to embrace the path of disarmament and peace. He brought a fresh red rose to the lady, looked straight into her eyes and said:

"Sister, look at the beauty of this flower. Enjoy its fragrance. I know that you came here to pass on some message and I think you have achieved your purpose. Others at this gathering would like to share their messages here, too. It would be good if you would dress and join us."

She did and joined in the singing, all the while holding the red rose in front of her. Peter's imaginative use of love and beauty averted a sensitive incident and made this annual Doukhobor Peace Day and picnic a most memorable event.

On other occasions, Peter Oglow gifted dignitaries, including royalty, the governor general, the premier, the director of the Canadian Museum of Civilization, and many others. This fine arts skill was instilled from his father Tom, a Russian-born Doukhobor, who excelled in the craft of spoon carving.

Peter's central wish was for humanity: In loving life and nature, all of mankind should make an all-out effort to stop wars. This is the most urgent thing today, because if this will not succeed, then war will destroy humankind.

By Koozma J. Tarasoff, anthropologist, ethnographer, historian, writer and peace activist. (kjtarasoff@gmail.com).

Friends for Peace

It all started on a bitterly cold winter evening years ago, as the Iraq war loomed. I received notice that a Peace Song Circle was happening on Parliament Hill to protest the bombing of Baghdad. So I went, accompanied by my wife Carolyn, a friend and our dog.

No-one else turned up, as it was so cold. I remarked to Carolyn, "This is a good idea but it needs attention to detail and organization."

She replied, "Let's do it."

And so we did, creating the nucleus for Friends for Peace Canada. It quickly grew to a loose coalition of over fifty organizations in the city and we asked them to begin the peace process first of all within themselves, then to the community and out to the world.

Our mandate evolved from peace advocacy to projects on the ground. We gave annual Peace Grants to local and international organizations making a real difference, as well as working in concert with other coalitions in the city for environmental and social justice issues.

We organized five thousand participants at the Peace Song Circle on Parliament Hill in Ottawa, held on a miserably wet, cold spring day in 2003. A sea of multi-coloured umbrellas on a rain swept morning welcomed all those gathered. The pouring rain was strangely welcome, for it symbolized the tears of Iraqi children, my tears, your tears, transformed into hope through singing for peace with one another and experiencing deep peace. From there, we knew the wise actions to take.

The Friends for Peace Day became an awesome, diverse, unique Ottawa experience. It is made possible by the generosity of volunteers, supporters and the diversity of Ottawa who show up to have a good time, be educated and inspired. It creates an epicentre of intent and action, intense at times as people are moved to both tears and laughter. It is fun, poignant and direct. The intensity and joy ripples through the diversity, all generations, faiths and cultures in our northern city.

It has all grown in ever increasing concentric circles. The foundations of mindfulness through the fifty organizations we partner with have taken root in our northern city. All adhere to some form of the Friends for Peace mandate: peace, planetary care and social justice.

I felt that these efforts could infuse global networks from the epicentre created in my home city

I had received many invitations to be a global speaker and teacher, yet realized that a concentration on my home city of Ottawa was the primary focus. I responded to the many international invitations with a gracious decline.

I was inspired to devote my time and energy to moving things just a little bit in my city, so that more good things could begin to happen spontaneously.

As I soon discovered, there were many good friends across the city more than happy to make this possible.

Dr. Ian Prattis is Professor Emeritus at Carleton University in Ottawa, Zen teacher, peace and environmental activist. Born in the UK, he has spent much of his life living and teaching in Canada. His moving and eye-opening books are a memorable experience for anyone who enjoys reading about primordial tendencies. Beneath the polished urban facade remains a part of human nature that few want to acknowledge, either due to fear or simply because it is easier to deny the basic instincts that have kept us alive on an unforgiving earth. Prattis bravely goes there in his outstanding literary work.

Our Mahatma Walks the Walk

In the spring of 1970, I reported for my first administration position at the CUSO Thailand office in Bangkok. I had previously volunteered for international work camps in Costa Rica and the Philippines. I had also been an inner-city youth worker and later an English teacher in Thailand.

When I entered the office of Murray Thomson, my new boss, I was struck by a huge picture of Mahatma Gandhi. I quickly learned that this picture symbolized the values of Murray Thomson. He had spent his career working for social justice, non-violent social action, political and institutional development and nuclear disarmament. He also had extensive experience utilizing the Quaker method of consensus decision-making.

My values were a little different. I grew up in the United Church of Canada. My hero is still Dr. Bob McClure, the Medical missionary, who provided medical care for needy patients all over the developing world. As a college student, I sought opportunities to assist those in need in developing nations.

After helping build a school playground and basketball court in Costa Rica, I was part of a group that successfully raised funds to help finance the college education of one of our Latino work camp colleagues. After returning from six months of volunteering in the Philippines, I spoke from the pulpit of Central United Church in Calgary and raised money which helped to finance an operation for the crippled child of the Director of the Agricultural Rural Center where we had built a school dormitory and planted thousands of rubber trees.

As Murray and I began working together, I was impressed by his ability to get people to work together by listening to their concerns and building consensus. When presenting a joint paper at a UN conference on "The Role of Youth in National Development", I was shaken by a fiery young Filipina who scolded us all for being fat cat bureaucrats and too old to understand the needs and concerns of youth.

As soon as she finished, I asked Murray to let me leave before our presentation to visit some poverty-stricken students and their families in N.E. Thailand. We were selecting scholarship recipients and taking pictures for fund raising. I wanted to do something useful so as not to be a fat cat bureaucrat. Murray sensed my passion and let me go.

Murray established The CUSO Thailand Committee (CTC) with volunteers, host national (Thais) and staff. We met regularly to set program directions and approve projects. I often complained about how long it took to reach consensus. Murray wisely helped me understand that if everyone had their say, and their concerns dealt with, they would be more apt to support the implementation of the venture.

I have utilized this valuable "Mahatma Concept" over the past 43 years. Emerging from the CTC were a series of scholarships for needy Thai students and gifted Thai educators, and a dormitory for a rural teachers' college. The most high-profile organization put together by Murray the Mahatma was the Thai Hill Crafts Foundation, with Thai Royalty, CUSO and Thai staff. It was amazing to watch Murray the Mahatma create it and also point me to various funding sources. It was still operating successfully under Thai leadership when Glen Dunkley (a former CUSO Thai Hill Crafts Foundation employee) and I visited it in Chiengrai in 2006. Any non-profit organization that lasts over 42 years is remarkable.

Murray the Mahatma and I do not agree on the role of CUSO in political development in a host country, nor was I to involve myself in political activism in North America. I respect his nuclear disarmament values and activities but they are not for me. I have written letters for Amnesty International but would rather work on people development as a coach, teacher and career counsellor.

I also hung a huge picture of Mahatma Gandhi in my class room as a tribute to our Mahatma who accepted us as we were and sought out ways to work together for common goals.

When students ask me about the Gandhi poster, I tell them about our Mahatma Murray who showed us the way.

By: Jim McFetridge (CUSO - Thailand 1967-1973; Ottawa 1973-1975).

Peace – an Everyday Activity

Peace-making has not been kind to eastern Sri Lanka in the past generation or more. Home for centuries to people of three religions, two languages, and wide-spread poverty, the region has seen more than its share of tension, conflict and war.

This is also home to A. Sornalingam, known simply as Sorna, a Tamil with three languages, whose wife is Sinhalese. He lives in the region's major city, Batticaloa, beside the ocean and among the palm trees. Some, including Sorna, see it as idyllic, except for the human destruction that has ravaged too many families during his lifetime.

Sorna has worked for 30 years with a national civil society organization to improve the lives of people in this and other regions of the country. His focus is to strengthen local village groups and organizations so that they may design and execute their own activities to raise living standards and build solidarity among the diverse groups.

Despite three major religious communities – Buddhist, Muslim, Hindu – plus some Christians, most people have lived historically in relative harmony. But poverty and social injustice have been evident and tensions constant; violence is always close to the surface. Sorna sees his role mainly as addressing these conflicts, by mediating and negotiating on a daily basis. His underlying goal is to increase trust, mutual respect and cooperation among people in the different groups.

The long Sri Lankan civil war took these tensions to horrendous new heights: killings, kidnappings, disappearances, and a total disregard for human rights by all sides brought untold fear and pain. Sorna had to protect his family, the communities, and the development work under his responsibility.

He chose to employ honest communication and persuasion with all parties – government, LTTE (Tamil Tigers) operating in the area, communities and their leaders, and people in the villages.

He dealt with life-threatening circumstances for himself and those around him. People disappeared – some were confirmed dead, some were not.

Both the government forces and Tiger rebels were threats; the fighting was brutal and long-lasting. And yet, he still managed to bring most people in his orbit through with their lives intact and the will to rebuild and reconcile. This will among people and communities also served them all well in rebuilding after the 2004 tsunami that brutally hit eastern Sri Lanka, where the water surged as high as the palm trees.

Sorna could easily have moved to Colombo and taken an executive position with a prominent civil society organization, or perhaps in the government.

But he has chosen to remain in his humble surroundings to work directly with the communities who need his support and mentoring. In spite of the horrendous loss of life through the civil war and the frequent communal conflict over a longer time, Sorna's presence, his words and actions have no doubt saved many lives and alleviated the suffering of many more.

His work has built harmony and cooperation across conflicted lines and improved the satisfaction of life, directly and indirectly, among thousands. In his quiet and unassuming way, he has made peace an everyday activity.

By: Richard Harmston, Board Member, Canadian Peace Service Canada, (www.civilianpeaceservice.ca).

Peace after Aceh Tsunami: a Co-operative Revelation

I flew from Ottawa to attend a wedding celebration of my niece on 26th December 2004 in Bandung, Indonesia. Alas, this festivity was severely disrupted by the overwhelming news about the giant Tsunami that raged along the coastlines of the Indian Ocean, which followed a 9.2 magnitude earthquake.

My great anticipation of a celebratory wedding morphed into a gloomy atmosphere of hope and despair after seeing the enormity of the natural disaster. Aceh in Indonesia, which is the worst hit, lost 220,000 lives. More tragic was the fact that this disaster occurred during a period of an armed conflict between a separatist movement called "GAM" (Free Aceh Movement) and the Indonesian army, killing over a thousand civilians, and with close to 500 still missing.

My inner compassion, and a lifetime career with co-operatives, took me to Banda Aceh, the Capital City, in less than a month after the catastrophic Tsunami, where I could still see dead bodies being lifted from the streets near the Ule Lhe beach and the Krueng Aceh River. I first went there with my friend Lydia from the Canadian Co-operative Association, and returned again soon thereafter as envoy of the International Co-operative Alliance to reconstruct and rehabilitate co-operatives shattered by the tsunami.

Reconstruction was no doubt very onerous. We had to transport needed supplies to fishery co-ops in Lhok Ngha and Lhok Suedu along the western coastline of Aceh through damaged roads and bridges. Not to mention the difficult task of having to attend to emotional needs of traumatized survivors.

However, the more difficult prospect was to reconstruct those in the eastern coastline facing the Andaman Sea, because human rights violations by government troops and the GAM rebels ensued with impunity. We were unable to travel to the Sigli in the district of Pidie as frequent ambushes were still taking place during the first half of 2005. Recovery efforts for two peaceful fishery co-ops, i.e. "Bahari Karya" and "Panti Raja" in Pidie district, were basically stalled.

Notwithstanding the enormity of the Tsunami, it fortunately opened a critical opportunity to end the conflict because human lives in the entire province would have been more severely affected and endangered should the warfare have persisted. Mediated by former

President of Finland M. Ahtisaari, GAM finally dropped its demand for Independence and an agreement was reached and signed on August 15, 2005.

Towards the end of 2005, our work of reconstructing five pilot co-operatives destroyed by the disaster became fairly conducive. One co-operative in Bireuen even had a number of previous GAM rebels as members, creating beautiful ornaments made from leftover and unused weaponry, under the fine leadership of Teuku Nasarudin, one of the GAM leaders who made a wise decision to develop and rebuild communities through co-operative means rather than to engage in politics. He truly believes that co-operatives are powerful instruments to promote and sustain PEACE in communities, and so it has been!

By: Robby Tulus, Asia-Pacific Regional Director (Emeritus) for Canadian Co-operative Association (CCA) & International Co-operative Alliance (ICA), based in Ottawa.

The Canadian Peacekeeper

In December1987, I was on United Nations duty in the Golan Heights, and starting to feel the loneliness of the situation. As you know, on Christmas Eve, CBC Radio hosts a special broadcast of "As it Happens". They ask service members at remote locations around the world to send special messages of love and longing back to their families. Carols are sung. Jokes are told. A great show.

What you probably don't know, is that CBC phones these locations well before the show. Personnel are chosen, put into a tiny room and their voices are taped, then magically edited for the show that has folks from around the world seemingly sing together and send home their messages on Christmas Eve.

That year, I was one of the lucky five from my camp. I remember being handed the phone. My turn, but what to say? In my mind's eye, I saw all that I would be missing: my family gathered, laughing and chatting, gifts, smiles, and parties with so much food you would bust. The joy of togetherness. The true enormity of it moved me so close to tears that I couldn't speak.

"What's your message for home?" the fellow on the other end of the phone asked repeatedly. Then I knew what could remedy my longing. "I want to wish you all a Merry Christmas," I blurted out. "Go out tonight and look up to the stars. I'll be looking at them too and somehow we will be together for Christmas Eve". That was my message. The fix. It wasn't great, but the best I could do. Well, Christmas Eve came around.

As luck would have it, I was on duty. A buddy and I sat at the camp gate in darkness on a very stormy night and watched for anyone trying to enter. I proposed a wee little Christmas present:

"I have the key to the Headquarters. How about you go and call your family. Then I'll do the same".

"Brilliant!" he said and set off, key in hand and smile on face.

He returned about 45 minutes later in obvious bliss.

My turn.

It took over 30 minutes before the phone finally rang. I was surprised to hear my wife say "I can't talk to you right now, you're on the radio. Call back in 10 minutes".

Then, dial tone.

I walked out with disappointment in my heart and rain pouring down my back. I thought of my family all listening to the radio, all having a good time. I was cold and lonely and wet.

Then I remembered my message. Jeesh ... how was I going to see the stars in this muck?

I raised my face and spoke, with utter frankness, to the heavens. I remember my words.

"I haven't been talking with you lately. I don't know if that's good or bad, but I know you've been here. I need some help. You know that message I left? Well, I'd kind of like it if I could spend just a little time with my family. Would that be too much to ask?"

What happened next is the honest truth. There were no lightning bolts, no iridescent clouds, no booming voices, nothing "Hollywood".

Instead, the rain stopped. The clouds parted around an unseen boundary in the limitless beauty of a starry sky.

For about 30 minutes, on the Golan Heights, I felt the peace of being caressed by the Divine.

Then the clouds came back. The rain resumed. But, it was a warm rain. All part of that gift for me, my family and my soul:

While serving as a Canadian Forces member on peacekeeping duty, I spent a Christmas in abundance.

With a Maple Leaf on my shoulder, I was honoured by so many.

With privilege, I was afforded the opportunity to share Canadian values. With humility, on a rocky road in the midst of a hostile land, I was bathed in love.

It was a good Christmas.

By: Timothy D. Brodie, C.Med, Q.Arb, PCC, CEC, MMM, RCMP

The Gulf War – Invisible Victims of Armed Conflict

Basrah, Iraq, 1990. The surprise invasion of Kuwait by Saddam Hussein spawned an exodus of Kuwaitis, Palestinians, as well as other workers, mainly from Iran and the Philippines. Various UN agencies reduced their staff. As weeks went by, a steady stream of looted luxury and other commodities destined for Baghdad headed north on Highway 8. Workers from the Philippines were housed in makeshift camps in various suburbs of Baghdad. Staff of the headquarters of the United Nations Iran Iraq Military Observer Group (UNIIMOG), monitoring the 1988 cease fire between Iran and Iraq, reported on the appalling conditions in the camps, including women being forced into prostitution.

In the meantime, with depleted staff, UNHCR was unable to monitor, protect and assist vulnerable populations generally, and in particular, the Iranians who were encamped around Az Zubayr, awaiting the opening of a temporary border crossing between Iran and Iraq so that they could eventually go home.

For Sector South, our vague and imprecise task was to "monitor and report" the condition and treatment of those crossing into Iran. The first of two-man patrols on twelve-hour shifts, 24/7, noted that Iranians and others who had been dropped off by taxis and mini-buses had no shelter from the sun where daily temperatures climbed to 50 degrees Celsius or higher, no water and no privacy for women seeking toilets - forcing them to venture into suspected minefields. The Iraqi authorities resolved this after repeated UNIIMOG interventions.

Equally thorny, was extortion by contracted drivers who demanded additional payment to cross into Iran. Direct intervention by UNIIMOG patrol members was required since Iraqi authorities refused to take action.

The most vexing problem was the Iraqi military. Under the guise of expediting crossing procedures an officer accompanied by soldiers would go down the line of cars, obtain vehicle registration and other documents to begin "pre-clearance" but by the time an Iranian reached the crossing point and his car and his belongings were judged to be valuable, the car and chattels would be confiscated since the driver would be unable to produce the documents that had previously been collected. Their cars and belongings were deemed to be stolen goods or contraband. They would now have to make the crossing on foot.

Normally on a UNIIMOG patrol one member would remain with the vehicle on radio watch while the other would patrol on foot. Due to widespread abuse both members of some patrols would patrol on foot, showing up unexpectedly, to observe and take notes.

The threat of accountability had a marked effect on Iraqi behavior, but the unfortunate reality was that not all Iranians and others could be protected since some UNIIMOG patrols remained in their vehicles for the entire 12-hour shift and merely observed cars and people inching towards the crossing point.

This reflects the varying degrees of pre-deployment training on pressing issues now facing UN peacekeepers in a markedly more complex environment. For example, Peace and Security; Protection of Civilians; Sexual and Gender Based Violence; and Conflict Related Sexual Violence. Canada has played an important role in pioneering such training, through the Pearson Peacekeeping Centre (PPC) from 1994 to its unfortunate closure in 2013. Today, there are over 80 peace-keeping training institutions, the genesis of many also due to the PPC.

Canada now has an opportunity to revive its role in peacekeeping (especially with low-income countries, including critically needed support for pre-deployment training); and also in peacebuilding, to reduce the need for UN peacekeepers. Then we can truly assert that Canada is back!

By: Ted Itani

The *Kumbha Mela*

Fifteen and a half million people, mostly Hindu pilgrims, collected on the banks of the Ganges River at Ahallabad. The year was 1977, and it was the *Maha Kumbh Mela*, a festival that happens only every twelve years.

Once I made my way to the plateau overlooking the *mela* grounds, I could hardly believe my eyes. Eventually, I walked down and into the crowds, walked for miles taking it all in. The *Naga Babas*, naked with matted hair, crouched beside the holy river to make sure they'd be the first to take the ceremonial bath each day. I saw a fellow who'd been buried up to his neck for nine days. He said hello in English as I passed. I saw a *Baba* with a withered arm since he'd held it aloft for many years.

There were elephants, horses, cows and, of course, dogs running all around. There was a spirit or a pervasive vibration, so to speak, of spirituality, of oneness. I watched the people, the animals, the life, and it occurred to me that I'd never see a spectacle to match the *Kumbh Mela* again in this life.

It had rained hard the night before. So there was no dry place to sit and eventually, exhausted, I sort of plopped myself down right in the middle of a muddy path, leaned against a tent pole to rest, to meditate. If I fell asleep it was not any form of slumber I'd ever had before. But, when I awoke I found myself in the centre of a circle of yogis chanting mantras near a fire that lit up the night.

The peace in the camp of those yogis was palpable and so incredibly welcome. It was truly remarkable. They meditated, chanted, played their *dotars*, softly drummed and by the dawn a mist created a surreal and otherworldly effect. One of the yogis placed a bowl of curd and sweets in front of me that tasted as rich and wonderful as if it had come from a five-star hotel.

I've carried the memory of that night, the deep sense of peace, wellness, oneness, through all these years. Having been embraced so fully by complete strangers was profound. It was as if they were saying: "There's no such thing as strangers, not really."

By: Nathan Vanek

Mahatma Gandhi and Nonkilling Vision

Mahatma Gandhi saw his humanist approach to politics transcending the notion of a nation-state. To him and many Indian leaders, the good governance that provided equal opportunity to everyone in making their livelihood with dignity and respect was key. What was the grounding of the Gandhian experiment, six decades after India's Independence, was now being reflected in subterranean undercurrents around the world toward the end of the 20th Century. Aspirations demanding the Universal Rights of Man were enshrined in UN and UNESCO charters.

The UN declaration that the first decade of the 21st Century's be devoted to building a "Culture of Peace and Nonviolence for Children of the World" (2000) was a path breaking initiative in this direction. It exhorted the Gandhian vision that violence and wars were not necessary and the 'Right to Live' was a fundamental right. Principle 13 of the Nobel Peace Laureates Charter for a World Without Violence (2008) called for a killing-free world "in which everyone has the right not to be killed and responsibility not to kill others." Political success and the notion of war were no longer seen just in terms of how many wars a nation could win or how much weaponry a nation had amassed.

The concern was now also about people, civilian casualties, and how to prevent the deaths of men, women, and children from deliberate killing. Further, most conflicts now resulted from local issues - as 7000 cultures worldwide coped in their own ways with the technological and material onslaught of unevenly distributed wealth and knowledge. Even some military generals from NATO countries accepted that there were no longer clear-cut military victories like those in the Second World War.

Violence prevention and conflict transformation now required well-resourced institutions for peacebuilding at local, national and global levels. And yet, beyond the UN, in the absence of such an infrastructure of peace, responsibility for peace work fell to ad hoc and ill equipped voluntary organizations. Serious attention was needed from individual governments to provide well-resourced peace education, human and economic rights enforcement. Also, the curbing of arms buildup and, most of all, a trained cadre of peace professionals with skills and expertise in the prevention, mediation and reconciliation of conflicts at home and abroad. National government structures were also needed to recruit, train, and deploy specialized peace professionals - equivalent to tax-payer funded, military professionals.

A Ministry or a Department of Peacebuilding and Disarmament, for example, headed by a Cabinet Minister could enable all the above, and help to balance the advice received by a Head of State from a Minister of Defence and Minister of Foreign Affairs. Similar institutions could be created at local levels to inspire development of peace cities and peace provinces.

The impact of Gandhi's thinking showed unending creativity for such nonviolent peace structures and actions. Thus, as pointed out by Dr. Dhirendra Sharma, the ancient Indian Vedantic tradition of Ahimsa (to hurt others is to hurt oneself) first found organized, political application in the twentieth century by Mahatma Gandhi in South Africa and India, followed by Dr. Martin Luther King, Jr. in the USA. It was an important tool in post-war decolonization, and was applied more actively in the late 1980s as means for bringing about change in the former Soviet Union by civil society groups under various nonviolent leaders.

By: Balwant (Bill) Bhaneja, Ph.D. retired Canadian diplomat, peace activist, cofounder of Annual Ottawa Peace festival and the Canadian Department of Peace Initiative movement, http://canadianpeaceinitiative.ca, excerpted from his book "Quest for Gandhi: A Nonkilling Journey".

Towards a Global Peace Education (PEP)

Canadian astronauts who had the opportunity to travel in space, all came up with the same observation. As they looked down on our little planet travelling alone through space, each independently realized that we have no other place else to go and must therefore act accordingly.

Hence, the importance of establishing global peace. Clearly, we need an agreement on global peace equivalent to the Paris agreement on global warming before we ruin our only home. But how long will it take and how long have we got? And how can we use increasing access to the printed word around the world? The first war recorded in human history occurred in the Middle East some 5000 years ago and it appears that we have never stopped.

Role models have obviously played an important part in this. For most of us our parents are our first role models. Around the world people almost universally speak the same language as their parents. Our analysis of the time required for substantial global change must, therefore, recognize the old saying, "Like father like son." Or, perhaps, "Like grandfather like father". Regretfully, global change for peace thus takes more than one generation. Role models and family values continue to have an important place throughout our lifetime. As we age, our personal horizons gradually expand to include not only family but neighbours, friends, teachers and more. (Sadly, terrorist organizations know all too well how to use this to their advantage.)

As a personal example of generational influence, during my early years in Calgary, Alberta, our family attended the Baptist church but after graduating from university and moving to Peterborough, Ontario, I married into a Presbyterian family and some years later my wife and I had two young children. We began attending a Presbyterian church where eventually I began teaching Sunday school to a class of students of about twelve to fourteen years of age. On one occasion, and much to my surprise, I was requested to deliver the sermon to the whole congregation on the occasion of their annual layman's day.

Wishing to be sincere I carefully selected topics and examples that were close to my own heart and beliefs. Quite appropriately this emphasized how parents act as primary role models. When the service was over I thought I could walk out quietly through the lobby and go straight home but to my surprise it was now full of church members, including the minister himself, all wanting to offer congratulations! I was surprised and still remember that as a special moment in my life.

Another example occurred when one Sunday afternoon I passed through Checkpoint Charlie from West Germany into Soviet controlled East Germany. To say the least, the scrutiny on going in was intensive. Realizing this, I very carefully put my Canadian passport into an inside pocket where I could frequently touch it just to make sure it was still there! Instead of taking it for granted as perhaps we usually do, I began to realize how valuable being Canadian really is. Around the world, many people regard Canada as the best place in which to live.

Over many recent years, my interests have consequently focused on the development of a document called The Global Peace Accord. Nation states that join can use it to document their own description. They can then see themselves as if in a mirror and seek to improve, not only for themselves, but also to encourage other nation states to do likewise. The accord is thus a tool to encourage global peace. A section is being added to this to improve the point-score evaluation for nation states who adopt this.

To do more than just end war, we also need a Global Peace Education Program (PEP) that will actually build peace. New Zealand has already made a start and perhaps we can benefit from their example.

By: Jack Scrimgeour

Peace on the Job

The first person I represented as a shop steward was Connie*, someone I had known for years in the workplace. A series of incidents had taken place in Connie's office, culminating in all but one of her colleagues signing a petition against her—something I had never heard of happening. Connie had been called to a meeting with her manager and a staff relations rep and I was asked to be there as her advocate.

They wanted her to go on leave for a period of time and she was balking. It was obvious to me at the meeting that Connie was in some kind of crisis. As things began to deteriorate, I asked for two minutes and motioned for her to join me in the hallway. I advised her that it would likely not go well for her if she continued to resist and in all probability she would find herself being escorted from the building by the security staff. I suggested to her that that would not be ideal and she agreed. When we went back into the meeting, she told the manager and the HR rep that because I had explained things to her in a calm manner, she was prepared to do as they had asked.

So began a protracted and sometimes difficult first involvement as a union rep. In that very first case I had my feet to the fire many times. I sometimes felt as though I was part of the cast in a Shakespearean drama! In the end, Connie was transferred to another workplace and eventually retired.

This happened in an environment where, when managers were assigned to our area, it was said they were going to the Eastern Front. In other words, the employees knew their rights and were not afraid to exercise them, so were difficult to manage. The union was almost in its infancy in our workplace at that point, and we had all been involved in one way or another in writing the first contract. That meant that the culture had to change from one of top-down management to collaboration, mediation, give and take—and that was a hard nut to crack for many years.

In the time that followed that first case with Connie, through contract negotiations, through mediation, through grievance procedures, I learned a great deal about people on both sides of the table, including myself. Among other things, I learned that some emotions had to be left in the hallway if progress was going to be made, and of course one must almost always compromise if a workable solution is to be found.

Over the years, labour relations were strained and sometimes difficult, and the challenges were many. It was not until a new manager came on the scene that things began to improve—and they improved dramatically.

I developed a rapport with this manager—based on an intelligent exchange of ideas, a mutual respect, and, best of all, humour.

Together we resolved many issues before they resulted in grievances. Even during contract negotiations, we had countless "off the record" conversations that resulted in issues being resolved through back channels and then formalized at the bargaining table.

This is not to say that it was only the two of us who effected change; there were many others who contributed to making the workplace less antagonistic. I am forever grateful, though, to this particular manager for his generosity and open-mindedness.

The culture of the workplace gradually did change, and we achieved labour peace. The Eastern Front was once again a term of history.

By: Elizabeth Hogan
*Name has been changed

Peace, Common Sense, and Being a Lawyer

There's probably some kind of computer software program that will review documents for not just grammatical and format issues, but also for things that just don't make sense or are incongruent, that don't "compute" and so, must have been written in error. And if that program does exist and if it were to review this story, I'm guessing it would have difficulty getting past the title. Jokes about lawyers and their single-minded quest for money and victory regardless of the cost? These jokes run rampant. One would be hard-pressed to find a Netflix special or movie portraying lawyers as level headed, calm, applying common sense to the problem at hand, let alone portraying the profession as peaceful.

But we do exist!

I am a settlement based lawyer which, essentially, means I choose to assist people in conflict to reach their own resolutions rather than ask that a third party impose a decision for them to adhere to. Not only does this provide parties the opportunity to consider their own unique interests, goals, fears, and expectations in reaching an agreement, but they generally have a greater chance of success in the implementation of what they agreed to do than in following an order issued by someone whose only knowledge of those individuals has been during a time when they typically show the worst of themselves.

And this is especially true in the context of family breakdown, separation, and divorce. The greater the love that began the relationship, the greater the pain, grief, and anger in the ending.

Many people hear the word divorce and instantly conjure images of the warrior lawyer stepping forward to protect the husband/father/wife/mother in distress. Of course with any image of war, there is then the warrior lawyer on the other side of the proverbial line in the sand, holding firm the position that it is their client who is the one in distress and in need of a protector.

And somewhere in the midst of the noise, dust, and confusion of the battle are children. It is estimated that 35% of Canadian children are affected by divorce and that statistically these children are more likely to have addiction issues and problems with peers, suffering at twice the rate than children of intact families with anxiety, depression and self-esteem issues. Knowing this, the question lawyers who practice family law must consider is how to help parents to mitigate the negative impact on their children resulting from the decision to live lives separate and apart from each other. It doesn't take a rocket scientist (but perhaps just someone with a bit of common sense) to recognize that the answer certainly isn't by feeding the conflict and escalating the war.

Across Canada there are lawyers who are thinking about this question and committing to the use of peaceful process options, such as mediation and collaborative law. These processes support the family in crisis rather than using the law in a way that then becomes the cause of the crisis. They create room for other professionals so that the families' needs can be met, whether those needs are education on budgeting for two homes compared to one, the need for coaching on how to communicate respectfully and effectively, or the need for experts to provide objective opinions that the parties can rely on in making difficult decisions.

I am honoured to be part of this group and to be practicing as a peace-making lawyer so that there can be less trials and more smiles!

By: Charmaine Panko, L.L.B., C. Med., Q. Arb. Panko Collaborative Law & Mediation

The People's Treaty

Antipersonnel landmines once were one of the most commonly used weapons. They were in the arsenal of most militaries, including Canada, and widely used in conflicts around the world. For those reasons it had been considered impossible to ban landmines despite the fact that they caused so much death, injury and misery for tens of thousands of civilians around the world.

That all changed on December 3, 1997 in Ottawa. On that day, 122 countries came to Canada to sign a treaty banning antipersonnel landmines. The impossible was indeed possible and the ban on landmines became a reality.

The treaty was the result of a unique partnership of a small group of like-minded states led by Canada, international organizations such as the International Committee of the Red Cross, and civil society under the leadership of the International Campaign to Ban Landmines (ICBL). For its efforts driving the movement to ban landmines, the ICBL was awarded the 1997 Nobel Peace Prize along with its then Coordinator, Jody Williams.

Hundreds of thousands of people had been killed or injured by landmines in the preceding decades with the vast majority of those casualties being civilians. With the changing nature of conflict since the Second World War risks to civilian populations were greatly increased as the resulting high levels of casualties attest. In dozens of countries people started to organize to find ways to reduce the impact of landmines. Initial efforts were focussed on getting militaries to restrict the use of landmines and to get governments to provide better support to survivors. When the ICBL was formed in 1992, the focus changed to banning the weapons largely because efforts to restrict, regulate or control use had been ignored. Organizations large and small began campaigning both nationally and internationally in support of a complete ban on landmines.

Naturally they were labelled as dreamers, unrealistic, or naïve. However, the ICBL and its members in more than 50 countries were not deterred. They lived or worked in communities that were adversely affected by landmines, many from conflicts that had ended years or even decades ago. They persevered bravely making their own personal stories public to force and sometimes shame governments into action. The fact that the treaty was opened for signatures in Ottawa just five years after the founding of the ICBL clearly demonstrates the power of the actions and campaigning by civil society.

Individuals through non-governmental organizations under the umbrella of the ICBL pushed governments into action and led the international community to negotiate in record time a treaty banning the use, trade, transfer, production and stockpiling of landmines. The treaty was also the first disarmament treaty to include victim assistance in its obligations.

Although individuals and civil society were the key force in the creation of the landmines treaty, only governments can sign international treaties. To me, that seemed unfair and didn't really acknowledge the extraordinary impact of the efforts of ordinary people. Mines Action Canada (MAC), as the Canadian member of the ICBL, played host to all the international campaigners arriving in Ottawa in December 1997 and organized a series of public events to promote and celebrate this unique, life-saving treaty. As a volunteer with MAC at the time, I suggested we have a separate parallel signing where the general public could come and show their support by signing The People's Treaty. This evolved into a major public event where thousands of local citizens came to the conference site to sign The People's Treaty. It also went national and international.

To date, more than a million people have signed it in dozens of countries. These people have all endorsed the steps their governments have made in protecting innocent civilians from landmines, an inhumane and indiscriminate weapon, creating some peace in their communities.

By: Paul Hannon, Executive Director, Mines Action Canada

The Trees in Bosnia

In 2003, the war in Bosnia had been over for six years, and the main dangers to peacekeepers were land mines, crazy and drunk drivers, and horrible road conditions.

Driving through Bosnia, I saw the saddening sights I had anticipated: rocket holes in the minaret of the mosque in Prijedor, collapsed bullet riddled houses, and large cemeteries full of white, recently placed headstones.

However, I didn't expect how the countryside always looked deceptively festive—as though all the trees along the rivers bore colourful streamers. In reality, the low water levels exposed shredded plastic shopping bags used for garbage caught in the branches. These surprising views of pervasive poor sanitation emphasized the state of the country to me, and the need for us to provide a secure environment for peaceful institutions to become effective.

In my role as a strategic planner, I had joined a group of British soldiers to observe how they patrolled their area of responsibility. We travelled from a central base to Gornji Ribnik, a village in "The Anvil", an area that had seen heavy fighting, and remained a source of ethnic tensions.

Photographs of hard-faced young Serb fighters killed in the war hung in the police station—not a good testament for the neutrality of the police, known country wide to be susceptible to corruption. In a conference room, the Royal Scots Corporal leading our team asked the chief about events in his district since their last visit.

Through our interpreter, a Corporal from the Parachute Regiment, he proudly spoke of catching a poacher the week before, who had cut trees from the land of a local Croatian farmer. People had often sought money this way due to the high unemployment and ubiquitous organized crime. Spotting a pile of freshly sawn logs from the window, I wondered why they hadn't been directly returned to the farmer.

I wanted to leave the interview to the soldiers, so through body language I tried to encourage them to look out the window. Perhaps nervous with a Canadian Major observing, they focused on the conversation and missed my darting eyes and slow head tilts. I began to feel that the interview was a pantomime carried out between players who didn't know or trust each other.

At the end of the interview, I stepped out of my observer role and asked if the trees outside were the ones stolen. The chief sheepishly replied, "Yes, we haven't returned them yet." I asked him to give the name and address of the farmer to the soldiers, as we wanted to visit him on our next patrol to learn more about the poaching problem.

After we left, the soldiers told me that if they lived in the town instead of visiting once every few weeks, details like this would not escape them. Under the circumstances, I didn't fault them for not noticing the trees for the forest.

This was a good case for a new approach—towns and villages with resident peacekeepers building relationships by getting to know the local authorities, people and problems, and able to call in assistance when needed.

Soon, this new method became the way NATO maintained the peace in small communities across the country.

By: Nicholas Curcumelli-Rodostamo, Lieutenant Colonel (Retired)

Quilting for Peace

During my Grandma's eighty-seven years of life, she quilted over two hundred quilts by hand. If anyone spoke of quilting, her eyes lit up and she was ready to get out her thread and needle. For her, hand quilting was both a highly creative and technical process. She meticulously designed the look of each quilt, drew the pattern, selected the many colours of material, cut each piece, sewed them together into the top of the quilt and added embroidery and appliqué as required. She pinned the top to wooden quilting rods, added the middle layer of warm batting and then attached the bottom, a coloured material to match the top. Then, she ever-so-lightly traced an elaborate design template on top of the quilt and began the long process of stitching. Finally, the edges of the quilt were bound into a completed masterpiece.

Grandma passed down the art and science of quilting to her daughters who taught it to theirs, including me. She told us her mother taught her to quilt when she was "knee high to a grasshopper" and told us "it's never too early or late to learn to quilt". She happily invited anyone who wanted to join in – gathering around a quilt meant friendship, comfort and love. It's no wonder she was so thrilled that each of her children and grandchildren contributed at least one stitch to the quilt the family made for her and my Grandpa for their 50th wedding anniversary.

Each quilt tells a unique story that she lovingly stitched into a work of art. She carefully selected a design specific to the occasion or person it represented – for the weddings of her ten children or the births and main life events of her thirty grandchildren and twenty-nine great-grandchildren. She made quilts for friends, special events and needy in her community. A true artist, she designed many quilts after being inspired by an image that sparked her sense of creativity and need for a new challenge. She reminded us many times that "the first rule in quilting is that you never count the number of hours". With around 2,000 pieces per quilt and an average of 800 hours to complete, her quilts truly were labours of love.

They were also her symbols of and instruments for peace. My Grandma didn't have an easy life. She grew up with what she called "hard times" and had some unthinkable things happen to her. As an adult, she was the mother of ten children, a farmer's wife and worked in fields and gardens. Whenever there was a spare moment, she spent it creatively. Even while suffering from Alzheimer's disease during the final years of her life, she quilted upwards of twenty quilts. Quilting was therapeutic and helped her comfort others. It connected her to the past and the future and offered her a sense accomplishment, pride and joy.

After my Grandpa and her retired from farming, they toured throughout Canada, always saying it was the best country in the world to live. As we celebrate Canada 150, I am reminded of what she called "one of my favourite quilts". She designed the quilt for the Canada theme at the local fair, naming it "Our Home and Native Land". She cut each province and territory by hand using many vibrant colours and a combination of appliqué and embroidery for islands, the Great Lakes, Mounties, flowers, animals and buildings. She was so proud when it won first prize!

Quilting was my Grandma's unique way to share her love and joy through the stories in her quilts and the energy they continue to hold. It was her way to find immediate and lasting peace. Peace for herself. Peace for her family. Peace for her friends and neighbours. Peace for her country and a better world.

By: Sharon Henhoeffer

Stephen Lewis – Selected Quotes

"No funding for peace talks unless women are at the table," Lewis says. "...this is a most serious gathering, and it may also be perfect timing, coming as it does right at the outset of an administration of which so much is hoped and so much is expected. And there is for me --- and for the organization I represent, AIDS-Free World --- another unanticipated happenstance. I had not met Ambassador Hunt before today, nor --- however embarrassing the admission --- did I know much of the Institute for Inclusive Security, or indeed, the work of Women Waging Peace that preceded it (albeit I'd certainly heard the name on many occasions).

But I have to say that reading the material that was sent to me spawned an instant sense of solidarity, and my colleagues and I really felt drawn to the advocacy on behalf of women that lies at the heart of the IIS. It's an advocacy that we not only endorse, but that sustains our own work, and frankly I feel more than a little foolish to have come to this discovery so late. And by the way, I'm not shamelessly currying favour; I'm too old to curry favour."

"As I read through the avalanche of briefing notes that Jacqueline O'Neill sent to me on behalf of the IIS, two things struck home.

First, the simple, unvarnished truth that men make war, and women lead lives without resorting to violence, so it makes unassailable logic to have women at the centre of peacemaking and peacebuilding initiatives. They are indispensable to negotiating peace agreements that last, and indeed, will never be sustained without the leadership of women.

But the other item was in a way transformative. In a Christian Science Monitor op-ed back in October, 2007, written by Carla Koppell, Director of the Initiative for Inclusive Security, she argues, and I quote,

'We could reserve seats at the table for those who have not borne arms but have a stake in peace. Most radically, mediators could invite non-belligerents to the table first and have them set the agenda for talks.'

It means, says Carla '... that those who haven't picked up weapons get to choose priorities.' I love it.

Of course it's radical: it would induce cardiac arrests in every warlord from Sudan to Zimbabwe.

But it's brilliant in the way it captures the quintessential fact that in every existing or anticipated peace negotiation, in every conflict everywhere, the women are missing.

So here we have a world awash in conflicts from Afghanistan to Iraq to the Middle-East. It never ends.

And because it never ends, we will always, as an international community be engaged in seeking peace where blood and terror reign."

Selected quotes, reprinted with permission, from "Remarks by Stephen Lewis, Co-Director of AIDS-Free World" (www.aidsfreeworld.org), presented at the 10th annual Policy Forum of The Institute for Inclusive Security in Washington, DC, on January 21, 2009.

The speech continues with recommendations for the then new Obama administration, including: refuse to fund or support any UN-sponsored peace negotiations without women as leading participants at the table; Full implementation of Resolution 1325; Provide or share funding to finance the full troop complement from the African Union to protect the people of Darfur; force negotiations through the Security Council with, again, the full participation of women as a prerequisite; Protect the women of the Democratic Republic of the Congo (the DRC) -"Guns are a complement to rape. The levels of dementia and brutality --- and, horrifically, the transmission of the AIDS virus --- endured by the women in the course of the sexual violence make bullets a mere addendum to atrocity"; Oppose all amnesties (for the militia) in such circumstances; Implement UN Security Council "Responsibility to Protect" ('R2P'). "When a government is unable or unwilling to protect its citizens from egregious violations of human rights, then the international community has the responsibility to protect." (E.g. in Zimbabwe). Create and share in funding a new UN international agency for women. ...akin to UNICEF for children. "In truth, an agency for women could well rescue the reputation of the United Nations."
[N.b. UN Women was created in 2010].

The Violence Vaccine

I had the courage. I had the pluck. I did not run away. And therein I feel, if not happy, self-respect.

But on this fine day in June 2016, one week after my first chemo treatment, I sit in a cancer ward in Victoria, British Columbia. Yesterday, as my white blood cell count dropped from the chemotherapy, I took very ill. My fever climbed rapidly and I have an infection that could be life-threatening. So once again I both admit I was a fool, and yet I marvel that I could be such a fool. That as I try to give this death sentence a philosophical spin, turning it over and over to find some nugget of wisdom, or a breakthrough insight about the mind and body – and my god question – I come up rather empty-handed. Except to say that an ounce of prevention is worth far more than a pound of cure. It is worth the whole shooting match!

There is also the cold fact of dying, of my death. My journey has had its moments when I willingly put my life at risk. Perhaps no more than when I went to meet Joseph Kony deep in the bush in southern Sudan, I knew I might not come back alive and I had left that sealed letter for Ann. What enabled me to put my life on the line was my mission. I was working to free thousands of abducted child soldiers from the horrors I knew they endured, and I was working for peace. My death would have been in the service of a purpose much higher than living my own life. And so it is for thousands of others who work for peace, who stand in harm's way.

But this death by cancer has no higher purpose. I will simply die without much ado in the eyes of the world. And my death will not benefit anyone.

So I had been bitter about this. That all of my life will end in a whimper, really. Death for no purpose. But then, is this not how the great majority, the thousands who die daily, die? There is no purpose to getting old and frail and one day or night dying. We just do it.

There is purpose in our lives, of course. And some people have the genetic material and good fortune to live to a very ripe old age, enjoying life. And then they die. But at the end of the day there is no purpose in their death. That my death comes far too early for me and my loved ones is a bitter, sorrowful thing, needless to say.

And I see no value in levelling blame at anyone but myself. If I am my brother's keeper, surely I must be my own keeper too.

And while there is a chapter to my journey that I could write, shrouded in the darkness of death by cancer, I will leave that to others.

What needs to be done now is that which is life-affirming:

- Refuse to accept that violence is inevitable in human relations;
- Take actions to eliminate the glorification of violence;
- Say "No" to illegitimate uses of force;
- Keep pressure on governments and leaders to intervene in cases of violence;
- Support society to build skills and mechanisms to prevent violence; and
- Fight this cancer to live my life as long as I possibly can.

By: Dr. Ben Hoffman, Peace Professional, from his book "The Violence Vaccine".

Three Women

Ten years ago I got to know three intelligent, kind and well-spoken middle-aged women, through the numerous human rights and peace activities in which I was active. They were there, wherever I went, and appeared to be close friends. Nothing unusual about any of that! But, what was somewhat unusual was that each of them practiced a different religion. And since I did not, I needed to talk to them about what brought them together. The Jewish lady was professor of social work, the Christian had a nursing background, while the Muslim was professor of engineering. I happened to run a weekly radio show in Ottawa, and invited them to tell my audience how a Jew, a Christian and a Muslim see each other.

J, who was active in Temple Israel, told us about the three branches of Judaism: Orthodox, Reform, and Conservative. She was impressed with the values she saw in the other two: ethics, humility, truth, justice, and charity. She saw far more in common with her two friends than she saw differences. C, active in her church, also talked about the values which she shared with her two friends, such as the Ten Commandments, also shared by the different divisions of Christianity. When challenged, she admitted that there were some in her faith, a minority, who look for differences, rather than similarities. M, a devout Muslim, urged us to start by recognizing the similarities. She pointed out that it is precisely because the similarities are so huge, that people can spot the differences more easily. After all, we have the same God, and pointed out that in her Quran, God addresses people with, "Oh human kind" not with "Oh Muslims." She also pointed out that Buddhism and Hinduism have some similarities.

"How did dialogue groups help you understand each other?" I asked J. "It was by how they conducted themselves that I learnt about Islam and Christianity. That is the image I have retained about my two friends. As a child and teenager, I was involved in inter-faith dialogue between Christians and Jews through the National Council of Christians and Jews Brotherhood of New York. I also got to know Muslims, dated a Muslim man, and almost got married to one, and studied the Koran. How I got to know Muslims in Ottawa is through the group which you created, namely Potlucks 4 Peace! As a result, M came to my synagogue for an information session, which one might call 'Islam primer for Jews' and it was so powerful to see parallel after parallel of shared values."

C answered my same question this way: "The way I learnt about the other two religions, about which I knew very little, is when J & M took me by the hand, leading me on a path of discovery about being devout. But they did it through example, by how they live their lives and how they treat people. It was a great source of enlightenment to someone who grew up not knowing a single Muslim, and only a few Jewish families, part of the Canadian experience, where there is some interaction within the Judeo-Christian community. But it is time to extend this to the Judeo-Christian-Muslim community. All have much in common. I hope others would take on these challenges."

M described her experience of talking at the Synagogue: "I was terrified about even entering the place. But later the experience was delightful. Some people from my Muslim community scolded me by saying 'How can you do this? These people hate us.' And I said 'No, they don't.'" As radio host, I challenged them: "You don't need a religion in order to be kind to others. All you need is to believe in human rights. You could be an atheist too and respect and love others!" J replied: "The issue of HR grows out of religion. You are creating a false division. To be a good Jew is based on what you do, not on what you believe." C added: "But religion gives you a spring board. It helps, but is not necessary."

By: Dr Qais Ghanem, (qghanem2@gmail.com), Author, radio host. In 2009, his radio show won the Radio Award of the Canadian Ethnic Media Association (CEMA).

"Several arrests have been made..."
Aljazeera, 29 August 2015

The news comes on as we turn
the van

       ...The bodies of 71 refugees were found in a truck...

west off the highway

          ...abandoned on
          a motorway...

oh the syrup of light on limestone bluffs

       59 men, 8 women and 4 children...

rolling waves of aspen and spruce

       including a young infant...

sunset slant across rapids and rock

       A police official said...

runnel of water, brush of breeze

       it was likely that those in the truck suffocated...

through open windows

       and had been dead for up to
       two days...

as we drive on our holiday wander down

       before the refrigerated truck...

Settlement Road.

       was noticed.

(Wikipedia, 28/02/2017 – "The Colonization Roads were created during the 1840s and 1850s to open up Ontario and used by settlers, much like modern-day highways, to lead them towards areas for settlement." Some, like this one in Haliburton, still bear the name Settlement Road.)

By: Susan McMaster. Her publications include books, magazines, anthologies and wordmusic recordings with First Draft and Geode Music & Poetry. She's founding editor of Canada's first feminist magazine, Branching Out, and past president of the League of Canadian Poets. This poem will be in her forthcoming poetry collection, Haunt (Black Moss, Autumn 2017).

Teaching Nonviolence

From the day I was born, everything around me was international. As a child born in Rome of Croatian parents, I was wrapped in a shawl made by the daughter of Leo Tolstoy.

When I was two, my family emigrated to Argentina, and I attended an Irish boarding school.

In 1965, I earned a scholarship to study at Cazenovia College outside of Syracuse, New York, and earned a BA in Liberal Arts.

I then went to live in London for four years and began to travel around the world, to Afghanistan, India, Brazil, and Thailand. Through a flatmate in London, I discovered Buddhism, which became a guiding light for my life and the beginning of my journey through nonviolence.

When I returned to Argentina in 1976, I landed in what the Argentines call "the dirty war," a period of terror in which tens of thousands of those suspected of being guerrillas or sympathizers were kidnapped off of the streets by the army. They were either killed or held in clandestine prisons. I remember those years as "business as usual," but with a river of blood running underneath. When my friends began to disappear, I knew that I could be next.

Suddenly at one particular moment, I knew I was in danger and it was time to leave.

I went to Brazil, to the city of Salvador Bahia with its old colonial buildings, African music and culture and peaceful coastline. There I lived for three years in the Sri Aurobindo ashram, a spiritual community where I, translated books from English into Portuguese, lived in an intense community and made lots of bread.

When I came back again to Argentina in 1982, I was changed forever. But the people of Argentina had also changed forever. Neoliberalism had taken over. The country was in total shambles and the economy was bankrupt. It has not recovered.

In 1989, through a series of serendipitous circumstances, I came to Canada and landed in Quebec. There I studied transpersonal psychology, worked as a physical therapist and taught self-development classes and meditation.

Through another series of connections, I was asked to go to a Cree community in northern Manitoba to be a resident assistant in a women's shelter. I went. That would bring about yet another paradigm shift in my view of the world and in me. I realized I wanted to dedicate my life to teaching nonviolence. For me, this was the best way to express my concerns, my need to serve and my longing for a compassionate world.

After a year, I returned to Quebec, called a friend who was a Franciscan monk, and asked him where I could study nonviolence. He told me about a group based in California, the Nonviolence Service *Pace e Bene* (peace and all good). I bought their curriculum, "From Violence to Wholeness", and phoned them to say I was going to organize a translation of the book into French. They agreed and were surprised when it got done in six months.

They invited me to meet them, and promptly hired me as their international program coordinator. I had found my path.

For the past 20 years, I have been a part of that organization, travelling and teaching nonviolence in countries in South America, Europe, Australia and elsewhere. In those years, I met extraordinary people with whom I share a relationship of love and respect.

In 2005, my team at *Pace e Bene* wrote a handbook called "Engage: Exploring Nonviolent Living", a work that Michael Nagler, a scholar and practitioner of nonviolence in California, described as a "toolkit for salvation."

Today, along with a Dutch colleague, I am writing the sequel to that book.

By: Veronica Pelicaric, as told to Carl Stieren.

My Babusya

During her life (Ukraine -1889; Canada -1969) MY BABUSYA demonstrated "Peace" in numerous personal ways. She did not get medals, she did not stop wars, did not participate in the reconciliation of belligerent sides, or alleviate in any concrete way the fate of people who were victims of human monstrosities... did not become one famous figure for her contributions to "Peace."

She accepted life's tribulations and joys with deepest humility, diligently avoiding judging and criticizing others, be it their origin, colour, religion, personal beliefs or choices. "Hate" was the "H" word not to be used. *Zhid* was not to replace *Yevrei* when addressing Jews in Russian. Derogatory names anti any peoples, jokes, remarks, accusations were to be left out. Babusya, never imposing, was honest, compassionate, and respectful of others. She loved life and lived in "Peace", within "Peace", towards "Peace". Her motto was: "To be in a state of "Peace" with God, with oneself, with one's neighbour".

From Tsarist Russia, her family ended up in Harbin, Manchuria, China in 1906. Harbin became a Russified city because of Russia's involvement in the construction of the Chinese Eastern Railway.

Eventually Babusya married (1912) and had two children. Her husband passed away in 1941. A short time before his death their 16-year old son left for New York to study violin at the Juilliard School of Music. All contact with him ceased because of WW II. Babusya's parents left for the Soviet Union. Babusya lost complete track of them and of her six younger brothers. Babusya suffered from cancer and underwent numerous surgical treatments. Her daughter married in 1941 and left for Mukden with her husband.

Babusya remained alone in Harbin.

I was born in 1945 and that year my Father was taken away by the Soviets to a concentration camp. Babusya became the breadwinner. She taught in a Russian school for a meagre salary. With lack of electricity, water, heat and edible goods along with pressure from Chinese for "foreigners" to leave China, in 1953 Grandmother, Mother and I were sent to Paraguay, an underdeveloped country run by dictator, Alfredo Sroessner.

Only Babusya continued to believe that "All is for the best in the best of all worlds". Finally, owing to Babusya's pursuits and efforts, Mother and I settled in Montreal, Canada (1956) where she joined us.

In spite of the inhuman political and economic turmoil of wars, revolutions, confiscation of properties, and currency devaluation, Babusya's struggle for survival was shown in her altruism, realistic positivity, in her ability to persevere, incite a smile, to be thankful and envelop in hope, faith, LOVE. Always accepting, never complaining, she was present as an indestructible pivot around which our lives evolved. Devoted to her family, a faithful friend, a talented and committed teacher, educated, well-read, well-informed, a lifelong learner, patient listener, peaceful fighter, a believer, Babusya was truly a wise person.

She brought me up and I cherish her legacy. She taught me Russian, instilled in me a profound love for Russian traditions, history, culture, faith and a truly genuine feeling of deep gratitude and love for our new homeland – CANADA. Yes, she did contribute to "Peace."

Babusya was a proud fan of EXPO 67. "Thank God for everything," she would say. Rest in Peace, Anna Sergeevna Bonch-Osmolovsky, MY BABUSYA.

By: Olga Kiriloff.

Peace before War – Peace after War

Unlike friends at university who marched under the Campaign for Nuclear Disarmament banner, and who camped outside nuclear facilities in inclement weather, surrounded by police cordons, I followed a more personal path and raised money for Oxfam and went on spiritual retreats with other students. Did I mean to choose personal peace over world peace? Not intentionally, it was merely a result of my safe upbringing.

Looking at long-term results of all this, the CND marchers perhaps spent their time more fruitfully – there hasn't been a nuclear war, and I'm not a priest!

Having never participated in a war, nor started a war (to my knowledge), nor ended a war, my professional experience and viewpoint is akin to one of the sweepers who arrives at the festival grounds the day after the big event, picking up the economic and administrative debris, to help bring the grounds back to normal. The cleanup events were, however, in exotic places like Colombia, Bolivia, Pakistan, and Cambodia.

In Cambodia, in 1996, I led a study regarding approaches for implementing massive reductions in the public sector over two years. The study was located in the Cabinet Office of the Council of Ministers. As consultants, our team worked to design approaches that would mitigate the economic and social turmoil of turning thousands of bureaucrats onto the streets with cash payouts designed to encourage new business start-ups and a new generation of entrepreneurs. Given that the streets of Phnom Penh were full of war veterans, many with missing limbs, already trying to learn to eke out a living in this new post-UN-administration environment, our team and the Council of Ministers did not see eye to eye with the IBRD/IMF field representatives on the timetable for the reductions. But this was the era of Structural Adjustment policies, so the IBRD/IMF took a very hard line on reducing government expenditures as part of the program of peace and reconstruction following the Pol Pot era.

So here we were, part of the cleanup crew long after the Khmer Rouge had been ousted, when an incident occurred, which caused my personal-view and the world-view of peace to collide. A colleague and I had been invited to a dinner, held in the courtyard behind the Council of Ministers building, to celebrate Cambodia's National Day. The venue had a stone tiled floor, was open to the sky, had round tables seating 10, and more than 100 people in total, everyone in festive mood.

Suddenly there was a loud bang as a litre-sized beer bottle fell onto the ground and exploded. I looked around in amazement. My Canadian colleague and I were the only two people I could see above the tables. Everyone else, including senior officials and ministers, was on the ground or crouched under tables. The message was clear. These people had suffered through war. They had lost family and friends. They had lost their homes. Memories of war were still fresh, even after a few years of peace. Outwardly peaceful, they carried the memories of war inside, along with hair-trigger reactions to sudden surprises.

This was a sobering experience. Not because of my naiveté in the face of potential danger, but because I'd not really understood the continuing effects of the trauma of war on people I'd been close to during the previous months. My Canadian cocoon had sheltered me from the reality in which large swathes of humanity live. I was with them, but I wasn't walking in their shoes. It made me realize that my personal, confident peace view, needed to be tempered with their worldly, fearful peace view, for me to be an effective colleague or friend.

By: Harry Monaghan

Tough Guy Tragedy

After retiring from Medicine Hat College in Alberta where I served as a recruiter, career counselor, instructor & registrar for twenty-eight years, I moved to the USA with my American wife to renew my much earlier life as an English teacher and coach. In order to promote harmony and to stop student violence, I discussed the following stories with my Arizona students.

One of the most successful football teams in California history had a star player on both offense and defense, T.K. Kelly. He was a tackling machine as a middle linebacker and a fast and powerful running back. He received a full-ride scholarship to Oregon. Many coaches said he was better than other local players, at the same age, who later became NFL starters.

Shortly before leaving for college, Kelly attended a send-off party. At the party a jealous punk called him out with insults. His friends told him to ignore the insults. Unfortunately, the insults got worse so Kelly, the football star, stepped outside and beat the crap out of the insulter. The insulter went home, got a gun, came back, then shot and killed Kelly. A book was written and a movie (When the Game Stands Tall) was made about this tragic tale.

After telling my classes this story, I required that all students sign a no-taunting pledge. I also gave the students an opportunity to write down what they would do to help make our classroom a happy, safe and positive place.

I was very forceful on this topic due to a sad incident that happened while teaching grade 10's. A very troubled young man had already been suspended once for fighting during lunch. I met his Mom during "Meet the Teacher Night." She was a single parent and a sweet lady who was trying her best but found him to be a very difficult challenge.

A little later, this troubled student was taunting and making fun of another student in my class for being too fat. The overweight student was very upset and on the verge of tears when his friend told the troubled bully to stop or else. It was getting loud enough for me to notice so I was able to get between them before any punches were thrown. Both students were temporarily removed from our learning community.

When they returned, we had a class discussion about what each of us could do to prevent this happening again. I told them about a tiny Filipina girl in my California class who held on to the arm of her boyfriend with both hands so he could not go after a guy who had pushed and insulted him. Then I gave them an assignment to write about what they would do to keep our classroom a safe, happy, and positive place.

The troubled bully didn't get it and said he wasn't taking "no crap" from anyone. This was on a Friday and all the next week the bully did not show up for class. When I asked why, there was a strange and mysterious silence. Finally, I got the rest of the story from one of my soccer girls.

Apparently, the bully challenged the guy, who stood up for his friend, to a fight in the desert. The bully picked the wrong guy to call out because the bully got beaten up so badly they had to call an ambulance for him. The bully was so embarrassed that he left the school and never showed his face again.

This was a very sad story that I determined would never happen in my class again, and it didn't.

By: Jim McFetridge

The Butterfly Peace Garden Batticaloa

BPG is an NGO, co-founded by Sri Lankan psychologist, Father Paul Satkunanayagam and Canadian artist Paul Hogan in 1996. PBG counsels and supports children traumatized by civil conflict and the 2004 Tsunami. Its mission is to be a unique, sustainable organizational model to serve traumatized children and adults of all communities, preserve their distinctive cultural identities and values, while partnering with progressive institutions and civil society through a creative, competent and dedicated team.

Trauma healing is achieved through the 'Garden Path Process', of contemplation/meditation and creativity to help children reconnect with self and the mystery of life. In Paul Hogan's words: "Our method of 'earth-work, art-work, heart-work and healing' became the model for other peace gardens in Sri Lanka and Cambodia.

The Butterfly Garden was cited in U.S. Congressional records as an example of 'best peace practice' with war-affected children." In 2003, he received an Ashoka Fellowship. Stories about some of the thousands of children reached by the Butterfly Garden include:

- The particular girl always was untidy. She always had a frustrated look on her face. She considered her younger sister as her rival. She would always say that she would commit suicide and then she would go somewhere to hide herself. She was an adamant type. There is a big change in my daughter. She is always tidy now. She does not have the frustrated look. She is always happy. She now happily offers things to her younger sister." "But my worry is that she might change after the Garden events end", said the mother. She will certainly show good qualities.

- Children numbering 6-8 selected for the program from the Paduwankarai area had the habit of chewing betel. Their teeth were stained. Their environment was the cause for it. Their friends too were addicted to this habit. After they came to the Garden, they completely gave up the betel chewing habit. At the same time, they have begun to make their friends too give up this habit.

- Tharmapuram is a village which is located on the seaside about 2 Km away from the Kalmunai main road, in the Kirankulum area. Out of the 50 children who came from this village to the Garden events, 20 children are girls in the age group of 15-17 years.

There are children in the village belonging to this age group who have developed love affairs or married very young. This situation was worst in the village. However, the children who participated in the Garden events are pulling out of this appalling situation in the village and they are being saved.

- Ajith, a 12 year-old boy, was very quiet and never spoke when he came to the Garden. We all thought that he was dumb. Now he has become a very interesting talker. He also comes forward to give various performances. When we went to his house to observe the situation we found that, from his early childhood, he had remained isolated. Nobody listened to him. Therefore Ajith, who had been lost in himself and become silent, identified himself in the Garden and has begun a new life. He is progressing day by day. This is evidenced by his activities both in his house and the garden. This boy entered the Garden event half way. It was the other participants of the event who informed us about this boy. He never stayed at one place. He would not concentrate on anything. It was a common occurrence for his mother to lock him up in the house. But he would escape via the roof and the fence. Therefore, there was no place on his body which did not have any signs of injury. When he came to participate in the Garden event, he was in a pathetic state. Now he has changed completely. He is able to concentrate. He does not run about aimlessly. After the parents' meeting in the Garden, his mother has not only begun to be less concerned about him but has also stopped locking him up.

By: Rev. Fr. Paul Satkunanayagam, sj, Executive Director, Butterfly Peace Garden Batticaloa.

The Collective Unconscious was Smoldering

I was born in rural Pennsylvania in 1946. By 1964, I learned all the social mores of the day. The Beatles had taken over America by storm. There were rising stars everywhere, Bob Dylan, Joan Baez, and old stars, Pete Seeger, and Woody Guthrie. Martin Luther King was making waves by getting arrested for being outspoken about civil rights and human dignity. Andy Warhol and Simon and Garfunkle, Jefferson Airplane and the Velvet Undergound were speaking to the collective unconscious of a generation. Women rising up and burning their bras in public! How could I not be a part of that? Germain Greer, Metgar Evers, Norman Mailer and Leonard Cohen and Kurt Vonnegut Jr. and Eldridge Cleaver, Jerry Rubin and Abbey Hoffman. Jack Kerouac and Allen Ginsberg. The collective unconscious was smoldering and about to become blazingly aware.

Lyndon Johnson was pulling us deeper and deeper into the Vietnam war. Conscription became mandatory. In the news, it became evident that the governors and lawmakers of the land were not listening. Young men were being shipped home in boxes from a war no one understood, or cared about, on the other side of the world. Socio-political protest was on the rise.

I was not old enough to vote, yet was forced by law to register for the draft. We found out much later that rich kids like George W. Bush, Bill Clinton and Donald Trump, were exempted by various expensive schemes while we, the rank and file, were shipped out to Vietnam more and more frequently, wave after wave.

Some of my friends and I decided to be the voice of the people, the voice of the America. We went to what started out as peaceful protests. In Harrisburg, Baltimore, Philadelphia, Washington D.C. York, and Lancaster. It was not enough to watch this from the sidelines; I became an activist, and wrote open letters to several newspapers. On one occasion, I was thrown across the hood of a police cruiser and spent a night in jail. Some of my classmates wound up wounded, or dead. These were very dark times.

In anger, I stormed into my Selective Service Office and told them I would not bear arms and promptly ripped up my draft card and threw it on the floor. They sent me another one. I burned it very publicly along with about 50 others that day, at an anti-war rally. By this time, I was being tailed by the FBI. They were doing an inquiry on me because I had applied for conscientious objector status.

(Though I could have easily claimed my Mennonite heritage, this was about personal conscience and not religion.)

In April 1968, I realized that rather than spend a possible five years in jail, I could go to Canada!

About seventy-two hours later, just ahead of receiving my draft notice, I was in Toronto! There was soon a bench warrant out for my arrest in the US. I had left my bewildered family and all my friends behind. Rough start, but in 1974 I became a Canadian citizen.

In the ensuing years, I learned that Peace is a personal process. Through some long and sometimes arduous hours of inner soul searching, the anger subsided. Canada had taught me about true humanity; tolerance, good will, honesty, integrity, and service. About the triumphs of love over hate.

Though I may have started out with good intentions, I have learned that I had been anything but peaceful. In Canada. I've tried to live a principled life, learning that true peace comes from within and expresses itself in everyday life through little acts of generosity, kindness and sometimes, sacrifice. And that these actions, as well as being effective, are their own rewards, and embellish the lives of those who practice them.

I am forever grateful.

By: Ron Martin

Visionary Lawyer Speaks Up for Peace

Peter G. Makaroff (1894-1970) was always at his best working uphill against almost impossible odds, according to Carlyle King, his pacifist friend and English professor. Born in Kars, Russia, to a Doukhobor family, Peter came to Canada in 1899 and settled on the Canadian prairies. At that time, he could speak no English, but in less than 20 years he was recognized as one of Canada's outstanding young lawyers. As one who inspired me and countless others to work for human justice and peace, Peter rightly deserves the title of 'our Bertrand Russell' as well as 'our Socrates'.

Makaroff was fortunate to have shared in the successful fights to achieve important social advances in Canada such as universal hospitalization and Medicare insurance. He was one of the original CCF group with his revered friend, J.S. Woodsworth, its first leader, who was like himself, committed to democratic socialism and pacifism.

Makaroff served one term on the Saskatoon City Council, 1939-1940. This was the time when he literally turned the other cheek after being hit by a fellow Alderman because Peter dared to speak out against the institution of war.

Until his death in 1970, Peter Makaroff was true to his Doukhobor principles and concentrated on promoting the idea of establishing world peace through World Government. He came to believe that without a sound structure of humane enforceable international law, mankind could never hope to avoid a nuclear holocaust. He was a life-time member of the Fellowship of Reconciliation and the Saskatoon chapter often met in his law office. Also, he served as chairman of the Saskatoon branch of the World Federalists movement.

Like Socrates, Peter challenged members of his own profession to come up with some solid legislation that could facilitate peacemaking in the world community. I attended one of these meetings in Banff, Alberta in 1965, on Law and Order in the International Community. During the question period, Peter stood up and said:

"I wasn't going to say anything at this Conference. But after sitting here for two days, I must admit I am frankly disappointed with the discussion which was largely focused on trade relations. Such discussion makes me indignant and impatient. You should throw out all your precedents, and your law books, for they lead to naught. Instead, you should set up new approaches of international law for none exists today.

Successful as he was as a Canadian lawyer and public figure, Peter was fully bilingual in Russian and English and cherished his ties with Russian culture and the best aspects of Doukhobor heritage, which for him meant a Tolstoyan Quaker-like day-to-day moral behaviour and rejection of violence and militarism. He played a vital role in promoting and helping organize several peace projects in Western Canada, in which I was involved. His motivation was to 'awaken mankind to the dangers of war'.

In July, 1964, he joined A.J. Muste and other peacemakers in protesting the chemical, biological, and radiological warfare tests at Suffield, Alberta.

In November, 1964, he met with 400 peacemakers at the gates of the radar base, Orcadia, Saskatchewan in a firm resolve to strive for nonviolent action, for one world, and for peace and universal brotherhood.

In June, 1965, he joined Mulford Q. Sibley, Frank H. Epp and 1500 people in a rain-soaked peace vigil near the RCAF radar base at Dana, Saskatchewan, where he presented a statement to the commanding officer to take immediate steps to prevent universal suicide from the threat of war.

"The way to peace is peace!" he said.

By: Koozma J. Tarasoff, anthropologist, ethnographer, historian, writer and peace activist. (kjtarasoff@gmail.com).

Plutocrates ou non?

Bombardier a été critiqué, en 2017, pour avoir garanti à ses hauts dirigeants des primes de rendement en millions de dollars. Ces dirigeants font partie du 1% qui gagne presqu'autant que les 99% des autres habitants du globe. D'où les inégalités, la pauvreté d'un grand nombre et la colère et la rage de ceux qui ne bénéficient pas de justes salaires ou qui n'ont pas d'emploi, ce qui peut être à l'origine de graves conflits. Voilà qu'un petit nombre d'individus capture une grande part de la richesse mondialement disponible. Comment cela se produit-il ?

Dans les années 80, j'ai obtenu un diplôme en Administration des affaires (MBA). J'ai alors choisi de travailler, comme fonctionnaire, à l'Agence canadienne de développement international (ACDI). J'y ai apprécié, durant 20 ans, mon travail auprès des populations défavorisées en Afrique. Je crois avoir fait la différence pour des centaines d'hommes et de femmes par ma bonne gestion de projets et ainsi, contribué de certaine façon à la paix.

Ce MBA m'aurait permis d'autres choix de carrière. J'imagine le scénario suivant: je n'ai pas le sou, mais avec mon diplôme et des connaissances en finance, j'emprunte quelques milliers de dollars à la banque que j'investis aussitôt en Bourse. Avec un peu de flair et beaucoup de chance, le retour sur mes investissements serait tel qu'avec de brillants collègues en informatique (c'était le tout début de l'informatique) nous aurions pu créer une nouvelle entreprise de communication et d'informatique. Après quelques mois nous la vendons à profit.

Utilisant ma réputation comme bon gestionnaire, prêt à prendre des risques et un important capital en banque, j'achète différentes petites entreprises en difficulté. Je les restructure en congédiant un grand nombre d'employés puis je les revends à profit. Ma réputation de brillant gestionnaire est reconnue, habile à saisir des opportunités d'affaires, générant le plus de profit grâce à la réduction des charges salariales. Sollicité pour siéger sur des conseils d'administration de firmes réputées, mon influence, mon profit, mon pouvoir et mon cercle de connaissances n'aurait fait que grandir.

Après quelques années, avec une imposante fortune personnelle, gagnée grâce à mes efforts, mon flair et de la chance, je me retrouve parmi les gens prestigieux ceux qui constituent le 1%. Je n'ai fait rien d'illégal. J'ai créé beaucoup de richesse pour moi et un peu pour l'ensemble du pays soit en payant le moins possible d'impôts et de taxes. Pourtant, en supprimant des emplois, j'ai favorisé la pauvreté chez plusieurs, ce qui aurait pu être source de conflits.

Alors, où en est la justice sociale condition essentielle pour la paix? On peut avoir des individus très riches, entreprenants, et prêts à prendre des risques et qui investissent cette richesse dans l'économie, par solidarité et souci du bien commun: il s'agirait pour les 1% d'utiliser leur capital, leur pouvoir et connaissances, pour créer de nombreux emplois stables avec des salaires justes et valorisants. Certains de ces riches investissent déjà dans des PME et ainsi permettent à des jeunes de générer à leur tour de la richesse et de nouveaux emplois. Sans la réduction des inégalités, on s'en va à notre perte et à de très sérieux conflits mondiaux.

À mon tour, sans être millionnaires, je me suis impliqué pour combattre les inégalités en utilisant intelligemment mes petits surplus, en temps et argent. C'est une façon pour moi de contribuer à la justice et à la paix en répandent un peu d'amour et d'amitié pour ceux qui en ont besoin.

Par: Yves Morneau, Professionnel de la paix, CPSC, (www.civilianpeaceservice.ca).

Waves of Black and White – Kabul, June 15 2007

Early every morning and late afternoon, except Friday, you see them in waves coming round the corners,
  walking down the streets, books in hands,
  some skipping, some walking slowly,
  some joking around playing tag, and others holding hands in serious discussion.

These are the school girls of Afghanistan. Probably ages 10 to 17.
  They are dressed in black with white head covers.
  They may all look the same but they are not at all.

The black shamwar Kameez (top and bottom) differ in slight styles and the white head/body covers are also differing. If you get close enough, the shoes are different. Some are flats, some are higher heels. Some have highlighted their hair and the wisps show from under the scarves. Some have pony tails, others braids or loose.

  What a sight to see.
  These waves of black and white flowing down the streets of Kabul.
  Ripple after ripple ebbing in and out of the shops.
  Making a statement.

  The schools we attend have not been burned down as have our sisters schools. We are not meeting under a tree as do our sisters.
  Our teachers are not murdered as in other parts of the country.
  We are strong as are our sisters.
  We are moving down the street to school and back from school and one day we will move with our sisters.
  We are a wave of girls, women.
  We are a wave of humanity.
  We are moving.

By Paulette Schatz, Project Manager, Joint National Youth Programme, UNDP, Kabul, Afghanistan Mar 2007 – Mar 2008

How Canadian Military Values Guided Humanitarian Activities in UN Peacemaking Missions

This paper will show how Canadian values guided humanitarian efforts so they were properly coordinated. Thus needy people were looked after. I was deployed on UN duty in Croatia as the Senior Operations Officer in two separate but very dangerous Sectors in Croatia. I must say my position was UN-delegated, not a Canadian one. Therefore, I reported to UNHQ in Zagreb. The mandate in the Sectors was for peacekeeping. However, the warring parties seldom adhered to the peace agreements and many situations resulted in death and injuries. Civilian casualties rose as hostilities continued. The idea of UN peacekeeping suffered accordingly.

In September 1993, I was moved from Sector West to Sector South. It was the largest of the four UN sectors in Croatia with three battalions, including one Canadian. Besides the usual military tasks, Canadians were always mindful of humanitarian needs, based on our values.

On my arrival in Sector South HQ, I discovered the magnitude of the staff problem there, with their inability to manage much, as they were barely capable of conducting their military functions, let alone give any thought to humanitarian aspects. From what I heard about the Sector before my move, I was very concerned and quickly learned the HQ was in worse shape than I thought.

Despite the many humanitarian agencies in the Sector, there was no coordination of activities, no sharing of information or managing requests etc. After discussions with several UN staff, it was clear guidance was needed. This was not a military task, however, one I was prepared to help develop. I suggested a weekly humanitarian conference be held with all stake holders to discuss and coordinate activities so everyone was fully aware of just what support was needed.

I provided a room for the meeting. However, its management was the responsibility of the Sector UNHCR Rep. She needed coaching on how to run such meetings but was willing to learn. We drafted an initial agenda and discussed how to cover each item. I briefed them on security issues and coordinated requests for military support to help them in their humanitarian tasks. Each agency briefed about what they provided, plus about what they could do and were not allowed to do. After the first few meetings, humanitarian agencies began to properly provide coordinated support to the Sector.

As an example how things now operated: in November to December 1993, the Sector was hit by several very heavy snowstorms that blocked access into the Sector. Despite a lack of snow clearing capabilities, the system now in effect worked because all the agencies provided support, with the result that no civilian casualties happened due to cold weather injuries. Military medical staff visited medical facilities to help ensure supplies were available. It worked in Sector South because we managed to get all agencies to work together, unlike the situation that was in place prior to September 1993.

Thanks to our principles and values, the Canadian military showed that it is ready to assist humanitarian agencies plan and execute operations to care for people. It is a vital task, freely done, because the need is always there. It is important to remember that the military is just one agency that can assist but does not have the mandate to coordinate or run such activities. It worked in Sector South because we managed to get all agencies to work together

---

By: John Davidson (retired LCol Canadian Army 1959-1966)

Peace and Friendship Caravan International 1984

During the Cold War, a high school teacher, Sigurd Askevold from Creston, British Columbia, was inspired by Vera Brittain's Peace Pledge Union plea that 'above all nations is humanity'. Because nuclear war seemed to be inevitable, Askevold worked two years (writing 2000 letters and making many trips) to arrange a 50,000 km Peace Caravan to Western and Eastern Europe as well as across North America. This was no easy task — all visas had to be pre-arranged from Ottawa, as were accommodations, travel plans, and meetings with heads of states and cities.

On February 11th, 1984, we flew from Canada to Frankfurt, then traveled by car through the entire Communist Bloc, Austria, Greece, Italy, Switzerland, France, Belgium, Great Britain, the Netherlands, West Germany, Denmark, Sweden, and Norway. On the way home, the Caravan traveled through the eastern USA to Vancouver.

Our Odyssey would take us 4 months to complete. The 17 people who joined us, aged 11 to 73, came from Norway (1), USA (3) and Canada (13) and included 5 Quakers, 2 Doukhobors, 2 Mennonites, and 1 Catholic.

Honourary Sponsor was Dr. Linus Pauling, the 1963 Nobel Peace Prize winner, plus Argenta Friends (Quakers) Monthly Meeting of Argenta Canada. Our Caravan was endorsed by the Doukhobor Union of Spiritual Communities of Christ, Bishop W.E. Doyle of Nelson, BC, Canada, Moderator of the United Church of Canada Clarke MacDonald, the Mennonite Brethren, and several other Quaker Friends Meetings in Canada and the US.

From the Frankfurt airport, we went to the City Council were we were hosted royally. Next day, we took a train to Salzburg where we picked up four new Peugeot Talbot diesels and a trailer to haul our luggage. At home, we had constructed signs 2'x6' to mount on top of our cars. The signs were interchangeable in 6 different languages, 2 saying **50,000 Km for Peace**, 1 saying **Above All Nations Is Humanity**, and 1 saying **Peace and friendship International 1884**. Lufthansa Air transported these signs for free.

Our message to the leaders of nations and city councils was handed out in a 1-page printed mission statement. We urged a massive exchange of youth with permission to travel freely and get to know their so-called enemies. Also we urged the development of twin cities and towns. All of this was an effort to shift our thinking towards a caring, civilized and peaceful society where friendship and trust overcomes fear. We said:

It is only on this person-to-person basis, across borders and oceans, that we can, in the end, overcome fear and distrust existing so deeply rooted between the East and the West. We must learn to live and let live and realize that other nations must be allowed to live their way of life, so that eventually, we will all be winners. It is everybody's responsibility. Perhaps it is not too late.

In travelling through the Communist Bloc we were deeply impressed by the sincerity of the people in their wish for peace. We had many beautiful moments and shed many tears. On entering Kiev when we stopped at a red light, the driver beside us motioned for us to open our window, and handed us a red tulip.

At our reception held for us by the City of Vancouver when we were leaving, a CBC reporter asked me why I was going on this trip. I said, 'If the world goes to Hell, and it looks like it very well might, I want to be able to say that I tried to do something about it'.

Alex Ewashen, Creston, BC. Retired auctioneer, singer, peace activist.

Welcoming Refugees to Ottawa

In 1980, my family participated in the sponsorship of a refugee family from Vietnam. The sponsorship of the Vietnamese family was made possible through the congregation of Knox United Church in Nepean. We assisted in making the first meal for the family in Ottawa, my father having recently taken an "Asian" cooking class.

My father also helped with the orientation to public transit and with the school registration of the children. Shortly after arriving, the family prepared a dinner for us. Years later, they invited my parents to their daughter's wedding reception. I was a teenager at the time but remember the experience of reaching a helping hand out to strangers.

In 2016, this time as an adult with a teenaged daughter, I had the privilege of being part of another sponsorship group, this time of a family from Syria. My link to the group of sponsors was through my women's book club and their families. The Anglican diocese of Ottawa provided the umbrella support to many private sponsor groups, such as ours.

I assisted in orientation to public transit and extra language training. It was wonderful to see the Canadian children of our sponsor group help to prepare the rental apartment for the family and set up a room with books and toys for the Syrian children, shortly before their February 2016 arrival.

On a wonderful warm weekend in May, the Syrian family invited us to Britannia beach for a potluck picnic and served delicious Syrian food. My husband made hummus for the occasion which seemed to be a favourite of the young daughter of the family.

I hope the experience of refugee sponsorship will lead my daughter to similarly reach out in the future and extend a hand of peace whenever needed.

By: Allison Phillips.

Zakat

Beyond the roses, which detonate from earth in explosive
crimson, the mosque is illuminated by morning light.

Blue and white tiles incandescent, a flourish of lilies against which
the faithful move – women in white burqas like doves,
men in hand-woven shawls encumbering shoulders.
These believers stroll, step out and beyond the shadows
condensed on the ground, dark residue left by gunpowder.
Their lips still flavoured by suhoor, bodies not yet craving
nourishment but braced for cleansing, their hearts
divining purity from worldly activities, inner souls freed
from harm. At one corner, a young boy in a wheelchair,
his legs scarred stumps, extends a hand for zakat.

I conjure the pressure of his soles that day he walked
across a field – perhaps lagging behind playmates
or tending to goats – while from below its surface
the trap sparked forth, entangling him in its fierce release
of metal and energy, shattering him in a split second
of confusion, blood and pain. He smiles at me,
his palm opening, as if in prayer, an aperture for the coins
that now burden my pockets. Exposed to the sunlight
they have the effervescence of fireworks igniting the sky.

As I release them, they are the plumage of the birds
the seller in the courtyard has bartered into the hands
of pilgrims. With these offerings we all are released
from the heat and pain of this charred earth,
our voices, like wings, vibrate in the air, repentant with chant.

By: Blaine Marchand, Award winning poet, author and program
manager. 'Zakat' is from his 2008 book Aperture, based on his
international development experience in Afghanistan

What Moves Us to Work for Peace? A Reflection

The occasion of white culture's observance of Canada's 150th birthday invites me to pause and consider several questions. What would move a veteran of an elite U.S. paratroop unit to become Canadian and spend four years of the third act of his life writing "Canada: The Case for Staying Out of Other People's Wars?"

What would send him across Canada at his own expense preaching the book's message that Canada did not come of age at Vimy; that Canada can and must end her fealty to the U.S. and that the need to do that has never been more urgent?

What would move someone to a law career of representing oppressed farmworkers, throwaway kids, and men facing the prospect of ritual execution? How could someone who unashamedly enjoys creature comforts find himself living in a family's tool shed in the middle of a Nicaraguan war zone?

Well, I am that guy, and this is my answer. It is the simple goodness of ordinary people going about managing their daily lives.

It is the family of Alexandra Picado, who showed me how to live in poverty with dignity in the midst of a U.S. proxy war.

It is the people of Ireland, the North and the Republic.

It is very much the families in the Middle East, who tenaciously struggle to live and feed their children in the midst of violence being perpetrated in my name.

It is even those who are misguided, like the ordinary soldier, devoid of hate, who falls victim to the recruiter's lies.

And yes, it is my fellow Canadians. Easy going, paying more attention to the NHL draft than the reality of the bloated military budget that robs them of opportunity; still under the impression that Canada is a peacekeeper; and yet living their lives with malice toward none.

They are frustrating, but they have not yet lost that basic sense of community that is apparently a thing of the past in the U.S. I believe that if we can learn to speak and listen to them, we can tap into the inherent decency of ordinary Canadians and advance the cause of peace.

A chance conversation with Joan Baez in 1969 took me the final step to a commitment to nonviolence.

Another chance encounter gave me a life partner whose passion for social justice equals and sometimes even exceeds my own.

I am the descendant of a leader of the Choctaw Nation. First Nations spirituality suggests to me that the Creator could have been behind these and other happy accidents that have characterized my life path.

But however it was that I got to here, I know that I owe it to ordinary folks to keep on keepin' on.

Don't we all?

By: William S. (Bill) Geimer, Barrister & Solicitor (Ret.), Professor of Law Emeritus, Washington & Lee University, Sooke, British Columbia

The Family Meeting

Peace begins in the family. It's badly needed when facing the challenge of navigating the emotional shoals of a parent's end of life care. My mother was frail and fading fast. Yet we seven middle aged kids knew she was in denial about this reality. "End of life? I'm nowhere near that! Care? I want companionship, not nursing!" she insisted. We said we needed to talk about it.

We gathered in a circle for our family conference in a dimly lit hotel bar with its Sunday pong of stale beer. Some of us sipped Tim Hortons lattes, others drummed on the arm of our faux leather arm-chairs.

Twirling my wedding band, I recognized my nervous gesture. Seven sets of legs were tightly crossed. Seven bodies leaned in, with all our eyes cast down.

Under the no smoking sign, Mom lit her next cigarette from the stub of the one before.

Our question: How could we support Mom, but head off the peril that lay ahead for Judi as the daughter on the front line?

"Won't it be wonderful?" Mom began, "living two floors down, we can visit in our pyjamas!" I shuddered.

"I'll decide," she declared, "but I want your input."

She started the pencil on its way. Who held the pencil had the floor. It was our moderator. Our family discipline was not to interrupt. Round one was sincere, but false. The gist was that we just wanted Mom to be happy.

It was John's turn. As the eldest and also a priest, we siblings knew his opinion mattered most to Mom. John pointed the pencil at Judi. He paused for effect.

"It is a lousy idea." Now his homily began and I sighed. It would be hard to stay patient with his habit of a lifetime. But John always laid bare hard truths. He talked about his women parishioners in emotional collapse. Burn out was so common when the only identity of the daughter became 'carer'. Some even became addicts, something John called co-dependants. They enabled their loved one to be less capable. It was dysfunction for everyone involved.

He held Mom's gaze. "So no way you should move in with Judi, for her sake. She needs boundaries."

The only sound now was his slurping the dregs of his coffee.

My face flushed with rising rage. I seized the pencil.

"You are dead right John about daughters bearing the burden of care." I glared at my brothers one after another. "She's up to her neck in it." My eyes locked back on John, "and none of us is doing enough to help her."

Judi tapped my arm and mouthed, "Zip it!" She hated conflict. But I mouthed back a silent "no" and plunged on.

"You sons? You go on with your lives as if nothing was different, then tell Judi she's doing too much? Disgusting!" I shoved the pencil into my youngest brother's hand. He passed it on with a chagrined "pass." It moved on. We grappled with the problem. It was Judi's turn.

"Caring for Mom is my calling," Her eyes pleaded with John. "As a priest, you know how vocation can be hard."

She was eloquent now, admitting it was getting more challenging, but also insisting that there was bliss along with the grit of her role. John took the pencil, put it down, and took Judi's hand.

"Do what you think is best," he said, "and I will support you."

We went once more around the sibling circle, confirming how we would help Judi in her calling. Mom dabbed her eyes with a tissue I had passed her. The last word was from Judi as she hugged Mom.

"I'll love to have you living downstairs. Welcome home."

By: Janet Dunnett, Author: The Dwindling

Peace has Broken Out

Peace has broken out –
children's faces are singing in the sun:
their fathers will come home now
to redeem their sleep from fear.

Only the warmongers knit their brows
into nightmares full of foul intrigues.

Peace has broken out –
The sun is singing in the women's eyes:
the men will bring their hearts
home now craving sweet love.

In America, Canada and Israel
arms dealers break into a sweat
over their offshore accounts.

Peace has broken out –
the wool sings it on the ancient loom,
the hammer drums it into tin and copper,
the chisel carves it into wood.

Only the brutal guns are idle now
resting smug on their laurels of death.

Peace is occupying the town:
the muezzin proclaims it from the minaret,
traders tout its pleasures in the bazaar,
lovers dance again to the beat of their passion
and the river runs red through dawn and dusk
washing away blood from bitter memories.

A dry wind blows hot from the desert,
keeps the green blades honed in the palms.

Let peace sift the sand beyond fertile valleys
to fill the life's hourglass with song and dance.

So that the dead shall not be dead in vain
let the arms dealers languish in the prison of their greed,
let Wall Street bankers and brokers bankrupt
their humanity with derivatives and bonuses:

May they choke on their iniquities
so that the truly living can rejoice again
in the serene air that sings of freedom.

© Henry Beissel, 2011.

What Goes Around Comes Around

In summer, my sister, brother-in-law and I enjoy hiking from their cottage. My brother-in-law plans the hike in advance, consulting maps and digging up whatever history he can find about the area. Both the planning and the activity have become a ritual for us all.

We had been walking a long time and were almost home when two men and a woman approached us and told us we could not trespass on the land, as it was their traditional camping and fishing area. Although they didn't say so, I assumed they were indigenous.

Their words and manner were intimidating. My brother-in-law did all the talking; my sister and I were both silent. He spoke softly and well, explaining that we had no idea we were trespassing and that we were respectful of the land and nature. He said we were on our way home and asked if we could continue on our way until we reached the cottage. The conversation went on for quite a long time; the others did not seem to be backing away at all.

During a rather uncomfortable silence, the man who started the conversation looked at me and said, "Do you play the violin?" I said "yes". He said he remembered me playing at a fund-raising event his organization had held the previous year. I was flabbergasted. (I'm not good at all at recognizing faces). He welcomed us to his land and wished us well on the rest of our hike.

Like I said – what goes around comes around.

By: Peggy Florida)

Towards a Peaceful Cambodia

Once a peaceful kingdom, Cambodia has been the site of genocidal conflict (20-30% of the population killed under the Khmer Rouge), has seen ten years of occupation by the Vietnamese, and an ostensible return to peace in the early 1990s. However, some 25 years later, human rights violations, mal-governance and unequitable development still pose major challenges to genuine reconciliation and peace.

My first trip to Cambodia was as an international development worker (CIDA) in 1998. I paid a private visit to The Peaceful Children's Home in Sre Ampel (near Phnom Penh), which together with its sister Home in Battambang, provide a permanent and supportive environment to some 100 Cambodian children and youth.

In 1994, two prominent Cambodians, Son Sann (1) and his son, Dr. Son Soubert (2), created the Khmer Foundation for Justice, Peace and Development (KFJPD) to help Cambodian children and young people emerge from two decades of conflict.

Managed by the KFJPD, the Homes took in "unaccompanied" child returnees from refugee camps on the Thai border. Over time, the Homes came to accept children who were orphaned, abandoned, rescued from the street or from human trafficking.

The founders were well aware of the disruption caused by decades of conflict to the family unit, to education, and to basic human values. Although operating on a modest budget, the Homes set out to address these issues and, on a small scale, to produce a new generation of ethical, peaceful productive young Cambodians.

The children and young people at the Homes visibly aspire to peace. The Peaceful Children's Homes was the name chosen by the first group of arrivals in 1994.

On my first visit, a young girl asked me if we "had war in Canada". A teenage girl told me she wanted to help people by being a doctor, while a young man stated that his career plan was to become "an uncorrupt judge". I was struck by the awareness and depth of their experience of conflict, governance and peace.

I returned to Cambodia often, regularly visiting the Homes. Back in Canada, I recounted my experiences to family and friends. In 2006, Laurent Côté, a 13-year-old Ottawa violinist suggested that we organize a fund-raising concert for the Homes, calling his initiative Kids Helping Kids.

Twelve years later, this volunteer initiative continues under the name, In Concert for Cambodia.

The cause of helping children and youth in a country struggling for peace and development continues to attract successive waves of young musicians. Many are drawn from the University of Ottawa's School of Music program, while others are recognized virtuosos. All proceeds go directly to the KFJPD for food, self-sufficiency projects, health and education.

IC4C is proud to support the university studies of four talented young people from the Homes – in economics, agriculture, law and medicine – our modest contribution to Cambodia's peace and development.

Recently, I met many happy young adults, now with their own families, whom I remember as children in the Homes - including the current Director, Veuk Chum. Their peaceful and productive lives are the best possible reward for our efforts.

By: Flora Liebich, IC4C Coordinator

(1) Former Prime Minister, founder of the Buddhist Liberal Democratic Party, and leader in the refugee camps in Thailand.
(2) High Privy Counselor to the King of Cambodia, Formerly Deputy Speaker of the National Assembly and Member of the Constitutional Council

Training Peacemakers – not Soldiers

The year was 1945. Hitler was ordering 16-year-olds into the military, and Hans Sinn of Hamburg was one of them. He found that one group in the induction centre was being sent to Denmark, where he knew there was enough food.

Bad choice: it turned out to be an SS training camp, staffed by veteran sociopathic Nazis.

Hans and his friends waited for their chance to escape. When they heard of Hitler's suicide, they made their move. Walking up - unarmed - to the guard at the gate, they told him,

"You can stay here and die with them, or you can come with us and live."

The guard threw down his gun and joined them. Over rivers, through bombed-out ruins, they made their way back to Hamburg.

Disappointed with postwar Germany's lost chances for disarmament and peace, Hans left for Canada in 1952, "just for two years." In 1959, Hans returned to Germany to oppose rearmament and spoke about a form of "Peace Corps," getting it onto the party platform of a small party, the Gesamtdeutsche Union.

Back in Canada, on a walk for peace from Vancouver to Berlin, Hans stopped to speak in Montreal in January 1963. There he met a woman named Marian Bedoukian. She left her job and joined him on the march, and they were married in England. There, Hans spoke at the Campaign for Nuclear Disarmament convention about forming a Peace Corps. Returning to Montreal afterward, he became co-editor of Sanity magazine, the publication of the Canadian Campaign for Nuclear Disarmament.

In July 1965, he was part of the Grindstone Island Training Institute in Nonviolence, including the famous "31 Hours" simulation of nonviolent resistance to an invasion. In 1970, after his sons Anthony and Nicholas were born, the family left for Brooke Valley near Perth, Ontario. He joined a land co-operative, where he built the house in which he and Marian have lived ever since.

In 1981, on Grindstone Island near Portland, Ontario, a group gathered to found Peace Brigades International, or PBI. Hans was one of the 11 founders, along with Murray Thomson of Ottawa. Hans became an International Committee member of PBI International and later chair of PBI-Canada.

In 1984, he spoke to a hearing of the German Green Party in Bonn about a Peace Corps. In the early 1990s, he spoke in Berlin, at the Evangelical Academy in Berlin, which had developed its own proposal for a CPS. By 1999, Ziviler Friedensdienst had become the first fully operational Civilian Peace Service in the world.

In 2000, Hans again was a founder, this time of Nonviolent Peaceforce Canada (NPC), still keeping his active role in PBI. In the summer of 2004, NPC accepted Hans's plan to hold a Consultation on a Civilian Peace Service or CPS for Canada. On February 10, 2005, he was speaking to Canadian parliamentarians about it. In 2008, CPS Canada issued a 400-page White Paper, and has since accredited the first CPSC Peace Professionals.

In 2015, Hans had joined forces with Silke Reichrath to establish Brooke Valley Research for Education in Nonviolence after resuming work with former European friends and contacts. Their organization works to combine restorative justice and peace education with the tools of civilian defence and unarmed protection. One of their projects is to bring recognition to the Armenian Genocide of 1915 and after.

"But the major issue I see today is the prevention of domestic violence in Canada," Hans said. "Why are we spending a billion dollars additional military defense spending, in the face of the great unmet need and failing commitment at home to indigenous children? Peace begins at home."

By: Carl Stieren, 2005, edited by an unnamed editor at Peace Magazine, http://peacemagazine.org/archive/v21n2p13.htm and Evelyn Voigt (Revised July 29, 2017)).

You don't know what you've got till it's gone

Have you ever thought about the phrase 'peace and security' with reference to the major responsibility of a government towards its people? I had never really considered the two as separate concepts, much in the way that I hear 'bells and whistles' or 'dog and pony' or 'nickel and dime' as a single phrase rather than separate entities.

I was confronted with the reality of this responsibility, or rather responsibilities, when I was acting as an Advisor to a Cabinet Office Committee on program reforms in 1999 in a central African country. My work was carried out under World Bank funding, primarily to assist the government in developing monitoring and evaluation processes to enable the Cabinet to manage national and international program funds more efficiently and effectively. The overall purpose of the work was to begin to develop processes to ensure that funds flowed to effective programs and that no incremental funds flowed to ineffective programs.

If this sounds very grandiose, it was when the Cabinet committee discussed the overall funding and distribution mechanisms – but it wasn't when individual members began confronting their own program issues.

For instance, senior members of the security forces and judiciary would discuss with each other in sidebar meetings, how to safely transport the daily group of 'accused' murderers and other felons, from the prison to the court. The issues being, that their one prison bus (in the capital city itself) frequently broke down, holding up the court proceedings; or the bus was often attacked to free prisoners, the police being insufficiently well-armed or without adequate communications to respond in time.

Or, when discussions centred on how to respond to emergencies in the far corners of the country, with inadequately trained responders and a lack of the necessary equipment.

Or, more importantly, did more funds for these contingencies mean less funds for hospitals and doctors, affecting health security.

Prosaic, yes. Unimportant, no. In other words, as peace reigned outside the borders, security became the dominant government issue inside the borders.

It was then I began to confront the separation of peace and security in my own mind.

The country was at peace in terms of international relationships. But internally it was not secure. Not in the sense of armed militias or insurgencies, but in the sense of the government being unable to guarantee the safety of individual citizens.

While safely ensconced in Canada, it is easy to forget the security half of the 'peace and security' phrase.

But, imagine if you were afraid to book a holiday in Halifax or Calgary because of frequent civil unrest; because there were insufficient police officers; because security officials' response time took forever due to lack of good communications with Ottawa; because the government lacked the equipment to protect you.

Yes, the government has a major responsibility in peace and security, but our own citizen's responsibility in our community is just as important. So, as in marriage, whilst peace may be a dominant partner, security is an equal contributor to the harmony of the relationship.

And the partners in security are actually the government and its individual citizens.

We Canadians should celebrate achieving such harmonious relationships both inside and outside our borders.

"You don't know what you've got till it's gone..."

By: Harry Monaghan

Women's Leadership in Peace Building

"There is no peace without development, and no development without peace – and neither peace, nor sustainable development without the active participation of women in both processes." - Rosa Emilia Salamanca, Corporación de Investigación y Acción Social y Económica (CIASE), Colombia.

Women have always played key roles in armed conflict, be it as nurses, care givers, combatants or workers. Women also contribute to peace in a multitude of ways. Yet these contributions often go unrecognized and remain undervalued because they take place outside official, high-level forums, or because they do not fit with activities traditionally associated with peacebuilding.

As a result, skills, insights and energy are overlooked; and a misleading image of women as mere victims of conflict, and passive beneficiaries of interventions, prevails.

To celebrate achievements made by women in various disciplines, as well as raising awareness to readdress the gaps that remain in our society, a march for women in leadership was organized on Women's Day (8th of March 2013) in the village of Walewale, Ghana. The march was organized by the Langum Women's Association in collaboration with the International Volunteers from Canadian University Service Overseas (CUSO) and the Peace Corps.

The march commenced from the Walewale local hospital at 8:00 AM heading for the District assembly, with an approximate distance of 5 km. The march involved more than 100 people from various domains including school children, Government officials as well as other members of the community.

Moreover, considering the importance of the issue, the local band volunteered to play while the participants sang, clapped, danced and chanted slogans for the promotion of women's role in positions of leadership. The participants brought many messages to the event regarding women and girls' empowerment and it was also an opportunity to underscore the need for political commitment to accelerate action to achieve gender equality called for in the millennium development goals.

The march ended at 10:00 AM at the District Assembly, where the appointed District Governor of Walewale delivered a speech to the audience on the importance of having women leaders, and stressed that their contributions to peace processes need to be acknowledged with greater financial and political support. The other members of the Assembly also put emphasis on the relevance of providing women and girls with equal access to education, health care, decent work, and representation in political and economic decision-making processes to fuel sustainable economies and benefit Ghanaian society and humanity at large.

The entire march was recorded by the local TV channel and was also broadcasted live by the radio stations.

Overall, the success of the march was not just limited to creating awareness of women's role in leadership but a tradition began to conduct the march every year on the occasion of Women's Day.

By: Ankur Mahajan

You Are Welcome; You All Matter

I had the experience of my lifetime when I visited Ottawa's main mosque on February 3, 2017, to offer Friday prayer. I saw a chain of local residents around the four walls of the mosque to express their feelings that Ottawa Muslims are part of a larger community and are under the protection of fellow community members against any threat.

This act was deeply touching and a heartwarming response to the mass shooting on the evening of January 29, 2017, near the Islamic Cultural Centre of Quebec City in a mosque in the Sainte –Foy neighborhood. Six people lost their lives in this tragic event and nineteen others were injured when a lone gunman opened fire shortly after evening prayers.

I was in for an even bigger surprise when I entered the mosque the next day.

A distinguished group of parliamentarians, leaders of various faith communities and the Minister of the Environment Catherine McKenna had gathered inside the mosque to share the grief of Canadian Muslims and assure them that they were not alone in these anxious moments. Members of Parliament Chandra Arya, Anita Vandenbeld, Yasir Naqvi, Karen McCrimmon addressed the meetings and a message was sent from two prominent rabbis in the community, Rabi Bulka and Rabbi Scher.

There was a big wall size poster where students of Saint Elizabeth Elementary School had shared their feelings about the event. A young student had written, "You are welcome. You all matter". There could be nothing more eloquent, substantive and profound than this simple statement. It captured the Canadian spirit.

It does not mean that there have been no rough patches in inter-community relations in Canada; quite the contrary. Canada has had troubled relations with immigrant Indian and Chinese workers in the past century, and it is still trying to overcome major challenges in relation to the people of The First Nation. There is a long way to go, but the direction is clear and support for this cause is overwhelming.

It reminded of my first sojourn to Canada in1979. I sought admission at Queen's to escape persecution by Zia ul Haq's military regime due to a treason case registered against me in Pakistan. Queen's University provided a breath of fresh air. It was home to many starry-eyed young revolutionaries from as far away as Chile,

South Africa, Bangladesh, Ireland, Turkey, Pakistan, and Canada. The International Centre provided excellent opportunities to meet like-minded students and activists from organizations like the Kingston Solidarity Committee, Amnesty International, Catholic Church and others.

My main interest was in Development Economics, as I had cited in my application for seeking admission at Queen's. I was lucky to have Professor Marvin McInnis as my course instructor.

Early on, he told me "Let me be very blunt. There is no interest in development economics in our department". That meant that I had to set sail and anchor at a new port. However, the university could not transfer my credits without the clearance of my pending dues.

I sought the help of Frank Flatter, the Graduate Chair. Frank succeeded in getting a waiver for me. When I asked him how, he said, "I told the committee, if Fayyaz succeeds in finishing his degree, he will land a good job on his return home. In that case, he will be able and willing to pay us back. If not, we don't stand any chance of recovering the dues". I was amazed at his kindness, brilliance and sensitivity.

This was the strength of a humanist Canadian culture and values.

By: Fayyaz Baqir, O'Brien Fellow, McGill University.

War's Deadly Legacy

I couldn't believe what I was seeing! Thousands of deadly unexploded cluster sub-munitions dropped by the United States during the Vietnam War still littered the landscape as far as the eye could see.

Our guide led us on a narrow path about a foot wide. "Follow me in single file", he commanded, "and be careful not to trip! If one of us falls on a "bombie" (the local term for a cluster sub-munition), "we are all dead!"

In their quest to cut off the supply routes of the North Vietnamese - the so-called "Ho Chi Minh Trail" – the CIA oversaw a covert US saturation bombing campaign over southern and central Laos–dropping the equivalent of the payload of a B52 bomber (which can hold 100 - 500lb bombs) every 8 minutes for 9 years.

This was roughly one ton of ordnance for every man, woman and child living in Laos at the time, leaving Laos with the tragic distinction of being, per capita, the most heavily bombed country on earth.

The American weapon of choice was cluster munitions, an indiscriminate, wide-area weapon that has devastating impact both at the time of use and for decades afterwards because of their high dud rate. Clearing them is painstaking and treacherous work.

In the 42 years since the bombing ended, the Lao government and their international partners have cleared less than 2% of the estimated 80 million cluster sub-munitions that contaminate roughly one-third of the country.

To this day, bombies are regularly detonated by unsuspecting farmers working their land, and often by children attracted by what appear to be brightly coloured toys. The International Committee of the Red Cross reports that 98 % of all known cluster munitions casualties throughout the world have been civilian.

On that day in the late 1990s, I was an analyst and planner with the Southeast Asia programme of the Canadian International Development Agency, on my first mission to the region. Though I had served extremely poor parts of West Africa and South Asia, this struck me as more horrific than anything I had seen before, because it was the direct result of 'man's inhumanity to man' –on a grand scale.

Five years later, I jumped at the opportunity to manage CIDA's Mine Action Unit that provided funding and technical support to countries struggling to clear the detritus of war.

Several years later, I joined the then Department of Foreign Affairs and, in 2007-08, had the honour of leading Canada's delegation in the negotiation of the Convention on Cluster Munitions, a legally binding instrument that banned this indiscriminate weapon for all time.

After leaving the public service in 2011, I returned to Laos for several years as a UN advisor, working with the Government of Laos in the Unexploded Ordnance Sector.

I was and remain in awe at the courage and skill of the thousands of men and women who continue to risk their lives every day to clear their nation of the deadly remnants of war; and at the resilience and forgiving spirit of the Lao people who want nothing more than to forget the horrors of the past and to live in safety.

By: Earl Turcotte is a former development worker and disarmament diplomat, currently focused on nuclear abolition.

Peace Song

Music has been part of my life for as long as I can remember and was probably imbued within me while I was in my mother's womb in Southern Alberta. She and dad were both excellent singers and often sang together; born in Canada but preserving their Russian culture including a commitment to pacifism. Growing up in the Doukhobor milieu, my first exposure to song was Russian folk songs and Doukhobor hymns. These were meditative chants which brought peace and solace to these pacifist dissidents along their historical thorny path of exile and re-settlement.

The Shakespearean quote: 'Music has charms to soothe the savage breast', in their estimation, was quite literally true and is best expressed by the following abridged Doukhobor psalm:

> *Singing of Psalms is an adornment to our souls.*
> *They form a union of love, give you power of observing and strength of fulfilling all.*
> *It all indicates a great soul.*
> *It cleanses one's lips and makes one's heart glad.*
> *To the ones who have perfection it shows the way.*
> *Serenity of the mind is a herald of peace:*
> *The Psalms express prayer for future generations.*
> *To the elders it is a sign of comfort.*
> *To the young it is an improvement of their mind.*

From my formative years onwards, from the country school square dances to the concert stage, I never believed that music and songs were just entertainment. In my experience, as a performer and singer for seventy years, music has been a vital life force.

Moreover, music and peace were inextricably intertwined. Early activism with the Campaign for Nuclear Disarmament included rallies which provided stages for many peace songs, echoing the civil rights movement and anti-Vietnam war protests.

The folk movement featured seminal peace songs written by Canadians such as Ed McCurdy's Strangest Dream and Buffie St. Marie's Universal Soldier which ranked alongside Pete Seeger's We Shall Overcome and John Lennon's Give Peace a Chance and Imagine! Throughout the years, these songs sustained our demonstrations and strengthened our resolve through sometimes abusive encounters.

After several productive years as the Curator of The Doukhobor Discovery Centre in B. C. where I featured many peace manifestations ranging from the UN Peace Day to Hiroshima Day and many Doukhobor choirs with their emphasis on holistic living and pacifism, I also revived the early immersion in Russian folk music with my two brothers, which again included peace songs at various events and rallies.

The Doukhobor manifestation for Peace reached a zenith when they celebrated the 100th anniversary of the famous Arms Burning of 1895 on the Russian steppes which led to their exodus to Canada.

With pageant and song, the over seventy member company United Doukhobor Centennial '95 Choir and Drama Ensemble presented Voices for Peace, 1995 International Tour, travelling across Canada with presentations from B. C. to Ottawa including a performance at the Canadian Museum of Civilization, the United Nations in New York and then in Russia with their multimedia event. The project was a historic bridge between the different groups of Doukhobors in Canada as well as a Canada - Russia peace bridge.

Throughout my life, music with its expression of peace and harmony, has been an integral and sustaining force, which helped present our goals while being a sustaining force in daily life.

By: Larry Ewashen.

'Cooperative games? Are you serious?' A remarkable Canadian success story

The genius behind Family Pastimes Cooperative Games is former artist and teacher Jim Deacove, assisted by his partner Ruth. Their's is a remarkable Canadian success story.

Take Musical Chairs as an example. Traditionally, this simple, common party game was supposed to teach children good social manners, but it actually fosters aggression by eliminating the loser. 'People are now going to be more important than the chairs,' says Jim introducing his Musical Chairs, 'so the only rule change is that after each round we take away a chair, but we keep all the people. It's up to the imagination of the group to figure out how to make a place for everyone.' Here hugging can replace pushing and everyone can now feel good by winning together rather than being ousted out of the game.

The big idea, they felt was needed in today's world where competition and conflict reigns and threatens our health and that of our planet. Especially since research has shown that cooperation is a more effective tool than competition because competition creates anxiety and often dampens motivation. It comes down to deciding what kind of society you want to live in.

Many banks, many suppliers, many friends and relatives warned them that the business would never last with such an outlandish idea. 'Cooperative games? Are you serious? Do not, under any circumstances give up your day job as teachers,' they cautioned.

But give up their jobs they did. Since 1972, their home cottage industry near Perth, Ontario, has produced well over a hundred cooperative games for all ages, under the motto 'Play together, not against each other and everyone'.

By 2017, these included more than five wooden Table Games, six Manuals and over 125 Board games in a half-million-dollar friendly business. Almost 90% of the sales go to the USA, a country that glorifies competition and private enterprise.

How do Jim and Ruth make cooperative games fun and compelling, even if everybody wins and there is no need to put down others or create and destroy enemies?

The key, as in all games, is to have all the players work together on a common problem, rather than against each other. The rules of any game can be changed, as with Untrivia for example, or

Earth Game and Space Future. In the Harvest Time board game, people enjoy being neighbours who help each other to bring in the harvest before winter comes. In Mountaineering, participants help one another in climbing a mountain. Ploughshares addresses the issue of war and peace, with a search for a fresh alternative paradigm to our overfed and sacred military industrial complex.

As we consider the notion of human worth, one world, and building a world without wars, Jim Deacove's approach of nurturing young and old to be compassionate, sharing and caring feels a lot better than confrontation, violence, and greed.

We can begin to see the wisdom of following a better way for people to live and work and play on this planet. In this new world, Jim's Family Pastimes Cooperative Games can inspire young people to avoid a win-lose outcome, such as sacrificing their children for misguided cannon fodder.

Bravo to the power of sharing and caring and cooperation! These qualities give us hope that leaders of the world can, someday soon, come together on a common strategy for peace.

Thank you, Jim, for walking the talk and showing us the way.

By Jim Deacove, as retold by Koozma J. Tarasoff, Ottawa, Ontario. Anthropologist, ethnographer, historian, writer and peace activist.

Des ONG por la paix

Durant mes cinq dernières années, à l'Agence canadienne de développement international (ACDI), j'ai eu l'occasion de travailler avec des organisations non-gouvernementales (ONG) appartenant à divers groupes religieux et non-religieux des provinces canadiennes. Les projets financés conjointement par ces organismes et l'ACDI étaient pour le bénéfice de tous sans considération de leur appartenance religieuse. Qui étaient-ils et quelle motivation avaient-ils?

Des musulmans canadiens oeuvraient en Somalie pour la construction d'écoles. Des médecins juifs de Toronto collaboraient au Zimbabwé avec l'Armée du salut pour la gestion d'un hôpital. Un Indo-canadien qui avait perdu sa famille proche dans le désastre d'Air-India en 1985 a redonné du sens à sa vie en fondant un hôpital dans son pays d'origine pour traiter les maladies des yeux. Des Quakers ont mis toutes leurs ressources intellectuelles pour aider les responsables de pays africains à défendre leurs propriétés intellectuelles contre les grandes multinationales. Des groupes sans affiliation religieuse de la Capitale nationale ont appuyé des organismes haïtiens pour la reconstruction de leur pays après le tremblement de terre. Un groupe d'origine égyptienne de Montréal a pu aider ses compatriotes pour la construction d'écoles pour filles de toutes appartenances religieuses en Égypte.

Ils étaient tous impliqués dans un travail dit « humanitaire » pour les plus démunis. Les principes de solidarité, de bien commun et de collaboration qui les motivaient étaient basés sur la justice sociale. Le souci que tous avaient en commun était d'œuvrer à réparer notre monde sérieusement en désarroi et à combattre la bêtise humaine. Dans un monde où il y a tant d'égoïsme et de narcissisme, des hommes et des femmes, des bénévoles la plupart, s'appliquent à créer des liens avec d'autres personnes afin de rendre notre monde meilleur. Cela contribue à donner du sens à leur vie.

Je me suis levé tôt le matin en sachant que j'allais rencontrer des amis et ensemble, grâce à Skype, nous connecter avec des leaders paysans au Kenya afin de les aider à défendre leurs droits à la terre. Parfois, c'était avec un groupe de femmes au Congo qui voulaient se prémunir contre le viol et entreprendre des activités économiques rentables. Ici même, à Ottawa, en apprenant qu'une voisine avait eu une intervention chirurgicale. Des femmes vont se mobiliser et à tour de rôle apporter à la famille un repas durant sa convalescence. Combien, durant les inondations du printemps 2017, sont venus en aide aux sinistrés ? Il y a mille façons de se dépenser pour les autres, de se sortir de son petit confort par amour et ainsi créer la paix.

Il y a partout beaucoup d'amour parmi les gens de tous âges. Qu'est-ce qui peut amener tous et chacun à agir en bien pour les autres? Il n'y a peut-être pas de réponse unique. Admirons plutôt la bonté et la générosité qui se manifestent chez tant de nos semblables peu importe leur allégeance religieuse ou politique. Il y a une graine de bonté à caractère presque divin dans les gestes mentionnés. Je suis convaincu que mon travail à l'ACDI en aidant de ONG canadiennes et étrangères a pu de différentes façons contribuer à la paix.

By: Yves Morneau, professionnel de la paix, CPSC
www.civilianpeaceservice.ca

Manifesto in Times of War

Tell the enemy this:
that missiles can no more blow up the human spirit
than tanks can crush an idea.
Guns are the weapons of the impotent,
and I wouldn't trade one line of true poetry
for a thousand of them. The blood flows
in a poem while bombs can only spill it.
Shrapnel can shatter glass and shred the flesh
but it cannot silence the song in a people's heart.

Tell the enemy this:
that our missiles fly on imagination's wings
they're poems aimed to explode in the heart
with all the violence of love and compassion.
It may flatter princes to think the sword mightier
than the pen, but we have the last word.
The true poet pioneers paths of freedom
and places on the future's mouth a brotherhood kiss
with the rage of a rainstorm that makes the desert bloom.

Tell the enemy this:
that every man, woman and child wears a helmet
poets hammer from a metal harder than any steel
the metal of their faith in creation.
You can tear a person limb from limb
but you cannot sever a song from the listening heart,
and when your missiles long rust in scrapyards
today's tears will have watered the desert
to make yesterday's laughter blossom into tomorrow's love.

Tell the enemy this: Yes, we're still writing poems, and if your
grenades blow off our hands, we'll sing them into the future.

© Henry Beissel, 1986 (beisselhenry@gmail.com) was reply to a
poem by a princess-poet from Kuwait who rhapsodied the war effort
(against Iran), declaring this was no time for poetry and that she'd
trade a hundred poets for one soldier. He wrote the poem overnight
and it was read the next day in English & in Arabic–to the
consternation of the many army officers in the audience.

Welcoming in the Light

As I got off the bus and started towards home, a group of high school boys got off the bus at the same time and started walking behind me. I could hear their conversation and all of a sudden, it became quiet, almost stilled. Then I heard the sound of laughter. "Hey man, look at this." I heard one of them say. "Look at how he walks." I heard them shuffling behind me but didn't stop to turn around. I didn't stop walking; I just kept moving forward, one step at a time. Another one said, "Come on guys, come on!" The group of them crossed the street and started walking to match my pace. Only they were exaggerating my movements. One of them was dragging his feet as he walked, another was walking with both feet pointed inward taking huge, exaggerated steps. They looked like a group of zombies, walking in the daylight. It amazed me that, in trying to humiliate me, it just showed how cruel they were. I stopped, watching them. The zombie horde stopped, too. Normally, I have a lot of courage and bravery inside of me, but it always seems to leave me when I'm confronted with people making a comment about, or in this case mocking, my disability and disease.

Normally, the words just flow off of my tongue or out of my fingers, but in a situation like this, I never know what to say. It's like my words shrivel up and I can feel them drying out on my tongue. One of the people I know has suggested I carry card with me with info about Multiple Sclerosis and Cerebral Palsy, but even if I had those done, I wouldn't be able to hand them out to a group of teenage boys. I contemplated how I could respond to them. I wanted to shout at them and tell them that none of them knew what it was like living my life. The anger demanded I speak out, that I yell, that I make them feel as terrible they had made me feel. However, I knew that anger would hold no sway over them. That what they wanted was a reaction from me that would reward them for their mockery. I didn't want to do that, didn't want to lower myself to their level. So, I did the only thing I could think of: I took a bow. It involved no words but let them know that I had seen them, each and every one of them. They had the good grace to look somewhat sheepish. I didn't think it was worth it to say anything to those that wouldn't listen. All I can do is repay unkindness with kindness. All I can do is brush away the malice and welcome in the light. Tomorrow is another day and for that, I am thankful.

By: Jamieson Wolf (www.jamiesonwolf.com).

A la recherche d'une justice qui apaise

A sa sortie d'audience, elle était effondrée, en larmes: c'était donc ainsi que ce procès se terminait pour elle? Son abuseur avait-il songé une seconde à ce qu'elle avait vécu? À la souffrance, à la honte, au dégout qui étaient les siens aujourd'hui? Et que se passerait-il si elle le rencontrait par hasard, après qu'il ait purgé sa peine? Serait-elle à nouveau en danger?

Silencieuse et désolée à côté de cette cliente dont j'avais pour tâche de défendre les intérêts, j'étais incapable de donner des réponses claires à ses questions, impuissante devant tant de souffrance, d'inquiétude et de déception. Et pourtant l'auteur avait été reconnu coupable de viol, malgré ses dénégations, les montants réclamés à titre de tort moral avaient été alloués et nous avions toutes les raisons de nous réjouir de ce succès judiciaire...Le tribunal d'arrondissement de V..., en Suisse, avait fait son travail, il en était de même du Procureur et des avocats. Mais quel gâchis !

J'avais entendu parler d'autres approches de l'infraction qui mettent les besoins de la victime au centre des préoccupations, qui tentent de responsabiliser l'auteur et qui associent les personnes concernées à la recherche de solutions réparatrices. Ayant l'occasion de séjourner à Ottawa en 2015/2016, j'étais bien décidée à me renseigner sur cette justice dite restaurative, que je savais appliquée dans plusieurs provinces du pays.

C'est ainsi qu'a débuté une longue série de contacts avec des services nationaux (Unité de la justice réparatrice du Service correctionnel, Gouvernement du Canada,) ou provinciaux (Programme de justice collaborative d'Ottawa, Restorative Justice Victoria), des praticiens/praticiennes, des chercheurs/chercheuses ou des académiciens/académiciennes rencontrés à la Restorative Justice Conference 2016 de la Dalhousie University à Halifax. Au-delà de l'approfondissement de mes connaissances sur le sujet, ces échanges m'ont permis de découvrir une manière positive et optimiste d'aborder les problèmes, une volonté de partage des connaissances qui semble couler de source, une ouverture aux préoccupations d'autrui, en un mot une attitude générale qui stimule et qui pousse à l'action.

C'est cet élan, cette capacité de construire et de développer, dans le respect des particularités de chacun que j'ai ramenés dans mes bagages, à mon retour en Suisse.

J'ai compris, grâce à l'expérience canadienne, que si l'on veut être un agent de changement, il faut un esprit neuf et positif, il faut un optimisme qui nous convainc chaque jour de la possibilité de faire évoluer les systèmes apparemment les plus rigides, à l'instar du système judiciaire.

Si la jeune femme évoquée au début de ce texte avait pu s'engager dans un processus restauratif, sans doute aurait-elle pu se libérer de ces sentiments négatifs et destructeurs que sont la souffrance, la honte et le dégout, sentiments qui sans doute l'occupent encore aujourd'hui.

Et je me prends à rêver que d'autres victimes aient un jour en Suisse la possibilité d'un dialogue direct ou indirect avec l'auteur du délit, afin de lui faire comprendre ce qu'elles ont enduré, afin qu'il se mette lui-même en mouvement vers une prise de responsabilité et qu'il ressente le besoin de réparer le mal qu'il a infligé, dans le respect des besoins de ceux qui ont été frappés par son acte.

Car ce n'est qu'à travers ce dialogue sur les conséquences du délit que l'on peut espérer une forme d'apaisement pour toutes les personnes impliquées.

Par: Catherine Jaccottet Tissot, avocate et médiatrice à Lausanne (Suisse) durant plus de 30 ans. Aujourd'hui, elle s'emploie à promouvoir la justice restaurative dans son pays.

Finding Peace in My Mind

Each morning, we wake up and think. That's what your bed's for, isn't it? Even when I'm asleep, I'm still battling thoughts. For many people, every day is a new start. For me, every day is quite literally a new day and nothing more. This is a story of how I battle my mind every day to find peace.

Sometimes, everything becomes too much and sometimes I just need to feel the warm tears run down my cheeks. Some days, I may just sink my head in my pillow and let it all out even if it doesn't change anything. I don't want to live a life where every day is the same and every day I open the same books and do lots of homework which stresses me out. The same thoughts pop up and it's almost like I'm trying to find reasons to make myself sink my head in my pillow.

That's why I step outside and find a place where He is with me; a place that He created. I step into the green where the trees stand tall and the leaves crumble underneath. Instantly, I feel relaxed. My mind wanders off in thoughts but they seem to leave my body. Everything is still and quiet except the beautiful sounds of the nature around me.

In the place that He created, I am close to Him. Alone or sharing the moment with others, I feel peace. Being outside and taking a breath of fresh air, I close my eyes and put my hands together in prayer. I set goals to only hang out with people who make me happy and I try to think about happy thoughts.

Then my eyes open and I'm in my bed again, my thoughts returning home also. Maybe the thoughts will never leave, but as I get closer to God, peace fills my mind. I know that no matter what I have done or left undone and no matter what anyone else thinks of me, He loves me.

By: Ryanna Haché, age 13

Mommy and Daddy Not Fighting Any More; Just Peace

Note from parent: I would like to submit this story for my daughter Camila Garcia-Monahan, aged 4. She recited the story and I did my best to write it down using her own words. I explained the word 'peace' to her when she was very young and she never seemed to have any trouble grasping the meaning and significance. She's delighted that her story might be read by others or otherwise used by this project.

"Sometimes mommies and daddies fight, but that's ok because it's just an accident. I love to do things that are peaceful, but sometimes mommies and daddies fight. Sometimes they don't know how to stand up for themselves in a nice way, or sometimes they just need to be alone for a while. So everybody knows that fighting isn't nice, but I never knew what to do about it, until one day I finally figured out the answer.

One day my mommy said: "Please can you clean up the mess." And my daddy said: "No I have a million things to do."

Mommy said: "I also want you to fix the fridge, it's broken again." Daddy said: "You're the one with all that laundry to do in the basement."

Mommy said: Erg, you drive me crazy! Daddy said: Me? I didn't do anything. Then they were about to start yelling at each other, but I used my peace solution:

I began to sing a beautiful song about peace. It went like this:

"I love peace in my home. Peace is so beautiful and spreads out everywhere you go... and you can't just get peace, you need to work hard for peace...but peace is the number one thing you should know...yes peace is the number one thing you should know...and I would like us to come together....and we can figure this out, if we do it with peace and love..."

I sang so loud and held both my mommy and daddy's hands, and then, like I already knew, they stopped arguing and started smiling, and then they both said sorry, and then we were all holding hands.

Camila Garcia-Monahan (4 years old) as told to her mother, Katherine Monahan

Peace with a Kid who used to be a Bully

There were these bullies at my school and they were bullies for a long time. They would be very mean to me every day at school.

One time they called me a crap head and I responded incorrectly. I had done the incorrect thing many times before.

They also never wanted to play with me because they did not like me.

The bullying never stopped but one bully apologized for being rude to me. I apologized back for being a tattle-tail. I felt relieved.

It helped that one bully apologized but the other two were still bullies.

I don't think I will be able to make peace with the other two because they are very stubborn but it is worth a shot.

At least I got one to be peaceful but there is still two left to make peace with.

By: Nathan Haché, Age: 11

Returning my Friends to Peace – Senior Kindergarten in the Playground

Note from parent: I'd like to submit this story for my daughter Annabella Garcia-Monahan, aged 7. She recited the story and I did my best to write it down using her words. I explained the word 'peace' to her when she was young and she never seemed to have trouble grasping the meaning and significance. She's delighted that her story might be read by others or otherwise used by this project.

Last year, I was at school with my two best friends: Lulu and Jasmine. My friend Jasmine had an idea for a game she wanted to play, but my friend Lulu said "no" (I think because she didn't know how to play that game). So, Jasmine started to get really frustrated and kept repeating over and over that all she wanted to do was play that game, but Lulu really, really didn't want to play. Jasmine got so angry that when Lulu said "no!" again, she reached out and hit her as hard as she could on the arm! For a moment, nobody moved and everyone just looked really surprised, but then Lulu yelled and yelled as loud as she could. She's never yelled like that before and she was so angry. She yelled so loud "I TOLD YOU I DON'T WANT TO PLAY THAT GAME, AND I DON'T WANT TO PLAY WITH YOU....and DON'T HIT!!! Then both Jasmine and Lulu ran away in opposite directions crying.

These friends were now fighting and hitting and I didn't like it at all. They've been friends since they were 1 years old! So, I went to find Jasmine, and I waited for her to stop crying and then I told her to meet me at the sandbox in the playground (where we make tunnels). Then I went to find Lulu and told her to meet me at the sandbox in the playground too. Both Lulu and Jasmine showed up at the sandbox a few minutes later.

I brought them both close together and said "Jasmine, you shouldn't hit Lulu...and Lulu, you shouldn't yell at Jasmine". Afterwards I said "So when I count to three, say sorry to each other". Then I counted to three really slowly, and then they both actually did say sorry to each other!!! ...and then, best of all, they hugged each other!!! (And I didn't even have to ask them to do that part!!!). Then the bell rang.

Annabella Garcia-Monahan (now 7 years old) as told to her mother, Katherine Monahan

Misiwe Ni Wakoomahgunuk

To say, All My Relations, *Misiwe Ni Wakoomahgunuk* in Cree, recognizes our interconnection to each other, and is a prayer of oneness and harmony with all forms of life. In other words, we need to embrace the sacredness of our connection to all before we can truly obtain harmony. Oglala Lakota war leader Crazy Horse (1822-1877) was quoted,

"I salute the light within your eyes where the whole universe dwells. For when you are at that center within you and I am at that place within me, we shall be one."

I fell in love with this quote the second that I heard it. The truth, wisdom and respect that it carries resonated at the core of my Soul. You have light, I have light, let us embrace the light within each other and shine as One.

Crazy Horse fought in a battle well known in history to protect what is Sacred about this interconnection. I honour him. I have stood in prayer on those battle grounds.

We have had our own similar battles here in Canada. Our war leaders today are people like our land and water protectors, those who created Idle No More, people like Cindy Blackstock and Senator Murray Sinclair.

All who are like beacons showing us the way, telling us that we cannot stand by and pretend we are bystanders in the current injustices.

Reminding us that we are all able activists and as relations are accountable to protecting each other.

I join the fight against our federal government whom the Supreme Court found guilty of a human rights violation because they underfund Indigenous youth in care.

I work with these youth; they are the most vulnerable population in this country. Many from communities in northern Ontario that are in third world conditions, where there is a sense of hopelessness and despair, and youth suicides are high.

How does our country spend billions on its 150th anniversary, but in the same breath say that they do not have the money to rectify this disparity between funding, so our most vulnerable can have an equal chance of living?

How do I look these children in the eye and say this country supports them when it does not even think they are worthy of equality?

This is an injustice. But most importantly, and most alarmingly, it is a lack of compassion.

Their communities cry out and yet somehow, we as a collective turn our backs on the wellbeing of our fellow neighbours.

Every meticulous step I have made in my life, or path I seemingly stumbled upon, has been an effort to rectify injustice and help people find their light again.

Becoming a psychotherapist to work with Indigenous youth to help heal them, their families and communities, from the impacts of the residential school genocide.

Creating and facilitating programming that brought youth in foster care together to learn about, embrace and celebrate Indigenous culture, which for many years this country tried to eradicate with its aggressive assimilation tactics.

Becoming an advocate and educator developing workshops and training opportunities to support truth and reconciliation and help forge the needed relationships across the province.

Studying under the amazing Algonquin Medicine Man and creating a healing lodge to provide a sacred space where everyone on the medicine wheel felt that they could come together to learn and heal, regardless of their ethnic or religious differences.

There is a peace warrior at the core of each and every one of us.

Connect with that part of you.

Look up to the Star Nations for guidance, let your bare feet root to the energies of our Earth Mother, sit under the quiet of a tree and learn to listen from your heart, and feel the love and wisdom of Creator and the Universe.

And in this moment of sacredness, may you realize you are not separate from anyone or anything, and that the world needs you to realize your sacred part in creating a harmonious nation.

Allow your light to shine, see that same light in others, and together may we shine bright as one.

All My Relations. *Gitchi-meegwetch.*

By: Jenny Sutherland, M.S.W., R.S.W. Indigenous Treatment Program Coordinator, Connor Homes

Story List – Alphabetical

Story List – by Category
(in alphabetical order)

The seventeen categories, in alphabetical order, are: ADR, Restorative Justice, Mediation; Business, Private Sector; Children and Youth; Education; Environment; Family, Relationships; French; Health, Medical; Indigenous, First Nations; Innovation, Cutting Edge; International, Development Assistance; NGO's, Civil Society, Co-op, Unions; Protest, Activism; Spirituality, Inner Peace, Reflections ; The Arts; United Nations, Peacekeeping, Governance; and Women in Peace.

Environment

Family, Relationships

French

Health, Medical

Indigenous, First Nations

Innovation, Cutting Edge

International, Development Assistance

NGO's, Civil Society, Co-op, Unions

Protest, Activism

Spirituality, Inner Peace, Reflections

306

United Nations, Peacekeeping, Governance

Women in Peace

About the Creators of this Anthology

From left to right:

Koozma J. Tarasoff is an anthropologist, writer, published author, photographer, blogger, peace activist and representative of the Canadian Department of Peace Initiative. He's a scholar of Spirit Wrestlers/Doukhobor studies. Born in Saskatchewan, he now resides in Ottawa, Ontario. http://spirit-wrestlers.com.

Mony Dojeiji is a pilgrim for peace, international award-winning author, TV host-producer and independent publisher of books and artwork that inspire. http://walkingforpeace.com.

Evelyn Voigt is a poet, spoken word artist, author and co-founder of Civilian Peace Service Canada (http://civilianpeaceservice.ca). She sits on the Board of the Peace and Conflict Studies Association of Canada (http://pacscan.ca), and is recipient of a Queen's Golden Jubilee medal for her contribution to international development.

Gordon Breedyk is President, Civilian Peace Service Canada (http://civilianpeaceservice.ca), an NGO that assesses and accredits individuals for Peace Professionalism. He has a diverse background in the public, private and non-governmental (NGO) sectors both in Canada and internationally.

Musical Bonus

All readers are invited to enjoy two original and beautiful peace songs, courtesy of vocalist Geri Childs, and the country band Grateful We're Not Dead, which regularly entertains, free of charge, throughout the Ottawa Valley in seniors' residences and for charity events and fundraisers.

Please visit www.150CanadianPeaceStories.com to download these songs for your personal enjoyment.

To learn more about Geri Childs, please visit www.gerichilds.com.

To learn more about the Grateful We're Not Dead band, please visit www.gratefulwerenotdead.com.